SUMMERS IN WINTER

SUMMERS IN WINTER

Four England Tours of Australia
under Jim Lillywhite, Plum Warner,
Gubby Allen and Mike Brearley

ANTHONY MEREDITH

THE KINGSWOOD PRESS

FOR ANNA
IN ENGLAND
AND HER COUSIN DAVID
IN AUSTRALIA

First published in Great Britain in 1990
by The Kingswood Press
an imprint of Methuen London
Michelin House, 81 Fulham Road, London SW3 6RB

Copyright © 1990 Anthony Meredith

A CIP catalogue record for this book
is available from the British Library
ISBN 0 413 64310 7

Printed in Great Britain
by Mackays Plc, Chatham

CONTENTS

ACKNOWLEDGEMENTS

This book began with research into the story of James Lillywhite and I am particularly grateful to Laurie and Natalie Lillywhite for much friendly help concerning Laurie's illustrious grandfather; they also introduced me to the knowledgeable Bill Walton of the Priory Park Club, Chichester.

I must also pay tribute to the help of the late Sir George Allen, Anne Anderson, Milo Corbett, Paul Fitzpatrick, Christine Foster, N. C. Garrett (of Lillywhites), Helen Grigsby (of P & O), the late Joe Hardstaff, Chris Haslam, Rachel Mecham, Will Morris, Don Mosey, Russell Muir, Justin Murray, Bob and Nick Platt, Robin South, Timothy Stunt, John Woodcock, R. E. S. Wyatt and the many England tourists of 1978–79 who kindly answered my questions. Stephen Green at Lord's made available R. E. Foster's diary, Ozzie Osborne at Hove A. E. Relf's. I am also grateful to the Brighton Reference Library, the Canterbury Public Library (New Zealand), the Bruce and Chatham House Libraries (Stowe), the National Library of Australia (Canberra), the Library Board of Western Australia (Perth), the Windsor Hotel, Melbourne and the Bellevue Hotel, Brisbane.

The illustrations of Mike Brearley's tour are reproduced by kind permission of Patrick Eagar. The original sources of the other illustrations – whether photographs, cartoons or drawings – are mostly unknown, though some appeared in *Alfred Shaw Cricketer* (1902) by A. W. Pullin, *How We Recovered the Ashes* (1904) by P. F. Warner, *The 1937 Australian Test Tour* by Bruce Harris (1937), and *Tours and Tests* (1940) by Kenneth Farnes, all long out of print.

At the Kingswood Press Derek Wyatt initiated things and Tony Pocock has urbanely and most helpfully seen the project through to completion. My wife has borne my enforced absences from the social and domestic round with amazing fortitude; my mother has again been a perceptive critic; my young labrador, whilst otherwise chewing us out of house and home, has somehow, most sportingly, eschewed the manuscript. For all, my thanks.

Chatham House, Stowe   Anthony Meredith
June 1990

FOREWORD

by Tony Lewis

On a sunny day in Melbourne, at one o'clock on Thursday, March 15, 1877, Alfred Shaw of England bowled the first ball in Test cricket to Australia's Charles Bannerman. For the next hundred years during which time Test cricket proliferated to involve seven countries, the pinnacle of an England player's achievement was selection to tour Australia – indeed England's Test selectors built teams especially for the Australian trip which came around every four years.

Then in 1977 came the Packer revolution. While a superb Centenary Test was being played in Melbourne secret plans were under way to recruit the best cricketers in the world to form a commercial circus which would play, often in coloured clothing under late-evening floodlights, for the benefit of Channel Nine TV in Australia, the network owned by the entrepreneur Mr Kerry Packer.

By the time Mike Brearley's England side toured in 1978–79 the Australian fears were that their team, drastically depleted by the exodus of World Series players, would not be able to give England hard enough competition. They were right; England won 5–1 and the golden history to which every England cricketer wanted to belong became tarnished.

It was a second-rate series which had to compete on ABC television with World Series Cricket on Channel Nine. I recall being at a dinner party one night in Sydney where the host asked which side of his table I would care to be seated. I asked what was the difference. 'It is Wednesday evening,' he said. 'Sit on this side and you can watch World Series Cricket on the television up there on the shelf. The ladies usually sit opposite. They can do without the cricket.'

I replied that I too could do without cricket having followed Mike Brearley's boys all day. Enough was enough. 'I'll join the ladies.'

The lustre has never quite returned because the standards of play in the two countries has declined. The West Indies towards the end of the seventies and through the eighties emerged as an all-conquering force with their four-pronged fast bowling attack. Pakistan struck a rich seam of talent including outstanding players in three important departments – Imran Khan, the captain all-rounder, Abdul Qadir the leg-spinner and Javed Miandad the natural run-getter. England versus Australia was a series of diminished glamour.

The four-year tour is still intended to be a pillar of the England-Australian relationship but the teams meet many times in one-day competition all over the world. Commercialism was a key factor at the start of it all when Spiers and Pond sponsored the first tour of English cricketers in 1861 and the Mr Mallam who was sent to make the arrangements then would probably recognise the new marketing world now.

England against Australia, however, is built on the great deeds and great moments of a brilliant history. The tale of these tours is a statistical jewel box to many or a multicoloured weave of social history. Whether in the mind you travel for thirty-two days aboard the *Orion* playing deck quoits with Gubby Allen or listening dreamily to Bob Wyatt's collection of dance music or to his Beethoven, 78 records on a wind-up gramophone, or are pinned down in the corner of an airport at the mercy of Ian Botham's 'ghetto-blaster', they are all men with a shared mission . . . to beat Australia at cricket.

Writing one's own role in history is a delicious fantasy, once perfected by Sir Pelham Warner. But *Summers in Winter* takes a more objective view and loses nothing in candour or entertainment.

I

INTRODUCTION

LILLYWHITE AND LATER

Jim Lillywhite did not lead the first tour to Australia – that honour went to Heathfield Stephenson in 1861–2 – but it was Lillywhite who persevered with the unlikely idea of travelling 12,000 miles to play a few games of cricket, making no less than six visits in the 1870s and 1880s. This book, therefore, which explores the saga of tours to Australia and retraces the steps of four particular teams, takes Jim Lillywhite as its starting-point and contrasts his tour of 1876–77 with those of Plum Warner in 1903–04, Gubby Allen in 1936–37 and Mike Brearley in 1978–79. Each of the four tours is representative of a particular era. Each stands in strong contrast to the others and yet complements them too. Together they tell a compelling story of the development of one of our great sporting institutions.

The tour of 1876–77 is an excellent example of the privately-run, speculative ventures of Victorian times. It was Lillywhite's second visit to Australia and his first as player-manager. He had been inspired by his travels three years earlier under the leadership of the young W. G. Grace, and had become aware of the commercial possibilities of such tours. Using contacts from this earlier visit, Lillywhite took his All-England XI on an adventurous cricketing odyssey, during which he played two matches against the Combined XI of Victoria and New South Wales, games which have subsequently become known as the first two Test matches. The All-England XIs which toured under Lillywhite were an overseas extension of the activities of itinerant professional XIs which had dominated the domestic scene in the mid-19th century but which were now being challenged by inter-county competition. Lillywhite's XI played rough-and-ready cricket on wickets which were often quite atrocious. As they travelled, the tourists became local celebrities but there were no popular newspapers, radio or television to make them national heroes. In this respect there is a telling story of Jim Lillywhite. He was lunching alone in the public dining room of a Sydney hotel. Presently a man of similar features sat down at a nearby table and the diners, almost as one, rose and applauded. 'Who's the celebrity and what's he done?' asked Lillywhite. 'The gentleman is James Lillywhite, the English cricketer', replied one of the waiters. 'He was playing yesterday, took 7 wickets for 7 runs and knocked up half a century.' Lillywhite said nothing, but, when it was time for his departure, seeing his double still there, surrounded by waiters and enjoying the meal of a lifetime, he took his wallet from his pocket and quietly left his card on the table.

Such mistaken identity of the England cricket captain could not have happened on Plum Warner's tour of 1903–04, for the advent of popular newspapers, with photographs and line drawings, had made Warner's boyish features unmistakable to the Australian public. This was a typical tour of cricket's Golden Age, as slow moving as a Stanley Steamer but full of Edwardian ease and plenty. Significantly, too, it marked the end of private enterprise, for Warner's team was the first to go forth under the aegis of the MCC. Much had happened since 1876–77. The phrase 'Test match' had been coined, England had been beaten on home soil and the legend of the Ashes of her cricket had begun. In England the County Championship had established itself, in Australia the Sheffield Shield had started. Standards of play on both sides had risen dramatically and Australia in 1903 could claim the most exciting player of the Golden Age, Victor Trumper. The tourists now travelled round Australia in trains rather than by ship. Cabling by two news agencies, a very expensive process using a chain of receiving posts, allowed the main details of matches to be relayed to England in just thirty minutes, though full eye-witness accounts might only appear in English newspapers a month later.

After the First World War cricket seemed less flamboyant, more serious, professional and political. Gubby Allen's tour of 1936–37 followed in the wake of the body-line crisis which had so damaged relationships between the two countries. Not a match was played, not a speech made, which did not have Jardine's visit in mind. But above all Gubby Allen's tour was strikingly representative of those fiercely competitive struggles of the 1930s, when cricketers like Don Bradman and Walter Hammond were the idols of their nation – respected, revered and seemingly without flaw – and when wide public interest in Test matches produced greater crowds than at any time in cricket's history. No less than 943,000 attended the five Tests of 1936–37. Radio broadcasting helped communicate events at once and turn the Tests into items of international news interest. 'Realistic radio reception over great spans of distance is truly a modern-day miracle', noted one advertisement, proudly proclaiming that its radio would be bringing the Tests to over a million Australian listeners. Meanwhile enthusiasts in England could listen to early morning summaries of the day's play. For the first time the activities of the tourists, on and off the field, were reported home (albeit responsibly) by a small band of English newspaper reporters, who travelled across Australia by rail with the team. Warner's tourists of 1903–04 had also travelled big distances by rail but had used horse and carriage within the cities, whereas Allen's team could avail themselves of the motor car. Leading players were supplied with courtesy cars by manufacturers anxious for good publicity. Travel by air was considered unwise by the authorities in 1936–37, but nonetheless Gubby Allen himself managed to make two flights.

Forty years later, air travel dominated Mike Brearley's tour of 1978–79, when, in keeping with more egalitarian times, it was the Test and County Cricket Board and not the MCC which organized proceedings. Brearley's tour of 1978–79 was of particular significance in that it had to compete with the rival attractions of Kerry Packer. Whilst Brearley's official tourists played 'fair dinkum cricket', fighting for the Ashes, World Series Cricket wooed the same spectators in the big cities. The Packer initiative accelerated the introduction of more money into the game through sponsorship; most Test players, assisted by their agents, were becoming more alert to the possibilities of commercial exploitation. The extra money, however, was hard won. On the field, the players had to cope with the differing demands of 5-day Tests and one-day Internationals, whilst their temperament and technique were both remorselessly probed by the television camera. Off the field, the tabloid press considered cricketers' private lives of public interest. In 1978 both Geoff Boycott and Ian Botham would provide ready copy. The tour of 1978–79, therefore, encapsulates much of cricket's Brave New World.

2

JIM LILLYWHITE'S TOUR

1876–77

One early afternoon in mid-September the Southampton wharf-side reverberated with farewell toasts, some in broad Yorkshire, some in Nottingham dialect, as Jim Lillywhite's team of twelve professionals noisily embarked on the P & O steamship *Poonah* en route for Australia. In the ship's saloon glasses were raised to 'The Land of The Golden Fleece', whilst porters below heaved the final trunks and cricket bags up the gangway and Lillywhite himself hastened to disengage from a crowd of well-wishers. It was a particularly emotional departure, for the All-England cricket team would be away from England for eight months.

Amongst those shaking Lillywhite's hand was a young gentleman farmer from Chichester called Arthur Hobgen. Hobgen had put the money up for the tour and had hoped to participate himself, but his own poor health and that of his mother had forced him instead to entrust the management of the enterprise to Lillywhite. Hobgen, a useful cricketer who played occasional games for Sussex, was a leading member of the Priory Park Club, Chichester, where Lillywhite sometimes played as a professional. Alongside Hobgen on the quay was Lillywhite's wife, Ada. For the Lillywhites it was a particularly hard leave-taking. They had been married less than two years, had a daughter, Clara, and were expecting another child. Most of the other players' wives, however, had said their farewells at home, consoled a little, perhaps, by the £50 which the players had been advanced to see their families safe through the winter.

Bidding Ada a final goodbye, the English captain boarded the *Poonah*; cheers rang out and momentarily all eyes were on him. He was a short, stocky man, about 5 foot 7 inches tall, in his mid-30s. Dark, meeting eyebrows lent his face a certain patrician severity, as did the sideboards and moustache which on tour he would grow to a full beard. He was smartly dressed, with new bowler hat; beneath it there was the dark, gypsy-like tan of the professional cricketer.

The liner which he boarded was the admiration of all. Not

large by modern standards – 3,000 tons and 125 metres long – the *Poonah* had gained great fame only the year before when the celebrated tightrope walker Blondin had walked between the main and mizzen masts whilst at sea. A speed of some ten knots was possible. She was, however, liable to alarming pitch and roll in the heavier seas, so that very few of her 250 passengers would avoid sickness on the journey.

Now, as the *Poonah* left her moorings and began to steam away through calm waters and beneath an auspiciously sunny sky, those on the wharf sang out hearty cheers and Lillywhite's men, who had gathered on the upper deck, loudly returned the salute. The cheering continued on both sides until the tourists were out of vocal reach, when most of them, their efforts arousing a convenient thirst, retired to the saloon. Lillywhite's fellow passengers would not have been wrong in supposing from this noisy departure that they were in for a lively time in the next month and a half. Much would have been the talk about Lillywhites past and present and many would have been the cricketing digressions as the passengers sat down at dusk that evening for their first formal dinner together, for the name Lillywhite had been synonymous with cricket for the past fifty years.

The most famous of all the Lillywhites was Jim's late uncle William, a Sussex slow bowler of such excellence that he became known as the 'Nonpareil'. A leading figure in the development of round-arm bowling, William has been immortalized in his top hat, black cravat and thick, white braces in a famous Corbet Anderson lithograph. There were also three Lillywhite brothers, sons of the Nonpareil. The one-eyed James Lillywhite senior had played some county cricket before becoming a coach for many years at Cheltenham College. His association with the businessman George Frowd had led to a sports business that bore their name and to *James Lillywhite's Cricketers' Annual*, known, from its cover, as the red Lillywhite. His brother John was a leading professional batsman who had played in all the big matches of the 1850s before starting a sports business in London and editing each year *John Lillywhite's Cricketers' Companion* – the green Lillywhite. The third brother, Fred, though not a player himself, had invented a portable cricket printing press, initiated *Lillywhite's Scores and Biographies*, organized a tour to North America (the first English tour overseas), supplied Lillywhite's Scoring Books from premises at the Oval and edited *Lillywhite's Guide to Cricketers* (which, at his early death, was incorporated in the green Lillywhites).

But by 1876 the most famous Lillywhite of all was the captain of the All-England touring party, James Lillywhite junior (Jim). He had been born in the same hamlet as his famous uncle: Westhampnett, outside Chichester. His father, a brickmaker on the Duke of Richmond's Goodwood estate, grew anxious about his young son's obsession with cricket and, tired of seeing him practising with his cousins all winter long in a large brick shed, sent him off to stay with a schoolmaster in a nearby parish. Jim's schooldays at Birdham proved of lasting value to him, for he later married the schoolmaster's daughter, Ada. He was also indebted to the schoolmaster of Birdham for his facility in writing and arithmetic. A book of complicated sums from Jim Lillywhite's schooldays survives, the accuracy and neatness of which are impeccable, suggesting both an admirable attitude to work and a good brain.

At 17 Jim Lillywhite became a tile-maker on the Goodwood estate, but he was also playing cricket for the Goodwood and Priory Park Clubs. By the age of 20, in 1862, he was in the Sussex team and he was not to miss a match for the county for the next nineteen years. He was a slow-medium left-arm bowler and lower order left-hand bat. As a roundarm bowler Jim Lillywhite was tireless and exceptionally accurate. His cousin John wrote of his 'ease of action and delivery' and his 'power of deceiving the batsman by raising or lowering his arm and appearing to vary the length of the ball while all the time a uniform pitch is maintained.' He altered his flight cleverly: 'The only thing that varies is the curve described before the ball pitches.'

Jim soon became known as the Young Nonpareil. In 1868 he toured the USA with Willsher's team and in 1872 replaced Willsher as secretary of the United South of England XI, one of the last successful touring XIs, which boasted as its chief ornament W. G. Grace, then at the peak of his powers. Out of season, as a young man, Jim Lillywhite coached at Oxford, Harrow, Cheltenham College and Trinity College, Dublin, while he was also engaged by Lord Stamford at Enville. In the winter of 1873–74 he had sailed to Australia with W. G. Grace's party, only the third team of Englishmen to go there. Jim Lillywhite was always prepared to travel wherever cricket might take him. Although he lived all his married life in the same house – in the idyllic hamlet of Westerton, facing the Downs, on the Goodwood estate – for much of the time poor Ada was a cricket widow.

For all his travels, Lillywhite was a devoted family man and, as such, not cast in the mould of the professionals of his day. There was much reckless living, much enjoyment of the moment heedless of the morrow, much drinking, gambling and womanizing, and particularly so on tour when money, for once, was plentiful, and players' heads were often turned by local adulation. Many professionals too lived recklessly in the awareness that when their playing days were over, life might hold little for them. Such were the men who toured with Lillywhite.

It would not have taken many hours on board the *Poonah* before they polarized into groups. First there was a young, boisterous element, with George Ulyett, Tom Armitage and Andrew Greenwood of Yorkshire, John Selby of Notts and Harry Charlwood of Sussex. Of these Ulyett, at 26 the youngest member of the side, was the one destined for greatest cricketing fame, for he was to go on seven more tours and to play in twenty-five Test matches. Ulyett, a Sheffield man, who started life in the rolling-mill trade and ended it as licensee of The Vine in Sheffield, was cheerful in temperament and an inveterate practical joker. He was 'Happy Jack' and 'Our George' to the whole of Yorkshire which idolized him for his audacious hitting, outstanding fielding and fiery bowling. Tom Armitage, a stonemason by trade from Keighley, was enjoying his first and only tour, his underarm lob bowling having brought him into prominence that very summer. Greenwood, Charlwood and Selby were three of the chief batsmen. The latter was also a professional runner. Of short, muscular build, Selby had won some important short-distance races and was looking forward to making a big profit from his running in Australia. As a batsman he was renowned for his speed between

the wickets, a quality which did not always endear him to his less
athletic colleagues.

Then there was an older group with Ted Pooley of Surrey and
Tom Emmett and Allen Hill of Yorkshire, men who, though of
the years of discretion, had rarely found that virtue an easy
travelling companion. Hill was an effective bowler of fast off-
cutters, but not as celebrated as Pooley and Emmett. Pooley, now
aged 38, though declaring himself only 33, was the outstanding
English wicket-keeper. He had turned down an opportunity to
join the very first tour to Australia of 1861–62, because, as he
candidly admitted, 'Lor bless yer, guv'nor, I was doin' a bit of
sweetheartin' at the time'. Later, as a wicket-keeper, he set new
standards of liveliness and bravery, standing up to all manner of
bowling, in the custom of the day, and, not surprisingly, sustain-
ing many injuries. He lost three teeth, broke his nose and by the
end of his career possessed 'two fists that are mere lumps of
deformity'. Controversy and Pooley seemed inseparable and he
was frequently out of favour over allegations for throwing
matches for money and other crises related to betting and alcohol.
Tom Emmett, too, liked his drink and was a popular Yorkshire
captain in the days before Lord Hawke demanded a more sober
outlook from the team. 'After a cricket luncheon, his perception
was sometimes a trifle hazy', was one wry contemporary comment, though Emmett himself indignantly declared of his notori-
ous, heavy-drinking Yorkshire XI, 'I never saw woon of our
fellows coom onto field oonfit for plaay'. The delight of the
ladies, who called him 'Mr Punch', Emmett was a wild but lively
left-arm bowler (whose famous ball – the 'sostenutor' – pitched
leg and hit the top of the off stump), a forcing bat and a mobile
fielder in the slips and gully, who tended to hold brilliant catches
but drop easy ones because his tongue was too active.

In view, therefore, of the lively nature of the team, it is not
surprising that Lillywhite and Arthur Hobgen inserted a good
behaviour clause in the contracts. 'Should any of the players be
guilty of any extravagence, improper conduct or behaviour which
may conduce to the loss or detriment of the others, their pay shall
be stopped or deducted.' In other words, the players could get up
to as much mischief as they wanted *provided* that the team's overall

performance was not set at risk. Lillywhite was to be the sole arbiter, should any such case arise.

There was left, finally, the third, most reponsible group, of Lillywhite, Jupp, Southerton and Shaw. Surrey's Harry Jupp, nicknamed the Young Stonewall for his careful back-footed play which had made him one of England's leading batsmen, was, in contemporary description, 'a broad-shouldered, powerful, thick-set, muscular man'. A brickmaker by trade originally, he had been licensee of the Sun Inn at Dorking, his home town, before moving recently to a pub in Lower Norwood. Now aged 34 and a most popular individual, he had been presented with an expensive watch and chain shortly before sailing by 'a few admirers of his great merit as a cricketer and of his character as a man'. *Lillywhite's Scores and Biographies* saluted his personal qualities: 'He is one of the steadiest and best behaved cricketers . . . His example might well be copied with advantage by many . . ..' Jim Lillywhite, however, had anxieties about Harry Jupp, for the recent loss of his wife had not only affected his form but also his state of mind.

Jim Southerton, the vice-captain and at 48 by far the oldest member of the party, was, like Jupp, known for his devotion to his wife and family and the speed with which he would return to them as soon as a match was ended. He was a hairdresser for many years before becoming licensee nearby at The Cricketers on Mitcham Green. Like Lillywhite, he was highly literate, and had made an agreement with *The Sportsman* to send back regular articles about the tour. Southerton had a balding head, straggly side whiskers and short, ample frame which made him look more like everybody's favourite uncle than a vigorous Test cricketer. He was a slow right-arm bowler who spun, or threw, big off-breaks; strangely, the older he became, the higher went his arm, so that he started as a roundarm bowler but by the time of the tour was nearer to overarm. An article which he wrote for the red Lillywhite contained some splendid wisdom on the art of bowling, which he compared to the art of fishing. 'You must have plenty of ground bait, and the ground bait in cricket is to continue to give the batsman *almost* but not quite every kind of ball that he wants. When he hits at a ball well and freely he is on the feed, and then is the bowler's time to drop a ball very like the last in appearance but with a slight difference of pitch, break and spin, and one of the field is very likely to play the part of the man with the landing-net.'

As a slow bowler Surrey's Southerton was still reckoned to be second only to Alf Shaw of Notts. Shaw was a sprightly 34-year-old, plump but not yet grossly fat, dapper with a handlebar moustache and side whiskers. He bowled slow off-breaks, remarkable for their flight and accuracy. In twenty-seven seasons he took over 2,000 wickets and bowled more overs than had runs scored off him! Shaw was a difficult man, canny and conceited, yet possessing a good business brain. But for cricket he would have spent his working life knitting stockings. As it was, he used his cricketing fame to good advantage, running a successful sports business in Nottingham with Arthur Shrewsbury, becoming landlord of a pub and finding employment with Lord Sheffield (who wrote the introduction to Shaw's book of ghosted reminiscences).

If Jim Lillywhite had hoped to settle down on the voyage and talk over his itineraries and financial worries with the likes of Jupp, Southerton and Shaw, he was to be disappointed, thwarted by the intervention of the elements, for, not far from South-ampton, the weather deteriorated. It became dull and foggy and the *Poonah* frequently had to slacken off her engines to cope with the poor visibility. Her fog-whistle shrieked constantly and, to make things worse, the ship began to roll. Soon most of the team were confined to their bunks, Lillywhite and Emmett suffering the most of all through the Bay of Biscay. Nothing, however, could daunt the spirits of 'Happy Jack' Ulyett who, according to Southerton, 'made ample amends at mealtimes for absent friends'.

After the miseries of the Bay of Biscay it was not surprising that all members of the team stretched their legs at Gibraltar, despite the heat, and visited the usual tourist sites. They also loaded themselves with fruit from the market before returning for the voyage on to Malta. The Mediterranean was a source of delight. For hours the players would hang over the rails, admiring the sight of a shoal of porpoises following in their wake. The calm waters also allowed them to use a confined, hot space beside the engine room for a game of 'small cricket'. Later, one side of the upper deck was enclosed with canvas and the team had great fun and some useful exercise with the aid of canvas balls and a home-made set of stumps.

To travel first-class by P & O was the height of luxury and, as such, an existence dramatically different from the players' everyday experience. Service was immaculate, comfort admirable (heavy seas permitting) and the food somewhat too plentiful for the well-being of professional sportsmen who were taking scant exercise. Few concessions were made for foreign locations; the food was as thoroughly British in the Red Sea as in King George's Sound. In an age when animals had to be killed on board (for there was no refrigeration) the meals were quite remarkable for their scope. A typical first-class P & O menu of this period started with the popular mutton broth. After this came a multiplicity of main courses and there was absolutely no limit to the number of dishes which might be eaten. There were roasted turkeys, sucking pigs, geese, duck, fowl, beef and haunch mutton; there were boiled leg of mutton, fowl and ham pies, kidney puddings, braized sheep's heads, stewed pig's feet, chicken sauté, curry and rice and even corned beef. The choice of puddings included fruit tarts, black cap puddings, sandwich pastries, apple turnovers, jam tartlets, sponge cakes, Brighton rocks, pancakes and rice puddings. For many years unlimited quantities of wine, beer and spirits accompanied a first-class ticket. Fortunately for Lillywhite this concession was withdrawn only two years before his expedition. But the wines were still of the finest – P & O were famed for their clarets – and there was still free champagne on Sundays and other days of celebration.

Awnings were put up to give the passengers more shade, the overheating engines were slowed for five hours, a piano was rolled out from the saloon for open-air songs and, somewhat strangely, a badminton net was put up 'for the use of the ladies'. The menfolk, meanwhile, when not watching the badminton, amused themselves with card-playing, quoits, bullboard and reading.

Some of the English cricketers were quick to exploit their fellow-passengers over the card table. Alf Shaw was shocked by these unsubtle, pecuniary antics. He himself had first been taken in by the sleight of hand of one of the Yorkshiremen: 'When I saw him call three "naps" in succession, and get home each time, I simply thought that luck was on his side. Subsequently, when some of the team played with another passenger until four o'clock in the morning – on the deck by moonlight – and one of them got the richer by £20, I considered it time to make remarks, and I did so.' The P & O management would have approved of Shaw's interference, for ship-board gambling was one of their biggest headaches. A memo of this period, from P & O's head office, declared 'It has come to our knowledge that great laxity exists in some of the Company's ships with respect to card playing for money and gambling in other forms. Such practices are not in accordance with the high state of discipline we expect maintained in vessels of this company . . . .'

Coaling took place at Malta and again, after fourteen days at sea, at Port Said. The players found the latter 'a small and wretched place, with nothing to be seen which could not be seen from the ship'. They soon returned. Then came a day of travel down the Suez Canal (which had been opened seven years before, obviating a wearisome overland trip through Egypt), a night moored on its banks, and continuation to Suez itself. Because of the need to wait for the Brindisi mail, the *Poonah* had to spend two days off Suez, which, to Southerton, was 'the most filthy, wretched and disgusting place we have ever been in'. To reach the town itself the passengers had three choices. They could walk three miles, or pay two rupees for a boat or hire an infamous Suez donkey. Most of the team chose the last resort, and, eventually, after an interminable journey during which Tom Armitage was thrown into a large, muddy puddle, they reached Suez, only to find its Post Office closed and its hotel seedy. Even the French bazaar and the famed gardens gave them no incentive to linger.

The Red Sea brought temperatures of 92° in the shade, but even so, after the squalor of Suez, it was a relief. 'It is the same sensation as if we were in a Turkish Bath', noted Southerton. 'Our fellows are satisfied that there is not the smallest fear of them putting on too much flesh at present, however good their powers of eating!' At Aden the *Poonah* took on board another 400 tons of coal and soon she was sailing through cooler, less still air. The team revived accordingly and Jim Southerton was in lyrical mood: 'Since we left Aden we have been astonished at times by the beautiful appearance of the sea at night, which has been highly changed by phosphorescent light, giving to the ship the appearance of sailing through a sea of splendid green-coloured liquid fire and smoke, and the waves that were thrown from the ship's side were something to remember.'

Evening entertainments were highlights of the voyage. Amateur concerts were very popular, lugubrious ballads and stirring patriotic ditties both sounding well in the warm night air, once vocal chords had been moistened. One evening a Trial By Jury was improvised on the quarter deck, with distinguished passengers playing the roles of judge and counsels for prosecution and defence, and the All-England XI providing the prisoner. George Ulyett was tried, and eventually acquitted, for attempting to steal a ship's funnel! There was professional entertainment, too, for there happened to be a light operatic company travelling to an engagement in Calcutta. So in the quiet of the Suez Canal the Royal Corinthian Comedy Drama Company entertained the passengers with 'Still Waters Run Deep'. Their manager had been much impressed by the voice of Sussex batsman Harry Charlwood, who was the boldest of the team's night-time singers, and insisted upon Charlwood appearing on the bill in a special spot between 'Still Waters' and a concluding farce. But as the big occasion drew near, Charlwood panicked and, when his turn came, he was nowhere to be found until, all too late, he was discovered in his bunk pretending sleep. The company later performed 'All That Glitters Is Not Gold' and 'Mr and Mrs White's Trip to Richmond', but, apparently, Harry Charlwood was never called upon again to sing.

With such entertainments as these, the nights, if not the days, went by quickly and a whole month passed whilst they sailed to Ceylon and the harbour of Galle, which they finally reached at night on 20 November. Galle was too dangerous to be entered other than in daylight, so for the remainder of the night the passengers waited on board the *Poonah*, its engines suddenly silent. For Lillywhite and those not going on to India it was time to pack up belongings in readiness to transfer to another steam-ship, the *Tanjore*. For some these final hours on the *Poonah* were an opportunity for an all-night party and there was no suppressing the witticisms of Emmett and Ulyett and the singing of Charl-wood and his cronies in the saloon. For others, however, it was a time for reflection. Jim Lillywhite himself used it as an oppor-tunity for musing over the succession of circumstances which had led him to Ceylon, for looking ahead to the days to come, for rehearsing anxieties and probing uncertainties.

How, Jim Lillywhite wondered, had he come to be here, on the *Poonah*'s rails in the cool of a tropical night, outside the hidden port of Galle? Part of the answer, he knew, lay in the close, uncomfortable working relationship which he had with the Grace family. He remembered his previous Australian tour and the confrontations which he had experienced with W.G. and his brother G.F. The Graces had both treated the professionals very poorly and when their boorish antics upset the Australians, too, it had been he, Lillywhite, as leader of the professionals, whom most of the powerful Melbourne committee men came to respect. In particular he had formed a friendly understanding with Jack Conway, the Victorian fast bowler and journalist, and it was Conway who had suggested to him that he should bring out his own all-professional XI as soon as possible.

But he had also made enemies in Australia. There was one especially, Joseph Pickersgill of Melbourne, who had publicly rebuked Lillywhite and his fellow professionals during the heat of the argument at the end of Grace's tour. He had said that 2nd-class travel was quite good enough for English professionals who travelled 3rd-class at home! Likewise they should make do with beer, he claimed, and not aspire to champagne! This same Pickersgill, on learning of Conway's plans to procure a team of professionals, had been in touch with the Graces and for some time it seemed that Fred Grace might bring his own, rival touring team.

Throughout the summer of 1876, therefore, both Fred Grace

and Lillywhite had discussed terms with potential English tourists. Lillywhite, however, was confident that few professionals would expose themselves to poor treatment from the Graces – 2nd-class travel, inferior hotels, and an early bat only if the wicket was especially treacherous. 'My team', he wrote to Conway, 'will stick to me like wax. I don't think they would come out for £500 each under G.F. with the recollection of the last trip still fresh in the memory.' Even so, as late as August, Pickersgill was making controversial statements to the effect that Lillywhite would not be bringing out a team. Lillywhite grinned at the thought of Pickersgill's discomfiture when eventually he had to announce the withdrawal of Fred Grace's touring plans.

Lillywhite liked the Graces, despite their insufferable behaviour. He knew them both very well and somehow one could forgive them anything. W.G. and Fred had been his leading attractions for the past few seasons with the United South of England XI, scoring prodigiously all over the country. He expected runs, however, for the kind of money he paid them. They had spent a busy time together just before the voyage began, as team-mates for the United XI (against XXIIs at Stockport and Wellingborough) and for the South versus the North (at Rochdale), and as opponents in a county match at Clifton (when W.G. indulged in a sit-down protest at one umpiring decision).

Lillywhite turned his thoughts, with difficulty, from the Champion, to the complicated set of financial arrangements which he had had to make before sailing. Ten of his eleven players would be given £200 for the trip; they would share the profits of two benefit matches, would be paid all their expenses and, at the end of the tour, claim their portion of the profits, a quarter of all match receipts after expenses had been deducted. Arthur Hobgen, who had underwritten the tour with £3,000, was to have taken 50% of the profits, had he accompanied the team. However, after his withdrawal he had most generously altered the arrangements, claiming as his share in the venture only 'half the one-twelfth share in the one-fourth of the net profits'. Lillywhite himself would now receive the 50% share, a big incentive for shouldering the entire burden of captaincy and management.

Alf Shaw was likely to become his chief helper. Shaw's shrewd financial sense was obvious. Lillywhite himself had recently suffered from it, for Shaw, knowing how much his services were needed to give the team credibility in Australian eyes, had held out for more money than the others and eventually was paid £300. Still, his presence was a comfort. He would be sharp enough to notice any Australian chicanery. Lillywhite realized that he himself was too mild a person to make an ideal business man.

His thoughts of finance were interrupted by the approach of dawn and the *Poonah*'s careful advance into the large harbour of Galle, fringed romantically with coconut trees and palms. He rejoined his team for breakfast – always a big meal – after which all manner of canoes and small vessels arrived to take the passengers ashore. Jim Lillywhite's first object in Ceylon was to try to discover the expected details of his tour itinerary from his agents, but in this he was to be disappointed and now it would not be until his arrival in Adelaide that he would know the outline plan. He was offered a cricket match there and then, however, for the captain of the Galle cricket club wanted to field a team of twenty-two against him, but, by this time, the All-England XI had scattered so Lillywhite could not accept the challenge. There were plenty of alternative distractions for him and his team. Southerton reported 'offers to pilot us to any place that we might wish to go, from the Post Office to the dancing girls'. Surprisingly, perhaps, most opted initially for the Oriental Hotel, 'the chief resort and in this place tolerably cool'. Leading from its verandah was a billiard-room, whose two tables the All-England XI soon appropriated. The younger players then went to explore the town on foot, whilst others, including Lillywhite and Southerton, ignored the dancing girls and invested the considerable sum of ten shillings in an 8-mile carriage drive to Wacmalla, through coconut groves to the Cinnamon gardens and back to the Oriental Hotel in time for 'tiffin' at 2 o'clock. 'They are celebrated for their prawn curry', wrote Southerton, 'and I think justly so.'

By late afternoon the re-united cricketers had transferred their baggage to the *Tanjore*. Those passengers remaining on the *Poonah* gave them 'ringing cheers' as they left Galle and so too did the

Poonah's sailors, who had been ordered into the rigging for the occasion. The two-masted and two-decked *Tanjore* was a little smaller than the *Poonah* but travelled a little faster (as much as 17 knots being claimed for her when running with the tide). Lillywhite's men liked their new ship, though they regretted the loss of an upper deck, for there was now no room for any more 'cricket'. The cooler weather, however, encouraged the taking of exercise. 'There will have to be some wasting by our lot who have led an idle life on board and partaken freely of the good things that life affords', noted Southerton.

Jim Lillywhite, always positive, later described the voyage from Ceylon to Australia as 'a very fine run'. Southerton, however, recorded it somewhat differently: 'We had an amateur theatrical and "Tanjore Minstrels" entertainment last evening performed under certain difficulties, as the wind changed and a heavy sea came rolling in astern, and made the ship roll very heavily, a state of things which has continued all today. . . .' Worse was to follow, for under heavier seas the ship began to pitch, whilst, after the crossing of the equator, there were also adverse trade winds and current. Most of the team lay prostrate in their cabins. 'Charlwood and Jupp were in the cabin adjoining mine,' remembered Shaw, 'and one day I heard such a groaning. Presently Charlwood commenced to pray, after which he turned to Jupp and remarked "Juppy, ain't I a good prayer?" I burst into the cabin, laughing, and asked what was the matter. Charlwood exclaimed "Alf, I'm dying." "Nonsense", I replied, "You're worth a lot of dead men yet." "Remember me to my wife and family", he said. "I shall never see them no more". Then he turned his face to the side of the bunk and groaned and prayed again. . . .' The worst sufferer in rough seas was always Tom Emmett. He was such a natural comic, however, with such an expressive face, that his fellows found it hard to take him seriously even when he was at his most ill and miserable. Once, on a later voyage to Australia, he crawled out of his cabin, ghastly green, to discover Lord Harris, his captain, a good sailor, enjoying a cigarette on deck. 'Glad to see you out, Tom, but you don't look very well.' 'Noah, me Lord,' croaked Emmett, 'Ah doant feel very broight.' He looked sadly at the mountainous seas. 'Ah doant think they've 'ad the 'eavy roller on, me Lord.'

The rough weather continued and led to a tragic incident on the *Tanjore* just after Cape Leeuwin, on the south-west tip of Australia, was sighted. One Sunday evening, whilst the passengers were at dinner, the ship suddenly gave a tremendous lurch. The four men on the wheel at the time, two English and two Chinese sailors, had been mastered by the rudder. It transpired that the Chinese, in fright at the rough weather, had let go their hold and one of the English sailors had been knocked down by the wheel as it went out of control: he died of his injuries the following day. The unhappy Chinamen were placed in irons and handed over to the authorities at Adelaide on a charge of manslaughter. It was not an auspicious beginning to Jim Lillywhite's time in Australia.

The *Tanjore* had made such excellent time from Ceylon that the cricketers arrived at Adelaide a week earlier than anticipated. Their agent, J. H. Bennett, was at the quayside at Glenelg to meet them and had just made arrangements for their overnight stay at the Pier Hotel. Their landing, however, did not go smoothly, for no suitable small steamers could be discovered to take the passengers off the liner. Eventually, after a wait of two hours, the players came across in a little boat, usually used for mail bags, which drenched them all in spray. Southerton noted anxiously: 'I hope this mismanagement is not chronic'.

Sadly it was to prove so. Jim Lillywhite soon discovered that the reason why his itinerary had not been available at Galle was that it was still incomplete. Only three fixtures had been finalized! Accordingly, with help from his agents Bennett and Conway, he pieced things together as he went along. Eventually the XI played nine matches in their first two months in Australia, a further eight matches in a two-month diversion to New Zealand and a final six matches in their five-week return to Australia. It was a haphazard arrangement which resulted in 7,000 miles of travel between their first and last match.

It is doubtful whether the cricketers, after two months at sea, could, that first night ashore, have cared much about their itinerary. Even the sober ones would have found the floor of the Pier Hotel swaying beneath them. Harry Jupp, for example, was so disorientated that he is said to have searched under his hotel bed for his bunk in some perplexity and, next morning, on seeing a window, to have exclaimed 'That's a new porthole, ain't it?'

Shortly afterwards members of the South Australian Cricket Association arrived to escort the team to Adelaide in a coach drawn by six grey mares. This cavalcade, the first of many, was accompanied by music, the Concordia band leading the way and drawing admiring crowds onto the streets in the six-mile procession. The tourists, in their turn, gazed at Adelaide in admiration. Founded only forty years before but already having a population of 60,000, the city with its fine stone buildings and wide regular streets proudly proclaimed its success as an agricultural centre and its foundation as a free settlement. Its Lutheran immigrants, too, had given Victorian Adelaide a moral tone which few Colonial cities possessed. As Alf Shaw looked about him, at the city and its cheering inhabitants, he was deeply impressed: 'It was all wonderful to me'.

Arriving at the Globe Hotel, Rundle Street, the visitors found themselves the centre of attention. Lillywhite handled the questions of local reporters resolutely but with less than total candour. Had they had a bad time at sea, he was asked. 'Not at all,' he replied, trying hard not to catch Tom Emmett's eye, 'We are all fit and in excellent spirits. No one has been troubled with indisposition on the whole voyage!' Was he optimistic about his chances of success? 'I confidently believe', said Lillywhite, 'we shall not be defeated by any of the colonies.' A large reception awaited them inside the Globe and soon they were able to test the hotel's advertisement that it had the best wines, ales and spirits in Adelaide. Jim Lillywhite duly replied to a toast of welcome: 'Such kindness as I and my friends have received this morning well repay us for making the long voyage. I too trust that our stay in the colonies will be an enjoyable one. I am confident that we will conduct ourselves in such a way as to meet the approbation of all. I thank my South Australian friends most heartily for your very kind and cordial reception.' If Jim Lillywhite entertained any misgivings about his public speaking, he could take comfort that W. G. Grace, his predecessor, was a notoriously abrupt performer. Lillywhite, though not equipped for the task by education, spoke with increasing fluency and certainly seems to have enjoyed speech-making. 'I spoke like Gladstone!', he enthused on one occasion.

These formalities over, there were nine free days before the first match, billed as 'A Grand Cricketing Festival, All-England v South Australians under the patronage of His Excellency The Governor'. The Adelaide Oval became a scene of frantic activity. Only five years earlier, when the South Australian Cricket Association was formed, the bumpy Oval with its thistles and weeds resembled its famous English namesake only in its dimensions. The Association, according to Alf Shaw, had been afraid to use a roller on the grass for fear of bruising and killing it and there was consternation when Southerton, lending the locals a hand, borrowed the corporation roller and pulled it across the centre of the ground with a team of four horses.

The Association far-sightedly used the arrival of Lillywhite to establish the Adelaide Oval on a proper footing and spent £400 on improvements before the match. For the Association, therefore, it was something of a gamble, as the terms struck with J. H. Bennett were couched entirely in favour of the visitors, Lillywhite taking two-thirds of the gross proceeds, the Australians paying all the expenses. The anxious Association, therefore, resorted to a high entrance charge of 2s 6d per day (and a similar amount for the reserved enclosure and for carriages).

These arrangements were vehemently criticized locally and it was said, with some justification, that the Association favoured social exclusiveness. Certainly it carefully vetted its membership, banned gambling on its ground and favoured upper-class English manners. The Association also attempted to attract to its cause the most influential and wealthy members of the community. That it succeeded can be seen by the city's ready acquiescence in the idea that the first day of the match should be a public holiday. The playing membership came from wealthy backgrounds, too, for the XXII chosen to represent South Australia against Lilly-white all had means enough to devote the entire week before the match to practice.

There was also a hint of Adelaide exclusiveness in the original suggestion that the entrance charge to All-England practices should be one guinea. Happily, this figure was modified (drastically, to 6d) and many South Australians were able to marvel at the Englishmen at work on three Oval practice wickets. The batting was declared 'very free, indeed vigorous and decidedly open'. Selby impressed with his 'easy grace and telling force' being 'especially great at leg hitting', whilst Jupp 'played a steady and very good defensive game'. Of the bowlers only the left-arm Emmett, with his deliveries angled in from wide of the crease, failed to please: 'The pace appears fast, but the exertion looks too great to last for long. His bowling is not by any means elegant.' There were suggestions too that he threw the ball.

Alf Shaw caused the most favourable comments of all, many admiring 'the easy grace with which he delivered his balls and the precision and certainty with which they broke the wicket.' One of the spectators was the 17-year-old George Giffen, who later wrote of Shaw: 'I remember going out one evening after the Englishmen had concluded their practice and finding on the pitch, which was rather soft that day, a patch about the size of a small saucer that the balls sent down by the great Notts bowler had worn.'

The English, confident of success, turned their thoughts mainly to pleasure, which Adelaide offered most generously. The team was allowed free travel on all the South Australian railways as well as free use of the city's public baths. There seemed to be all manner of entertainments. One evening was spent at the Town Hall, for example, watching a Professor Fay in an entertainment which pandered to current interest in spiritualism; another at White's Rooms, where a group of amateur minstrels played in honour of the Prince of Wales's 35th birthday; and another at the Theatre Royal, where a certain Madame Lo-Lo topped a music-hall bill with death-defying leaps of ninety feet through two balloons.

The proprietors of theatres, in return for the team's free

admittance, were able to advertise its 'patronage and presence'. Wealthy Adelaide enthusiasts also vied with each other for the privilege of entertaining the cricketers. They were taken to the racecourse, to a stud farm (where the pleasures of seeing Norfolk Trotters was eclipsed by that of drinking 'some of the best champagne we have had since leaving home') and for a ride out to Eagle-on-the-hill, their sponsor being 'anxious for municipal office and wanting to be brought prominently before the electors of his ward by entertaining the All-England XI'. It proved an exhausting excursion: 'After a refresher, and after the four horses had been taken out,' wrote Southerton, 'we went for a stroll down a deep gully to some waterfalls and by the time we got back we had more taken out of us than any day's practice we had had . . .' No doubt the Adelaide heat was debilitating, for the wind, as Southerton remarked, 'was almost hot enough to set fire to your clothes'.

The first match was advertised to begin at 1 o'clock and for at least an hour beforehand a constant stream of pedestrians and horse-drawn vehicles moved down King William Street and along the City Bridge Road so that by the start the Oval was very full with nearly 9,000 present. In addition, there was a large crowd outside the ground, watching from Montefiore Hill and the gum trees in the Park Lands. Dominating the scene was St Peter's Cathedral, completed only months earlier, though still lacking its tower and spires. Adelaide took an understandable pride in its picturesque new cricket ground: 'Our Oval is certainly beautifully situated, and the scene on Thursday must have impressed our visitors with the fact that the Great Southern Land is not altogether the arid desert it is sometimes imagined to be. Looking from the stand, the handsome villas on Montefiore Hill, the pretty little lantern tower and gables of St Peter's peeping over the belt of dusky eucalypti, and the changing hues on the distant Mount Lofty Ranges made up as pretty a picture as one could wish to behold.' There was pride too that the many ladies present were more seemly in their dress than the ladies of Victoria. 'There was none of that gaudy display of colours', wrote a reporter, 'I have noticed in the neighbouring colony and if the dresses were not rich they were at any rate, what is far more to the point, quiet and in good taste.' The conditions at the ground, however, did not suit Adelaide's preoccupation with the niceties of fashion. Dust was a constant irritation, not least when it arose in clouds at every passing buggy. 'A shoeblack might have made a small fortune', mourned the *South Australian Register*, as would 'a boy with a good clothes brush.' Thick layers of dust turned coats and dresses, which had arrived black or dark blue, into a uniform of yellow-brown.

The match began a quarter of an hour late at 1.15. Lillywhite had won the toss and Southerton had agreed to act as umpire when Jupp and Ulyett came out to bat in the wake of the twenty-two scruffy South Australians. 'The beauty of the scene', noted the *Register* severely, 'was considerably marred by the motley appearance of the XXII. Surely the attendance was sufficiently large and distinguished to deserve that the very small trouble and expense of dressing alike should be gone through for them . . ..' The English were less censored, though the *Register* did observe that 'their headgear was none of the most beautiful', for it was only in future ventures that there were smart Lillywhite team blazers, cravats and sashes; Lillywhite at this time favoured a comfortable, checked cloth cap.

Harry Jupp took first strike; J. E. Goodfellow was the first bowler. He received this honour not just because he was one of the best bowlers in the colony but because it was his publishing firm in King William Street which had produced the souvenir brochure of the match. Jupp looked round at the fielders. They seemed to cover every blade of grass. On the off-side there was a short-slip, long-slip, third-man, point, cover-point, forward cover-point, mid-off, long-off, long-off-drive, and short off-drive. Behind the wicket-keeper there was a long-stop, saving a single, and on the on-side there was a forward short-leg, square short-leg, fine short-leg, short on-drive, mid-on, long-on, long on-drive, long-leg and square-leg. With such an inhibiting field and with Jupp's penchant for caution, it was not surprising that the first (4-ball) over of the tour should have been a maiden. Progress was slow, Ulyett making some good hits but Jupp 'taking observations and keeping the ball well down'. They came in at 2.30 for lunch with 35 scored.

The Mayor of Adelaide presided at lunch and afterwards toasted the XI, paying tribute to Ulyett and Jupp before ending his speech with a call for three hearty cheers. Jim Lillywhite responded cheerfully. 'I never thought I should again get excited over a cricket match, but I have been excited today to see the great interest taken by the public. I never once anticipated such a company as that which is gracing the Oval by its presence at the moment and I trust it will have a treat afforded it. I hope all members of the team will do as well as the first two. The bowling which they have had to face I have heard from their own lips was very good. They had all their work set to keep it off their wickets without getting many runs. I am no speechmaker and in conclusion I will only say that I hope there will be as large an attendance tomorrow, when the XI will be seen displaying their powers in their greatest department of the game – their bowling.'

Play resumed in mid-afternoon and, with Ulyett soon out, Selby joined Jupp in a long partnership, which was briefly interrupted by the pomp and ceremony of the arrival of the Governor of South Australia and his entourage. It was not until 5.00 p.m. that the stand was broken and Jupp, 'in playing forward to a ball well up, failed to get over it in his usual scientific way' and was caught and bowled. His 35 runs, scored in 3¼ hours, elicited strangely fulsome praise: 'His innings was undoubtedly the most faultless one we have seen since he was here with Grace two years ago, when he scored 2 and 6. He excelled all his previous displays, and showed an ease, grace and elegance, and thorough knowledge of batting of which the South Australians hitherto had no conception.'

Selby continued to thrive 'with beautiful defence and occasional driving', but wickets fell at the other end and at the close of play at 6 o'clock All-England had scored 111-5: hardly, by modern standards, a full, satisfying day's cricket. However, the dust-spattered crowd streamed home happily, 'satisfied, but also tired with the close attention which nearly all had been paying to the game'.

The second day's play started around noon and, although the bank clerks and shop assistants were all back at work, there was still a good crowd of around 4,000. The England innings concluded at 153, Selby finishing with 59 scored in 4¼ hours 'in scientific and beautiful play – always steady, careful and along the carpet – and yet playing with it a considerable amount of dash.'

The South Australians began only fifteen minutes before the 2 o'clock lunch break, Alf Shaw opening the bowling with just two men on the leg-side, Lillywhite at short-leg and Ulyett at long-on. Wickets fell regularly throughout the afternoon, Shaw proving unplayable and ending with 14 wickets for 12 runs off 226 balls; at the close the South Australian XXII were all out for 54. Shaw himself attributed his success to the fact that 'the wicket was sandy and broke up quickly' but eyewitnesses suggest that it was a mesmeric piece of bowling; 'batsman after batsman who faced him retired without a run, a maiden followed maiden for half hours together. The great bowler repeatedly changed pace, pitch and break, to the utter bewilderment of the men who were facing him.' Shaw took his whole three-hour stint with such seriousness that, when Emmett caught the South Australian captain and 'the local umpire, believing the ball to be a "bum", gave the man in', he stared around him in utter disbelief and roundly remonstrated with the umpire before continuing.

There was another large crowd, about 7,000, on the third day, a Saturday. There was also another formal luncheon with speeches and a further visit from the Governor. The demoralized South Australians collapsed again and were bowled out for 53, Shaw taking 7 more wickets, but the extent of the South Australian confusion can be seen from the success of Tom Armitage's lobs, which took 7 wickets for 11 runs off 60 balls and made the anxious batsmen seem like total novices.

There was an even bigger difference between the two sides in their fielding than in their batting. The South Australians were slow to move and slow to bend, whereas the English fielding was 'simply perfection'. Pooley, enjoying every minute and showing off quite dreadfully, won the admiration of all and was rewarded for one catch with a bouquet from the pavilion, 'the receipt of which he gracefully acknowledged and then handed the trophy to the umpire, Southerton.' 'In the matter of fielding', wrote a sad South Australian, 'we have much to learn from the Englishmen; even every man seemed to be in the team for the purpose of doing his level best. I have seen some of our wicket-keeps refuse to move unless the ball was thrown into their hands. Pooley was after the ball anywhere he could get it first, and somebody was at the wicket in a moment to take his place. They all backed up each other, and fielded like machinery. They dashed in and met the ball; they did everything they could to save a run . . .'

That evening, on the stage of the Theatre Royal, Madame Lo-Lo presented the prizes which wealthy Adelaide enthusiasts had offered (an interesting variation of the modern man-of-the-match awards). John Selby was presented with a silver-mounted bat and Tom Armitage (somehow winning precedence over Shaw) with a silver-mounted ball. Shaw, however, together with Jupp, received an electro-plated pint tankard. There were also prizes for the Australians, a silver inkstand and a silver lever watch, incentives which had been on display in the committee-room all day, to be awarded to the best batsman and bowler from the Norwood and Kensington clubs. However, the committee seems to have been so overwhelmed by the magnitude of the defeat that it decided 'to take time to consider to whom the prizes should be awarded'.

The biggest prize, of course, for both sides was the financial one. The gamble of the Association had come off. The gross receipts for the match were £1,143 of which Lillywhite received £762 and from which the Association made £300. Thanks to Lillywhite's visit, its membership had trebled to nearly 600.

Jim Lillywhite, the match over, was now very anxious to reach Melbourne, to sort out the confusion over fixtures there, for Melbourne offered the biggest crowds and profits. So, reluctantly declining a farewell banquet but committing himself to a return fixture at the end of the tour, he determined on sailing that very night. A special train was arranged to take the team down to Glenelg and large crowds assembled at the Globe Hotel and King William Street Station to wish them goodbye. Around midnight about fifty South Australian cricketers gathered at the Pier Hotel, Glenelg, to drink the health of the departing Englishmen and there were the usual speeches. Amid the euphoria of the departure Lillywhite could not resist drawing a parallel with the bitterness caused by Grace's visit three years previously: 'I would like to propose the health of the XXII, between whom and myself not one difference has arisen throughout the match. That is more than can be said for some of the matches played in Australia during my last visit . . .' After further toasts the party then adjourned to the jetty and to great cheers Lillywhite and his men departed in a small steamer towards the lights of the *Claud Hamilton* and the next stage of their journey.

The fifty-hour voyage to Melbourne proved wearisome for all fifty passengers. The seas were rough and, with no cargo to give her stability, the *Claud Hamilton* rolled most of the way, so that all the cricketers were ill and unable to eat or sleep. Afterwards, however, most of the team enjoyed six free days in Melbourne. But Lillywhite himself spent most of the time in earnest consultation with his agents, trying to untangle complications over the Boxing Day fixture. The most desirable venue was the Melbourne Club's ground, the facilities of which were superior to any other. However, when Fred Grace had arranged to have its exclusive use, Lillywhite had agreed to use the East Melbourne Club's ground. Now that Grace's tour had fallen through, Lillywhite was most anxious to play at the larger ground where the profits would be much greater, but the East Melbourne Club, having spent money on improving its facilities, was threatening Lillywhite with litigation if he withdrew. Despite help from a lawyer, Lillywhite had not succeeded in resolving the problem when the time came to catch another steamer for the three-day voyage to Sydney.

There were other worries for the captain as his team boarded *The City of Adelaide*. Shaw, Selby, Hill and Jupp (one third of his party) were ill. Jupp was in a terrible way, suffering from sciatica or rheumatism and, on departure, Jim Lillywhite noted with alarm that his most experienced batsman could barely walk down the pier to the steamer. Things became even worse at sea and Jupp became so helpless from the acute pain in his hips and loins that he had to be helped in and out of his bunk. The little *City of Adelaide* was a good, clean ship and the cricketers liked the captain ('one of the right sort!'), but soon they were all in the throes of seasickness yet again as a southerly gale followed them up the coast. It was not until they reached the more placid waters of Port Jackson that Lillywhite's men emerged on deck and began to think about the match to come, a difficult fixture against fifteen of New South Wales, at the time the strongest of the colonies.

The arrival of Lillywhite's men in Adelaide and Melbourne had been at night time. Now, however, as they approached Sydney, they were arriving mid-afternoon and the players' excitement at seeing the dramatic beauty of Sydney harbour, as they steamed through the Heads, was equalled by the pent-up emotions of thousands waiting at the wharf for the first glimpse of the cricketers from England. All manner of small craft put out to greet the in-coming *City of Adelaide* and members of the New South Wales committee chartered a fast little steam launch, appropriately named *Britannia*. With bunting and flags waving gaily in the wind, she met the *City of Adelaide* as she was rounding Bradley's Head. 'They gave us some hearty cheers', wrote Southerton, 'which we returned as heartily. It was too misty and dull to see the full beauty of the place, but enough could be discerned to form some idea of it. As we drew alongside the wharf, we were welcomed by the assembled thousands with deafening cheers, and as we were landed and driven in a break and four horses to our hotel – Tattersall's, Pitt Street – it still continued.'

Among the welcoming crowd on the wharfside were a number of local reporters, keen to sketch first impressions for their readers. 'The team are a fine, jolly-looking set of fellows', wrote one, 'and, taken altogether, are not what might be termed "big" men. With the exception of Armitage, Allen Hill and Ulyett, who are fine, strapping cricketers, they are not much above medium height, but they are all well-knit, square-shouldered and apparently active.'

The *Sydney Mail* attributed part of the enthusiastic welcome to the goodwill felt by Sydney for English professionals in general and Lillywhite, Southerton, Jupp and Greenwood in particular, ever since Grace's tour 'when the professional element was contrasted with the amateur, not altogether to the advantage of the latter.' W.G. and his fellow amateurs were vilified at Sydney for the unscrupulous way they tried to make good on the field of play the heavy wagers they made off it. It had been a case, said the *Sydney Mail*, of 'the gentlemen and professional players reversing their respective social positions' and it concluded that 'Southerton and Lillywhite were the most gentlemanly and unassuming members of W. G. Grace's All-England XI.'

Sydney in the 1870s was a city of 130,000 people, only a fraction of today's 4 million, but a flourishing one nonetheless, which did not like to be reminded that convict transportation there had ceased just twenty years earlier. Fine new civic buildings were rising to rival those of Governor Macquarie; Lillywhite's men marvelled at the new renaissance-style Town Hall and the gothic Cathedral of St Andrew, gleaming in newly-finished sandstone. Sydney was a site favoured by nature, with its magnificent ports and the wealth of its hinterland, a city in which its people could take a justifiable pride; and nowhere was that pride more fully expressed than in the exploits of the New South Wales cricketers.

There were six free days before the England XI were to meet the New South Wales XV, but they practised little. Instead, they enjoyed all that Sydney had to offer. As in Adelaide they were given free rail travel and free entertainments. Like their modern counterparts, they were presented with free items of cricket kit. They were taken on all manner of drives, picnicked up the harbour, visited Sandringham, Botany Bay and South Head, and cheered on their countryman Robarts, a professional billiards player, who was giving away 600 in 1,100 to the best in Sydney and still winning.

Like Robarts, they too wanted to make a quick profit. Some of the players had brought cricket goods to sell, others had brought photographs. Sensing the interest of Sydney society, they quickly organized, with some like-minded Australians, a fancy dress ball 'in honour of the All-England and Australian cricketers', double tickets costing an exorbitant £1 (single gentlemen 12/6, single ladies 10/-). A fashionable band was hired, supper for five hundred organized and the Sydney Exhibition Building festooned with flowers and evergreens. Public opinion, however, began to swing against Lillywhite's men who were fiercely criticized as 'bent upon money-making'; the ball went on, but a mere four couples attended!

There was, however, tremendous local support for the strong New South Wales XV, conspicuous among whom were the Bannerman and Gregory brothers, the 23-year-old demon fast bowler Spofforth, a young wicket-keeper-batsman Billy Murdoch, and Edwin Evans, the current idol of Sydney, a medium pace bowler and stubborn bat. The Sydney cabbies, sensing the importance of the occasion, had doubled their fares. There was perfect weather, warm, genial sunshine tempered by a gentle north-east breeze. The Albert ground, Redfern, the home of the ambitious Albert Club for a dozen years, and Sydney's first enclosed ground, looked, according to a visitor, 'like an immense crowded circus . . .. Flags fluttered from a hundred points and the green trees and the green sward were exquisitely in contrast to the dust and heat of the outside city.' A public holiday had been declared and the grandstand overflowed with a thousand people. An unbroken ring of spectators, four or five deep, stood round the ground's wire fence, whilst the eastern terraces were packed with spectators sitting on the comfortable couch-grass. Card-sharps infiltrated the throng, plying their famous three-card tricks, until ejected by the police. 'There was plenty of the rough element', noted Southerton.

Wickets tumbled from the start. They usually did on the treacherous Albert ground, which was very bumpy and said to have been made up on a peat bog. By the end of the first day All-England had been bowled out for 121 and the New South Wales XV were 44–9. Betting, which had been heavy on both sides, was still in favour of the tourists. Wickets continued to fall on the second day, Lillywhite's men finding Edwin Evans almost unplayable as the ball jumped around, frequently chest high, one such 'bumpy ball' cannoning off John Selby's body onto the wicket. When the tourists' 2nd innings was over, New South Wales were left with 148 runs to win. There were still thirty minutes of play left but Jim Lillywhite, wishing for a good gate on the morrow, decided not to claim them. Cricket fever throbbed through the streets of Sydney that Friday night, as the crowd dispersed, spreading the news. 148 to win! There was said never to have been such excitement in the city before over any sporting event. The bookmakers worked overtime. Sydney in the 1870s was more renowned for betting than anywhere else in the whole British Empire.

The third day opened with the odds 3–1 against a home victory; as another big crowd assembled, the England players were alarmed to discover that the Australians had prepared a superb new wicket. This was within the rules, for captains often agreed to start each innings on a new strip, as Lillywhite and Joseph Coates had done on this occasion. As soon as the teams had left the ground on the Friday, a new wicket had been continuously watered; at dawn heavy rolling began and continued until the 1 o'clock start. There was much English anger that they had lost the opportunity of bowling at the Australians on a hard, bumpy wicket, but the mistake was entirely theirs.

A dour struggle ensued. Runs and wickets both came very slowly. The crowd grew more and more partisan. When the home side scored any runs, the spectators were delirious with joy, shouting and applauding until hoarse. When an Englishman did anything of note in the field, by contrast, 'ominous silence reigned supreme', whilst the visitors' umpire was singled out for particular abuse. The tall, bearded Dave Gregory, an authoritative figure (as befitted the father of sixteen children) had helped raise the score slowly from 27–2 to 40–2 when, in attempting to take a second run from a neat stroke to short-leg, he was given run out by Harry Jupp, who was umpiring despite his painful sciatica. This decision aroused a storm of yelling and booing which lasted many minutes. 'Go back, mate!' yelled the crowd in their thousands to Gregory. The howls of fury continued and a pitch invasion was only prevented by the admirable alacrity of Dave Gregory's departure to the pavilion. Later, as he made his painful way back to Tattersall's, Jupp was loudly and constantly jeered.

So intense and slow had been the play that a fourth day was required to bring a result, the New South Wales XV still needing another 25 to win with just 4 of their 14 wickets intact. Although so little cricket was left, so much money was at stake on the result that a crowd of 5,000 attended. Jim Lillywhite, in his own laconic prose, described the game's final moments: 'It having been arranged to play the match out, it was decided to commence at 4 o'clock on Monday. The XI were still favourites. A strong gale of wind blew straight down the wicket, which was much against the XI, as the medium-pace bowlers could not operate against it, and Lillywhite who had bowled very successfully on Saturday had to give way to Hill, Shaw delivering with the wind. A couple of 4s by Thompson caused the wildest excitement; but when he was run out soon after, the hopes of Sydney were considerably dampened, but no other wicket fell, and NSW won a magnificent match by 2 wickets.'

The jubilant spectators rushed onto the ground and bore the not-out batsmen, Powell and Garrett, on their shoulders to the pavilion, where the large gathering demanded the appearance of their favourites, Edwin Evans and Spofforth. After all the excitement of victory had calmed down, the players adjourned to the pavilion where champagne was produced and the Englishmen were toasted.

So Lillywhite's team had lost only its second match on Australian soil! So much for his proud forecast in Adelaide! He could, however, be consoled by his profits, for nearly 30,000 had attended the match and he had gained nearly £3,000, which would ensure the success of the whole trip. He also had the satisfaction of knowing that this match had taken twice as much money as all those played at Sydney by W. G. Grace on the previous tour.

There was, however, much concern expressed about the result. Rumours began to circulate in Sydney that the Englishmen had not tried to win the match. Such accusations were nothing new. A leading Melbourne bookmaker had been instrumental in bringing over Grace's team and, with the players heavily involved in wagers, 'the play of Grace and his team was looked upon with the utmost distrust' and accusations of their being bribed at Melbourne had caused something of a scandal. The possibility of Lillywhite's team being bribed at Sydney is a real one, particularly with the match so delicately balanced on the third and fourth days. Was it, indeed, with this final morning in mind that Alf Shaw wrote: 'Some of the members of our team, who need very small encouragement at any time to back their opinions and statements, were led to participate in enterprises they had better eschewed?' It is easy to believe so. However, there is one piece of strong evidence that the Englishmen *were* trying to win. It was a fine piece of fielding by Tom Armitage which effected a run-out on the last morning, which, but for Garrett's resolute batting, nearly ended things in All-England's favour. Armitage, a prodigious gambler, would certainly have been in the plot, if plot there was, to lose the match.

One is left, then, with Jim Southerton's own three reasons why the Englishmen lost. First, they underrrated the Australians. Second, they made a fatal error in not starting the last innings at the end of the second day. Third, they 'had been at Sydney long enough to make too many friends'. Their agent, Jack Conway, agreed with this final point. 'Was it', he asked, 'that many of the XI were not in their best trim, having spent what Falstaff calls the sweets of the night in the genial license of a tavern?'

The tempo of the tour now changed. So far the team had only played two matches after a month in Australia! In the next hectic month, however, they played seven matches. They visited Newcastle by sea, Goulburn by rail and travelled 400 miles overland to Melbourne. From there they journeyed to Ballarat and Geelong before returning by sea to Sydney, where they re-met the XV of New South Wales, lost disastrously and thereupon were challenged by a New South Wales XI. This historic encounter, for no English team in Australia had been met on terms of numerical equality before, ended in moral victory for Lillywhite. Soon after, he was sailing for New Zealand, with time at last to turn over in his memory kaleidoscopic impressions of the past month.

His memories of Newcastle were of hot, dusty days, mosquitoes and flies; there was Jupp's illness and the lucky presence of a young Englishman, Bob Kingsford, travelling with them and able to stand in as umpire. There was John Selby, making money for himself and team-mates by winning a 100-yards sprint against a local champion. Above all, there was an enormous attempt by the Newcastle temperance league to stop heaving drinking at the match.

Memories of Goulburn were necessarily dominated by the bare, loose wicket, the long grass in the outfield, and the two kangaroos and six hares acting as extra fielders. There was no one to roll the wicket and an absence of any measure with which to mark it out. Jim Lillywhite remembered too the Royal Hotel with its rock-solid mattresses (bad luck for Juppy) and its three billiards tables, the only source of amusement in that quiet little up-country town.

After Goulburn had come the big overland trek to Melbourne, first by rail to Bowning, then by Cobb's coach for 32 hours and 185 bruising miles to Albury, and finally 185 miles by Victorian Railways. The coach, said to hold eighteen, barely held their party of fifteen (which included agent, money-taker and stand-in umpire). Inside, it had three cross-seats, upright, narrow and uncomfortable. Outside there was room for two on the box in front and four at the back, all six constantly in danger of falling overboard as they jolted their way over unmetalled roads. Specific incidents came to mind from that nightmare journey. There was Alf Shaw, using his gun to bag a fine hawk, a guana and a 3ft lizard. There was the coachman borrowing an axe to cut a new bar after a breakage only eighteen miles from Albury. There were the jokes about being held up by Ned Kelly as they passed through that bandit's favourite territory. Fortunately he didn't show up. Then finally, there was their own comical appearance, as they were greeted on their arrival at Melbourne, smothered with sand and dust and looking, said Southerton, as if they had been working in a Roman cement factory!

Lillywhite would remember the team having its Christmas lunch at 1a.m. at the Old White Hart after their arrival in Melbourne. Exhausted, sore and bruised, they had but a few hours' rest before facing the XV of Victoria. He remembered too the torrential rain which ruined the Bank Holiday atmosphere at the Melbourne Cricket Club, the collapsed marquee, the screaming occupants, and the distressed ladies, trudging through the puddles, their dresses dripping with water. Only 20 runs were scored during that first day's play, but at least the takings were

£700, and more than covered the £250 he had had to pay the East Melbourne Club for not using its ground.

He remembered Midwinter, whose big hitting had helped the Victorian XV to victory, one 5 off Shaw clearing the spectators easily and going 120 yards. Midwinter was an interesting fellow, impressively powerful physically and said to be the son of a failed gold prospector. He remembered Frank Allan, too, the most idolized of all Australian bowlers, an impressively fast left-arm roundarm bowler. But his strongest memory of Melbourne was its fierce criticism of his XI. What had the *Australasian* said? 'Future speculators in cricket must bear in mind that we must have the very best article that can be imported. Had the two Graces been in the team . . ..'

Lillywhite turned his thoughts down pleasanter Melbourne byways . . . the 30,000 spectators at the superb ground, the new pavilion, the £3,000 profit, of which he was entitled to no less than 90%, a delightful luncheon at St Kilda's . . .

Then the railway journey on New Year's Day to Ballarat and its gold-mines. The welcome of the Mayor of West Ballarat and the peals of the Town Hall's bells in their honour. The welcome next day from the Mayor of East Ballarat and the drive round the town. Whose liquor was the better? The descent down a gold-mine, the new Kohinoor, and the ascent of some very dirty cricketers, plastered in pipeclay, not very long before start of play. And not a nugget, alas, for their troubles! Jupp's sudden disappearance into the bush, nobody knowing where, and his return several days later, with inflamed eyes. His wild, despairing look, when ordered by the Ballarat doctor to stay in a darkened room for two weeks. The dreadful wicket, the bravery of Armitage and Hill, batting on despite many bruises.

The train to Geelong, the farewell to Juppy, who was travelling back to Melbourne to see a doctor; the Corio Club's improved ground, its pride in the acquisition of running water; the delay to the start of the match, the wicket having been over-watered; the 264 runs of the All-England XI, their highest innings so far; the kindness of a Corio vice-president, who had shown them round the racing stables at his St Albans home and later given them the best supper – champagne, cigars and singing – they had ever had;

the golden locket won by Selby in another 100-yard sprint; the hardness of the Geelong hotel beds; the essential quietness of this pretty little place nestling around Corio Bay, memories that would remain with him for ever.

Then, the return by sea from Melbourne to Sydney, which brought the most painful memory of all, the utter humiliation of their second defeat at the hands of the New South Wales XV, and of being bowled out in the first innings for a paltry 35! It was possible, of course, to make excuses. They had arrived at Sydney sick and weary at 4.00am and had only had a day's rest before beginning the match. They were again without the services of their most reliable and experienced batsman, whilst they were facing, in Spofforth, a bowler of very special class. There was no escaping, however, that heavy drinking was responsible for lack of runs. Jim Lillywhite felt severely let down but, as one Sydney reporter pointed out, the greatest fault lay in his own complaisant attitude to what was happening off the field of play: 'A professional team, without some recognized head, empowered with authority and imbued with a will to control them, will never be a success from a cricket point of view. To play cricket successfully, it is necessary to have a clear head, a quick eye, and well-balanced nerves, qualities which I am compelled to admit were seldom exhibited by four or five of the All-England professional XI.'

There was one further aspect of the debacle which upset Jim Lillywhite as he entrusted his tour profits to a Sydney bank before the trip to New Zealand. Stories of bribery were again rife. All-England had been clear favourites, 2–1 at the beginning, and the result, as Southerton conceded, 'made the layers of odds look very blue'. As at Melbourne, where 'our losing caused some of our boys to have a roughish time of it', so at Sydney the English players were not popular amongst the bookmakers.

Certainly the batting in that dramatic first innings was, at the least, dreadfully stupid. Before a run had been scored Ulyett ran up the wicket to a fast, short-pitched delivery by Spofforth and was easily stumped by Billy Murdoch. He seemed to make no effort to regain his crease and Southerton was scathing: 'He made a dash up the wicket and was never near the ball, standing to see himself put out.' Then Greenwood was bowled by a full-toss and shortly afterwards Emmett and Charlwood both 'foolishly' ran themselves out. Pooley had already given a possible catch before he was clean bowled. Armitage, offered a loose ball from Spofforth, 'let the bowler off' and was shortly after clean bowled. Hill was stumped 'as he incautiously stepped out of his ground'. The English first innings, then, was a tale of self-inflicted wounds and the second went little better. Ulyett was bowled first ball and in no time at all the team was 7–3. Selby, the hope of the side, 'in attempting to hit one to leg, turned it into his wicket.' All in all, therefore, rumours of bribery were understandable.

There were two free days before the voyage to New Zealand, and New South Wales now challenged Lillywhite to a contest of eleven-a-side. His advisers ruled against accepting, reckoning that a defeat would destroy credibility for the rest of the tour. Lillywhite, bravely, chose to accept. Perhaps he wished to redeem himself with the Sydney public. At any rate some firm leadership off the field is at last discernible, for the team was taken away to the quiet watering place of Sans Souci, twelve miles from the bright lights of Sydney, where they spent a quiet Sunday and endured an early departure to bed.

The match caught the city's imagination and the crowd was accordingly as vociferous in its enthusiasm as in the first encounter at the Albert ground, loudly querying many of the umpires' decisions. Southerton was shocked: 'It was the most unruly crowd I have ever seen and the cricket people here seem afraid to say anything to them. Their conduct is at times disgraceful, even in the presence of the Governor.' This time, however, the England team stood firm. Ulyett, in particular, had a splendid game, scoring a vigorous 94, which turned out to be the highest innings of the tour and, bowling with real ferocity, made a number of direct hits on the batsmen. Even though Tom Armitage's 'full pitchers and daisy cutters caused roars of laughter' and 'he was evidently out of form and soon got out of temper', at the end of two days the England XI was close to a decisive innings victory. It was a significant match in the discussions which it now provoked. Already, since December, there had been plans for the England XI on their return from New Zealand, to meet a combined XIII of Victoria and New South Wales. But in the light of recent Australian successes it was now decided that the combined team should be an XI. Accordingly, as Lillywhite embarked on the *Tararua* for the 1,100 miles by sea to New Zealand, his Victorian friend Jack Conway was left behind to begin negotiations with individual players of Victoria and New South Wales. The fate of the first Test match was in his hands.

For five days the players were buffeted at sea. Everyone suffered, and Tom Emmett, who suffered most, declared that his face had been so drawn up in pain that it would 'never return to its natural beauty'. Eventually they sighted the snow-capped mountains of Hokitika and, sailing up the west coast of South Island, they anchored off Greymouth for a while, much to Jim Lillywhite's embarrassment, for the Greymouth Club committee came out in a steamer to prevail upon him to honour his promise to play the first match there. Jim Lillywhite, however, knew that if he delayed at Greymouth, he would miss the celebrations of Auckland's Anniversary Day, which, he was told, would help generate a lucrative gate, and so, with threats of legal injunctions ringing over the waters, he sailed on. At Nelson the team paused to embark in the *Wellington*, 'a very small dirty craft', and endured 'a good shaking up' over the final passage to Auckland, sharing between them a cabin of eight tiny berths. When the jaded travellers finally approached the wharf at Onehunga, on deck and well muffled in great coats against the early morning rain, their first reception at New Zealand proved a very enthusiastic one. There was much cheering and shaking of hands, the Hobson brass band sang a song of welcome, composed for the occasion, and a drag and six greys waited to take the heroes off to the Victoria Hotel in triumph. The cricketers, however, got in somewhat glumly. 'We wanted our breakfast', wrote Southerton, 'but found we had to go five miles before our arrival in Auckland.'

Only George Parr, in 1864, had before brought an English cricket team to New Zealand, and Parr had merely visited Dunedin and Christchurch, so it was a truly pioneering itinerary which Bennett had arranged. The first part of the programme provided the tourists with victories at Auckland, Wellington, Taranaki and Nelson and an honourable draw at Greymouth. Highlights were the magnificient scenery, the warm welcomes, the lavish entertainment and the easy money to be made from betting. The tourists, however, were unlucky with the weather and unhappy with poor pitches, low attendances and awful hotels and steamers.

The hardships of travel began as soon as they left Auckland (where they had enjoyed their stay, Lillywhite writing of 'a very pretty town, with about 20,000 inhabitants, who were very kind to us'), Lillywhite had paid the captain of the *Wellington* £70 to delay his departure to fit in with the end of the All-England match and no doubt regretted it as they sailed south to Wellington, spending the two nights curled up uncomfortably on the benches of the saloon, as the ship rolled in heavy seas. At daytime in thick fog and heavy rain it was not easy for them to appreciate the beauty of the wild mountain scenery which they were passing, numerous gorges running down to the water's edge, forming numberless bays. It was a dangerous journey, with sunken reefs and bald, rocky cliffs waiting for the unwary and it ended with a turbulent crossing of the Cook Strait. This difficult three-day journey, however, was forgotten in the drama of their reception at Wellington. As they approached, a steamer, coming out to meet them, fired off a gun from its bows, a signal for all the ships in the harbour to fire off a salute. There were at least 5,000 excited people waiting on the wharf for the 'masters of the willow', and there was the usual cheering, music and waiting drags. 'Who wouldn't be an English cricketer', murmured a lady passenger in awe.

Rain-swept Wellington, its wooden houses rising in terraces one above the other from the water's misty edge, did not impress them. 'It looked like one long street running round the end of a lake-like bay', wrote Southerton. Under leaden, ever-opening skies, its streets were quagmires.

From Wellington they sailed north to Taranaki, in humid weather, but on waters so troubled that the decks were for ever awash, the team confined below and the stewards in foul tempers.

It was so rough that there was a fear on arrival that they would not be able to go ashore in the usual little surf boats. For a while they bobbed off Taranaki, watching snow-capped Mount Egmont and listening with interest to tales of the iron-impregnated seashore. Was there, the XI wondered, a profit to be made from it? On landing, they compared Taranaki, with mild censure, to a quiet English country village.

They enjoyed better weather on the subsequent passage south to Nelson but the small steamer which took them on to Greymouth with its mixed cargo of pigs and poultry was distinctly unimpressive: 'We had to sleep on the seats, tables or floor, as best we could, and, as the steward was very drunk and the boat full, we again had not a rosy time of it.' Nonetheless, the reception at Greymouth suggested that earlier threats of legal action had been forgotten. A bonfire was lit, blue flares kindled, and rockets soared gaily into the night sky. Yet despite these encouragements, the town-loving Englishmen were disappointed to discover that Greymouth itself was nothing but a collection of huts and cottages, humbly hiding from an encroaching sea.

Dowdy hotels also came as an unpleasant shock. Wellington's Panama Hotel was squalid and Gilmer's Hotel at Greymouth offered 'very hard beds, or rather mattresses, as a bed out here is a great rarity'. The Masonic Hotel, Nelson, offered a few double beds only, so most of the party had to spend at least one night resting on rugs and 'shakedowns' in a large dining-room (where a group clustered round a piano and sang their way through the night). Worst of all, however, was the Ship Hotel at Taranaki. Its rooms, with wafer-thin partitions, contained such uncomfortable beds that Southerton in curiosity dissected one with a knife. He discovered that 'lumpy tow' was the reason why it was preferable to sleep on the floor. The bedroom windows had broken panes and were fastened by string. The ceilings, rain-stained and damp, had holes in them 'like chimneys'.

If the hotels were disappointing, so was the cricket. The opposition XXIIs offered no real resistance in the first matches and whereas the All-England XI raised some big scores (225 v Auckland and 248 v Nelson), opposition wickets tumbled. Taranaki, for example, were bowled out for 32 and 47, Greymouth for 50, Wellington for 31 and 38. The English slow bowlers were particularly effective, Southerton taking 13 Greymouth wickets in one innings, and Shaw the same number at Auckland. Shaw also took 13 for 11 against Wellington and no less than 28 Nelson wickets. When he did the hat-trick at Wellington, the match temporarily came to a halt as 'the fielders, in accordance with custom, dubbed up their shilling each for a new hat for the bowler, and then rushed away for refreshments.'

There was a temptation for the XI to treat the cricket light-heartedly. When a feeble Wellington player 'refused to move his bat', four Englishmen came up and stood a yard away from him. In the field at Auckland 'the larky style adopted by several of the All-England players' was remarked upon, while net practice one cold, damp day at Auckland was done in overcoats. The one-sided nature of the conflicts must have been demoralizing for the home sides and on the last day of the long, rain-affected match with Wellington, only sixteen of the twenty-two turned up.

Nevertheless there was much good cricket for the spectators to admire. Pooley's showmanship behind the stumps always took the eye. 'The rapidity with which he performs his work is simply marvellous', said one Aucklander. 'Pooley caused much mirth by his agility', wrote another. 'He played about as if the mere duty of keeping wicket was not half onerous enough to occupy his superfluous energy.' There was great interest also in the return of Jupp, who had sailed from Melbourne to meet the team at Taranaki. After an absence of eleven matches he played only his second innings of the tour at Nelson, where he batted all day for 30. It says much for the Nelsonians that 'his steady, dogged play was greatly admired among the spectators'.

The grounds were not easy ones for the display of cricketing skills nor were they well suited to a professional tour. The Auckland club had developed a pitch on the Ellerslie racecourse, four or five miles out of the city, and the grandstand was so far distant from the wicket that it contained only one long-sighted occupant. Though the pitch played well, the outfield was rough and in need of cutting. The Wellington ground, at the Basin Reserve, was small, less than 100 yards across, similarly rough and, after much rain, very boggy. The marshy ground one evening proved too much for the four horses of the team's coach and for an hour and a half the players heaved and pulled, to extricate themselves from six inches of mud. At Taranaki, they played on an ill-defined racecourse, the ground consisting of 'a ploughed field with a scanty growth of grass'. What grass there was grew in tufts about six inches high. The wicket at Nelson, by contrast, played well but the outfield was poor and the players not pleased to have to use the scorer's tent for changing. The committee had not bothered to get boundaries marked out and so the ball was frequently disappearing into groups of spectators with the batsmen still running. Most bizarre of all was the desolate ground two miles outside Greymouth on another isolated race-course. After journeying out on a wheezing train, the players, to reach the ground, had to cross a lagoon by means of a rickety wooden bridge; on the last day of the match the rain had washed away part of this bridge so that boats had to be procured to ferry the players over. All these difficulties the players faced with the true spirit of pioneers. 'In this wild-looking place', wrote South-erton, 'it looked anything but like an All-England match being played, but we were in it and had to go through.'

This stoic acceptance of physical discomfort did not bring much financial reward, the gates at most matches being very low. The failure at Auckland was the direct result of the bungling Bennett, who foolishly had fixed the game at the same time as the Auckland Anniversary Regatta. He also accepted venues where as good a view could be obtained outside the ground as within. Thus the Victory Square ground at Nelson was overlooked by an immense hill on one side, forming a natural grandstand. Bennett was told – and ingenuously believed – that the locals would not take advantage of this. One Nelson resident even put up a grandstand in his garden.

Inevitably the matches did not make much money. The takings of the first day at Greymouth, for example, amounted to only £32. 'A nice sum to come 14,000 miles for!' complained Souther-ton. But the losses were not borne entirely by Lillywhite, as, more often than not, the tourists sold their right to the profits in the smaller fixtures to local speculators, a useful insurance policy. The best bargain was the £600 received at Wellington, a sum which the purchaser, plagued with bad weather, could not hope to recoup. Negotiations for a match at Wanganui are instructive. Bennett had been negotiating to sell the match for £50, in addition to which he wanted all travelling expenses, including steamer passage, and 'the privileges of the ground', which in effect meant free food and drink throughout. In the end the Wanganui committee jibbed at the cost of the steamer tickets and Lillywhite instructed Bennett to cancel the fixture.

The low gates probably alerted the players to the need to look after their financial interests. To this end they travelled throughout New Zealand with two 'money-takers', one of whom, Alf Bramhall, took responsibility for the team's betting and the other, a cousin of the captain's called Collins, oversaw the collecting of gate money. Both men looked after the sale of souvenirs, such as a revolving card which opened up to show the vignette likenesses of the players, two at a time. The betting tended to focus on anything except the predictable outcome of the matches: the size of the crowd or the likelihood of a team reaching a certain total were popular items. For example odds of 6-4 were laid at Ellerslie that Auckland would not reach a score of 150. Income from betting could be augmented by special rewards offered for outstanding personal performances. The greenstone pendant, which Charlwood won as top scorer at Wellington, would have been much coveted.

John Selby's races provided the team with regular, lucrative betting. His opponents were well-supported local champions, the matches usually arranged through cricket contacts. Thus the captain of the Wellington XXII helped organize a race and also acted as the referee. With very large sums at stake, rules were carefully drawn up, often in a bar the night before the race. Selby usually won, but he seems to have lost, for tactical reasons, on occasion. He was, for example, severely beaten at Ballarat by a runner called Sharp, when the odds were low. This encouraged heavy betting elsewhere in support of local runners who had beaten Sharp.

Selby's most profitable run was against Ellis, 'the Auckland flyer'. It took place on the road from Auckland to Onehunga just before the team sailed for Wellington. At 8.15 in the morning, only forty-five minutes before the steamer's departure, several crowded drags stopped at the Junction Hotel, Newmarket. A course was selected on a straight piece of road, a trifle downhill, and a row of turf sods was placed in the middle of the road throughout the length of the 100 yards course. There was an umpire and a starter, the latter using a pistol and empowered to recall the runners if either man started too soon. A false start was to be penalized by a one-yard handicap. Stakes of £100 a side had been deposited the night before at the Victoria Hotel, the team's headquarters, and a further £100 per runner had since been wagered. As the men stripped, it was noted that Ellis was the taller and the stronger, though Selby 'exhibited plenty of muscle on the loins and thighs'. Odds were offered, just before the start, of 6-4 on Selby, but there were no local takers, for the Aucklanders knew that Selby had been beaten by Sharp of Ballarat. Besides, the Englishmen's late night carousing was the talk of the town. There was no way that Ellis, who had recently won the Sydney Cup, could be beaten!

Twice the pistol was fired for the start and twice Ellis bounded away leaving Selby standing on his mark. 'Ye needn't joomp about like that', shouted Selby, 'Eh don't mean to go till yo' stan' still.' Ellis, his concentration upset, then started too soon, and was penalized by a yard. They got away properly the third shot and Ellis tried vainly to lessen the gap. After fifty yards, however, it had doubled. At 70 yards Selby confidently glanced behind him, thereby losing half a yard of his lead, but he put on a tremendous final spurt and won by a comfortable two and a half yards, huge shouts of joy coming from his fellow cricketers at the finishing line.

'The scene in the saloon of the ss *Wellington*', wrote a chastened Auckland reporter, 'before that vessel left the wharf was a sorry one for Auckland eyes. On the table was a heap of notes and gold, and each member of the eleven as he came up added something to it. Selby was seated at the table with his pocket book out, totting up the amount.'

In Lillywhite's day a very discreet veil was drawn over the players' private lives, so one reads little of the ladies who no doubt flung themselves at these glamorous English adventurers at every port of call. But one lady, at least, a Mrs Radcliffe, briefly entered the story at Greymouth, and, like many a *femme fatale* before her, nearly wrought great ruin.

The next fixture after Greymouth's dreary racecourse was hundreds of miles away at Christchurch, against an XVIII of Canterbury. At Greymouth the team met Mrs Radcliffe, the landlady of Warner's Commercial Hotel, Christchurch, and it was she, it would seem, who persuaded Lillywhite to travel overland by coach, across the southern mountains, rather than round the coast by steamer. Quite *why* the Englishmen agreed to entrust themselves to a hated Cobb's coach over 200 miles of mountain roads it is difficult to tell. Perhaps they had had enough of local steamers, drunken stewards and stuffy cabins. Perhaps the delightful Mrs Radcliffe had made them an offer they could not refuse. Whatever the cause, the luggage was sent on to Christchurch by sea, Ted Pooley being given the job of looking after it, whilst the rest of the team (plus their agent, two money-takers and a young Christchurch artist) prepared to take the scenic route with Mrs Radcliffe.

There was an inauspicious beginning. At the agreed starting time of 6.00 a.m. one player was missing, 'fancying some other person's bed better than his own' and a search of 'various places of resort' delayed them. Meanwhile Lillywhite and Bennett organized the party's distribution between the two coaches, (each to be pulled by four horses), rechecking the cricket bags which had been flung on the coaches' roofs.

It could not have been long before the players began to wonder if they had made the right decision to travel by land. As the coaches made their way up into the mountains, the cricketers frequently had to jump down and walk, mile after mile, ahead of the panting horses. When they climbed back on board for the descents, those on top would cling on grimly to avoid being shaken off (Collins the money-taker providing a terrible warning, when he dozed off, fell into the road, and narrowly avoided being run over), whilst those sitting inside on the benches would hit their heads on the roof every time a wheel jumped over a pot-hole. The road, when not climbing up or running down a mountain, followed the courses of rivers, which frequently had to be crossed, sometimes by ferry, sometimes by ford. Flooded rivers, like the Taipo, half-a-mile across, presented a very real hazard: 'It is no easy matter', wrote Southerton, 'for a coachman to drive over such a track, the water rearing over the boulders as large as coal scuttles, over which the horses have to scramble and the coach wheels, now up, now down, with a thump enough to break them into splinters, and sending the inside passengers from one side to the other.' To increase their discomfort, by mid-afternoon it was pouring with rain and by nightfall Lillywhite and Ulyett, sitting on the box seats, were soaked through.

Eighteen hours into the journey, at midnight, as the rain continued to pour down, they reached the famous Otira river and gorge. Southerton and his fellows in the first coach were told to cross the swollen river on foot, by means of a narrow wooden bridge, which proved inadequate. One player fell through and was, with difficulty, rescued; the rest, finding the bridge broken off, were forced to wade through the rising river: 'There we were in the bed of the river, with the elements as bad as anyone can possibly imagine; on either side of us were mountains 3,000 feet high, the river rising rapidly, no one knowing which way to move in the utter darkness, and not a soul to hear us, shout as loud as we could . . .' At this critical moment the lights of the coach, coming through the waters, appeared from the darkness and Southerton's party, drenched to the skin, swam, rode or waded with it. Safe on the far side, they stumbled over boulders and stumps of trees towards a stone cottage, called the Otira Hotel, where they divested themselves of their wet clothes and leapt into the four small beds which, said Southerton, were all the hotel had to offer.

The second coach, containing Mrs Radcliffe, Lillywhite and six others, was less lucky. They had tried to drive through but a horse fell down and they found themselves stranded in the middle of the swollen river, which was rapidly rising. The coachman shouted to the players to alight and help him raise the horse. At first, in fear, they refused, but when he screamed that they were in danger of drowning, they jumped out in a hurry, Charlwood catching his foot in his ulster coat and falling in head first. Eventually they raised the horse and, amidst an ever rising torrent, the stranded coach was pulled, boulder by boulder, to safety. Ulyett reckoned that he swam most of the way across, but Armitage, carrying Mrs Radcliffe on his shoulders, must have found an easier fording place.

Inside the hotel at last, they demanded drink, consumed the sum total of the premises (three bottles of very rough brandy) and stripped off their wet clothes. Standing in bare feet on the swimming stone floor, they wrung their clothes in front of the fire which the first coach party had lit. They had nothing else to wear for their main luggage was somewhere on the seas with Pooley, whilst their cricket bags were wet through. With admirable stoicism they filled their pipes and smoked their way through what remained of the night. There were no chairs, but a few tried sleeping on tables, or even on the floor wrapped in blankets. It was to be significant later, though it seemed not so at the time, that Greenwood's soaking hat had been badly burnt, as it dried in front of the open hearth.

The next morning dawned bright and fine so the All-England XI put out their overcoats and shoes to dry. There being nothing to eat, the owner of the house set off with his horse and gun and returned in about two hours with a sheep, which the players helped cut up and roast. Ulyett meanwhile made some bread cakes, tending them with the only implement available, a hayfork. By noon it was raining again but the coaches set out once more in the early afternoon. However, two miles up the road they came across a landslide and were forced to return to spend a second night at Otira. Once more it was a question of making the best of a difficult time, smoking their pipes and playing cards deep into the night, for the floors and tables offered little chance of sleep.

The reminiscences of both Southerton and Ulyett fail to mention how Mrs Radcliffe, the Christchurch landlady, spent these nights. However, Alf Shaw, who usually followed Southerton's account slavishly for his own book of reminiscences, for once put in details entirely of his own: 'The lady passenger, whom Armitage so gallantly carried through the flood, was made as comfortable for the night as circumstances would permit by the woman who was in charge of the shanty'. It is possible, however, that this prim chaperoning is simply a gloss, pandering to the sensibilities of the readers of 1902. Moreover, the accounts vary mysteriously about the number of available beds, Ulyett recalling that five jumped into the only one. There, perhaps, one should hastily abandon conjecture of Mrs Radcliffe's whereabouts at Otira.

At a quarter to five the next morning the journey recommenced in pouring rain and it ended eighteen hours later on the plains of Canterbury. This was a further gruelling time, involving more ascents and descents of narrow, precipitous tracks (Charlwood so nervous that he took to running behind his coach), more hard walking (once across a plank with 100 ft drops below) and more river crossings, at one of which Tom Emmett and Harry Jupp came to blows. Jupp, riding inside the coach and comparatively dry, had taken exception to being asked to get out and wade across a deep river, whilst Emmett, who was already soaked to the skin, continued to sit on the box. Accordingly, Jupp climbed up and pulled Tom Emmett off his seat.

By late evening on the third day of their trek they reached Porter's Pass, with a startling view of a valley 6,000 feet below; one final descent brought them to Sheffield, the end of their sixty-hour coach journey. But even here their saga of misadventure continued, for there was no train ready to take them on to Christchurch, and they had to spend one further uncomfortable night, smoking their pipes or sleeping on a hotel's sofas and floor. One can imagine their mixed emotions next day at 9.30 a.m. as they were met at Christchurch station by the sportsmen of Canterbury and driven in state in a drag to Warner's Commercial Hotel, run by Mrs Radcliffe's husband. There they had a quick bath, a big breakfast, read letters from home (forwarded from Melbourne by Conway), and then returned to the drag to go out to play against the Christchurch XVIII.

Christchurch had been waiting eagerly for the arrival of the All-England XI. A new grandstand had been erected and eighteen good cricketers, the majority public school men from England, had been assembled. The Midland Canterbury Club had ninety members and Christchurch cricket was reckoned the best in New Zealand.

The England XI, by contrast, were not so ready for the fray, being 'cold, stiff and sore'. Some, like Shaw, could scarcely move. Pooley, who had twisted a leg badly at Nelson, was still unfit and umpired. Fortunately Jim Lillywhite won the toss and batted, before a crowd of 10,000, with betting of 2-1 in favour of England and 2-1 on Canterbury not being defeated in one innings.

Ironically, the sun was now shining brightly, but it is doubtful if the England players were able to appreciate the prettiness of the scene at the Hagley Park ground. Wickets tumbled at once, to the derision of the crowd. At 30–7 the match seemed lost, but the gallant Southerton held on with Allen Hill, a hard hitter, and a more respectable total of 70 was finally reached. At the close Canterbury were 27–4. That evening some of the Canterbury newspapers were less than kind about the Englishmen, which added to their overall tiredness and low spirits. Ulyett, however, persuaded his captain that a case of champagne would be in order. 'We 'ad a merry evening' recalled 'Happy Jack'. 'Next daay we went ont' field new men.'

Next day indeed All-England got back into the game and, in the last innings, Canterbury needed 108 to win. They failed by just 23 runs. 'It was a close thing', explained Southerton, 'for the Christchurch batting style was so different and so superior to anything we have seen on this side of the line.'

Altogether over 25,000 people watched the game. However, very few paid and the match was a financial disaster. Bennett had blundered again. Both at Christchurch and Dunedin cricket was played on public grounds, which could not be fenced off.

Despite the financial setback, the victory at Christchurch was a great triumph for the Englishmen, showing them at their resolute best. Sadly a betting incident was to mar this victory and, indeed, to overshadow the rest of the tour. It began simply enough. On the final night at Christchurch, with the home team still to bat, the England players as usual were looking for bets. A trick of long standing was to offer the unwary a pound to a shilling that one could name the individual score of every member of the local team. This Ted Pooley now offered, at £6 to 6 shillings, to a

Christchurch surveyor called Ralph Donkin, who was living at Warner's Hotel. Donkin accepted carelessly, whereupon Pooley forecast that every single member of the Canterbury XVIII would score o. He knew that it only needed one of the locals to be out for o for him to make money on this bet. As it happened, six of the home team did not score and that night Alf Bramhall duly gave Ralph Donkin £3 12s od and asked him for £36. The aggrieved Donkin refused.

There was, meanwhile, other betting interest. John Selby had arranged to run three races, after the match, against a member of the Canterbury XVIII, over 100, 250 and 300 yards, each for £5 a side. Selby duly won the first race by several yards but he lost the second race and was so distressed after it that he forfeited the last race. His backers in the England team would have lost heavily, and, having paid up themselves, were in no mood for tolerating Ralph Donkin's non-payment of Pooley's bet.

In the bar of Warner's hotel later that evening, around 8.30, Donkin found himself surrounded by a number of English players. Pooley threatened Donkin and swung a punch at him, knocking him back. When a friend of Donkin's came forward, Selby intervened. 'Hooold on, ol' chap. Two can plaay that gaame.' The towering Ulyett moved in, shaking off a burly local who tried to restrain him. Selby shouted to Donkin, 'We'll haave it out o' you before mornin'' and he and Ulyett began pummelling the unfortunate surveyor, until Charlwood, fearing that the brawl was getting out of hand, persuaded Donkin to leave the bar with him and go across the road to the theatre. A further scuffle, however, took place at the hotel entrance in Cathedral Square. Donkin was struck hard several times and tried to ward off his attacker by flourishing his stick. He was, however, thrown down to the ground and punched in the face by Ulyett, before someone else rushed in to break up the fight. Donkin went upstairs to his room to wash his bloody face and an English player tried to force his way in, but was persuaded by the hotel-keeper from breaking down the door. 'I'll have your xxxxing money before morning!' cried the Englishman as he departed downstairs.

Donkin by this time was thoroughly frightened and crept out of the hotel at around 9.00 p.m., having decided that he would stay away all night. The England players, hardly able to think straight after the fatigue and strain of the last few days and the worse for drink after a farewell dinner, broke into Donkin's room later that night and ransacked the room. Drawers were pulled out and clothes strewn around. Two of Donkin's felt hats were put in a basin full of water. Coats, waistcoats and trousers were ripped up, a black top hat was crushed. Some of Donkin's surveying plans were burnt in a chamber pot. Those responsible left no clue, apart from a hat, which bore marks of having been burnt by a fire. . . .

The next morning, at 7.00 o'clock, the team set out for Dunedin on a 24-hour journey by train and steamer. The match against a XXII of Otago started as soon as they arrived. In a remarkable display of resilience the weary Englishmen got to within 20 runs of victory when the match ended in a draw. Lillywhite himself, who had badly bruised a hand at Christchurch, took 12 wickets and the indefatigable Southerton took 8.

It had been a most successful match from every angle. Cricket was prospering at Dunedin, with three new clubs formed that year. The All-England XI's arrival had inspired yet another new grandstand, a scorecard printing press, and the usual luncheon booths, fruit stalls and fancy bazaars. Scottish influence was evident in the appearance in the luncheon intervals of a drum and fife band. Enthusiasm was enormous. The local hero, Dixon, scored 13 slow runs, yet was granted a triumphal return to the pavilion on the shoulders of his admirers and was later presented with a silver inkstand. Crowds of up to 5,000 attended and were more conscientious in their payment than those at Christchurch, so that proceeds added up to £460 and the Dunedin cricket club, which had prior assets of only £5 13s 9d, must have been well pleased. As at Christchurch a genteel, upper-class atmosphere prevailed.

This gay, if slightly prim, cricketing garden party came to a shocked conclusion, however, when news began to circulate at the end of the match of the arrest of Pooley and Alf Bramhall, charged with maliciously injuring property at Christchurch. The arrest seems to have been completely unexpected. Pooley had been in his usual good humour behind the stumps. He seems too to have taken the first news of Donkin's complaints with some levity, for Conway wrote: 'A warrant was issued for Pooley's arrest and an opportunity was offered him to compromise the matter. Pooley treated the matter with indifference; the majesty of the law was upheld.'

There was little that Jim Lillywhite could do but travel onwards without him. The arrest had been made between the end of the match at 5.40 p.m. and the team's departure by special train for Invercargill at 7 o'clock. There were no pauses in the schedule. The day the team arrived at Invercargill they started their 3-day match, and, on the third evening, having won, they were sailing back to Melbourne.

Ted Pooley and Albert Bramhall did not appear before the Christchurch Supreme Court until 14 April, over a month later. There were various legal delays, one being the need to wait for witnesses for the defence to arrive from Australia. Donkin brought as his witnesses two waiters and a chambermaid from Warner's Commercial Hotel. Witnesses for the defence included the Christchurch fast bowler and treasurer, T. S. Sweet, plus a bookmaker, a billiard-marker from Warner's Hotel, a bridge-keeper and Hugh Cassidy, the proprietor of a Greymouth coaching firm, who had himself driven one of the coaches on that epic journey across the mountains. It was quickly established that Bramhall had been wrongly identified and was not with Pooley that evening. He had, in fact, been settling accounts over score-cards and photographs with several New Zealanders. There was also doubt about Pooley's identification. The burnt hat suggested Greenwood's involvement. Witnesses agreed that Pooley was of the same build as both Greenwood and Selby. Pooley and Bramhall were therefore both acquitted, but poor Pooley had lost much. Even though the Christchurch players presented him with £50 and a gold ring, by the terms of the agreement with Jim Lillywhite 'every member of the team forfeited £10 for every day he did not play through his own fault'. By this reckoning Pooley would have been fined £220.

The worst loss of all was that All-England did not have a proper wicket-keeper when they came to play the combined XI of New South Wales and Victoria in the first Test match. It was also a setback for the punters, who, quite reasonably, had put early money on All-England. Indeed, with this in mind, the arrest of Pooley takes on sinister connotations. It is possible, for example, that an influential betting ring in Australia manipulated events in New Zealand to its advantage. Was it just coincidence that the arrest of Pooley took place in the eighty minutes between the end of a match and departure for another town? Was it just bad luck that damage in a bedroom of £5 resulted in a month and a half's detention? Why, moreover, should the trial have been delayed, allegedly whilst important witnesses were summoned from Melbourne, when, in the event, no such witnesses appeared? Was this simply a delaying tactic, to ensure that the All-England XI played their vital match in Melbourne with a weakened team? If, indeed, Ralph Donkin and his friends were 'planted' at Warner's Hotel to get the English team into trouble with the law, then the outcome of cricket's first Test match was seriously affected by organized crime.

If Melbourne betting syndicates *were* attempting to subvert the first Test match, then Bennett's travel arrangements aided them, for, after a terribly rough six days' passage, the Englishmen stepped ashore at 5.00 a.m. with the match to begin on the morrow. By contrast, the five Sydney players had arrived at Melbourne by sea a week earlier.

In Lillywhite's and Bennett's absence, Jack Conway had organized the match well, ignoring hostility towards it from Sydney and solving the problem of achieving agreement between the two rival cricket associations by simply ignoring them and contacting the players direct. He received a mixed response. Frank Allen, Victoria's leading bowler, preferred to patronize his local carnival (which caused him much unpopularity and a round of hissing at the Warrnambool races), Sydney's F. R. Spofforth, piqued because Victoria's Blackham had been preferred as wicket-keeper to his own friend Billy Murdoch ('the only one who knows how to take me properly'), declined to play (and was much criticized in Melbourne for his vanity), while Edwin Evans decided against the journey for family reasons.

Melbourne's response to the match was as ambivalent as that of the cricketers, crowds of 4000 and 5000, 10,000 and 2000 attending the four days. Nonetheless the match was certainly a big social event, the members' lawn resplendent with the fashionable youth and beauty of the day. The younger elements of the lower social scale were there in abundance too, outside, clinging to the gum-trees in Yarra Park – the very trees which Bannerman's fierce drives had peppered during practice earlier in the week.

Appropriately the ground looked at its best on the Saturday, St Patrick's Day, when green was the predominant colour in all the streets of Melbourne. 'Seldom has the MCC ground presented so pretty a picture', wrote the *Argus*. 'The smooth-shaven green was in such order that the ball, when smartly hit, almost invariably beat the fieldsmen in the race to the chains. The glistening turf stood out in lovely contrast to the dark solid mass of the onlookers thickly packed in a border.' Fine weather completed the bright picture.

The first Test, however, brought with it several big-match problems to cloud the summer skies. Receipts were seriously diminished by a spate of forged tickets and by an old anxiety, the embezzling of gate money. 'That we are robbed there is no doubt', wrote Southerton, 'and to a good tune, but in spite of all watching we cannot discover how it is done.' Detectives were hired by Lillywhite, but in vain. The Melbourne police too were busy, wrestling with traffic problems. Precise stopping places outside the ground were allocated to engaged cabs, disengaged cabs and omnibuses. The latter, for example, were to 'stand on the north side of the parade, along the fence, and to have the horses' heads towards the east, and to extend westward from 20 feet west of the entrance to Yarra-Park. . . .' Bureaucracy clearly was flourishing at the time of the first Test.

Traffic problems of another kind did nothing to help the delicate relations between the two rival colonies. At the same time as Conway and other members of the Victorian reception committee drove down to Sandridge Pier to meet the Sydney steamer, the five Sydney players were being brought up from the pier by special train! Nor did it help the cohesion of the team that these five – the Gregory brothers, Charlie Bannerman, Nat Thompson and Tom Garrett – were staying in their usual hotel in Elizabeth Street, splendidly isolated from their Melbourne team-mates. However, team unity was boosted on the morning of the match when the Australian players met to elect their captain and the vote went to Sydney's Dave Gregory when it might well have gone 6–5 to a Victorian.

It proved a close game. On the first day (a limited one, by modern standards, of not much more than three hours) Australia made 166–6, of which Charlie Bannerman scored a glorious 126 not out. The second day ended with things equally well balanced, All-England were 109–4 (Jupp not out 54) in response to the Australian innings of 245. By the third day the match had swung Lillywhite's way, Australia having slumped to 83–9, their first innings lead of 49 putting them only 132 runs ahead overall. However, a Sunday rest-day now intervened and the Englishmen began celebrating prematurely, their festivities carrying on into the Monday when the Australians quickly added an extra 21 runs and then bowled All-England out for 108, to win by 45 runs. At once rumours flew round Melbourne that several Englishmen were drunk and quite unfit for play and that one of their batsmen even had to be helped out of the pavilion by two colleagues and pointed in the direction of the wicket. There was much condemnation of the team's off-field behaviour, even as far away as New Zealand: 'The result will be heard in England', wrote the Auckland *Weekly News* 'with mingled feelings of regret, disappointment and indignation – with regret at the loss of prestige, with disappointment at the collapse of their confidence in English skill and indignation at the careless way the team have throughout the tour trifled with the reputation of the country . . .. Lillywhite and his colleagues are not likely to get a very enthusiastic reception on their return . . .. There can be no doubt that with sterner self-discipline and more self-respect they might have acquitted themselves much better than they have . . . How Pooley and Armitage will explain away their little escapades we shall be interested to learn . . ..'

Armitage's 'little escapade' concerned a very big wager of £100 with a 'well-known citizen of Sydney' which he had failed to honour when All-England lost. At first he simply prevaricated: 'Will send your money when we settle our benefit next week.' Later, his telegrams breathed brazen defiance: 'Armitage says, after your telegram, won't pay; do best.' He was accordingly chased round Victoria and South Australia by a succession of solicitors; Lillywhite was asked to intervene by leading figures in Sydney 'for the sake of the team's credit', but declined to do so. Eventually Armitage sailed home, the bet dishonoured.

There was, as usual, much betting on the match, particularly on the last day. At lunch-time, with All-England not apparently well placed at 50–4 in their quest for 154, the betting still favoured them and few backers could be found for the Australians. However, a little later, after the fall of Ulyett, much money was put on a home victory. It is probable that several of Lillywhite's men, and not just Armitage alone, had big money on an English win and certainly there was as great a tension evident in their performance in this match as at any other time on the tour. The English fielding seemed very nervous: Armitage, at mid-off, dropped Bannerman before he had reached double figures, a miss which Alf Shaw, the suffering bowler, could remember twenty-five years later: 'The ball bobbed up in the simplest fashion and struck Armitage in the stomach.' Shaw, however, who seems not to have had much time for Armitage, failed to recall his own two failures to catch Bannerman. The bowling was very wild. Ulyett often pitched less than half way down the wicket, though 'treating Bannerman to a full pitcher which threatened to cut his body in two', and Tom Armitage was so undermined by his expensive wager that his lobs got worse and worse. After attacking Bannerman's bails with donkey drops of such height that, said Shaw, one needed a clothes-prop to reach them, he changed to 'grubbers', which Bannerman and Cooper, sensibly enough, played with horizontal bats. Tension, too, seems to have caused an even greater degree of dissent than usual at umpires' decisions. Ulyett was outraged at his lbw dismissal: 'There can be no doubt', noted the *Melbourne Argus*, 'from the way Ulyett shook his head that he had no mind to leave and he undertook to prove subsequently to friends and listeners if they would only go down to the wickets with a tape-line that his leg could not possibly have been in the way.'

Despite some poor umpiring – the 4-ball overs being frequently miscounted – the first Test produced many remarkable performances, not least Charlie Bannerman's century, which earned him a post-match collection of £87 7s 6d. As in many great innings, a little early luck was helpful; on his very first ball Shaw missed his stumps 'by the thickness of a sheet of paper'. Thereafter a succession of bold drives and cuts tore the English bowling apart. His team-mate Tommy Horan, writing of the match twenty-eight years afterwards, remembered the crowd's tumultuous applause as Bannerman sent stroke after stroke crashing into the pickets: 'I was batting with him at one stage and Allen Hill, the fast bowler with a beautiful easy delivery, sent down one which Bannerman drove back hard along the turf. The ball hit Hill on the wrist and cannoned off it for 4. In a few minutes there was a dark lump on Hill's wrist the size of a cricket ball.' Bannerman's hitting was, in Lillywhite's words, 'truly terrific', but it was tempered with good sense. Lillywhite praised his 'perfect defence' and the *Argus* commented that 'the constancy with which the ball was hit along the turf showed that caution and accuracy were allied to enterprise.' Bannerman's great innings had reached 165 when he was hit by a short-pitched ball from Ulyett. Unfortunately the india-rubber had disappeared from part of his right-hand glove and Bannerman's middle finger was unpleasantly split to the bone. The England team waited for ten minutes, as a doctor tended the wound in the pavilion, and then called for another batsman. This reasonably chivalrous action was not reciprocated in the second innings when Bannerman bravely batted again. Ulyett contined to bowl short and 'Bannerman showed he now had a wholesome dread of that vigorous bowler's bumpy ones and suffered himself to be clean bowled in consequence.'

There were other Australian heroes. The Victorian wicket-keeper Jack Blackham fully justified Conway's faith. Southerton reckoned he had not seen better wicket-keeping. Blackham conceded no byes, yet needed no long-stop, except for the few overs which Dave Gregory bowled, or, rather, threw. The brave Blackham, utterly impassive after a bad blow on the side of the face when standing up to the fast-medium left-armer Hodges, contrasted starkly with Selby, the All-England stand-in for Pooley, who retreated in the direction of short-slip to take anything above slow-medium. Much was made of Horan's bad luck when caught by Selby 'at a place which is never filled except when there happens to be a wicket-keeper like Selby with more discretion than valour'. Generally, Selby was a very poor substitute and gave Tom Armitage, the team's regular long-stop, a hard time of it. The betting barons of Melbourne may have been well pleased, for Pooley's presence would surely have tipped the first Test Lillywhite's way.

There were several effective English performances, most notably from Jupp and Ulyett. Jupp's 63 was a gritty performance. Always the complete professional, he was at one moment baiting the crowd, feigning departure after cutting a ball onto the ground and into Dave Gregory's hands, at the next brazenly fooling the umpires, a favourite Jupp pastime. As he turned a ball to long-leg for two, his foot touched the leg stump and dislodged a bail. The Australians at once appealed to the umpires but neither saw what had happened and Jupp was certainly not going to enlighten them. The crowd's anger mounted as Jupp's innings grew and, at the close of play, Terry, a Melbourne professional who was umpiring for All-England, was set upon by spectators and 'bounced'. Jupp was well versed in all the game's subtleties. Towards the close of the second day's play, he attempted to shield his new partner Greenwood, protesting to the umpires, without hope of success, that the sun's re-appearance was blinding. His hand shielding his eyes from the imagined glare, he looked in turn at bowler, sun and umpire, the elaborate pantomime wasting valuable seconds, before he settled down, with consummate care, to face the next ball. This played, he moved down the wicket and – to the fury of the Australians – demanded his sun hat from the pavilion. Justice, however, was done. Greenwood's wicket still fell before the close.

There was great jubilation at the Australian victory but much ridicule of Lillywhite's men. The team was still smarting from these criticisms as they began a very hectic week, touring three goldfield towns north of Melbourne. Bendigo and Ballarat had sprung to life in the gold rush of the 1850s which led to Victoria's prosperity; they were simply squalid, lawless camps initially, but, by Lillywhite's visit, were in the process of becoming elegant cities, though the third venue, Ararat, was, to their disappointment, almost deserted. Most of its 4,000 residents (who included many Chinese) were too busy in the quartz and alluvial mines for cricket. Altogether it was a thoroughly miserable week. The weather was poor, bleak and cold, the crowds meagre. Only £13 was taken from the two days at Ararat, whilst the three-day fixture at Ballarat was abandoned after two days: 'The public not turning up, it was decided to play no more.' Mosquitoes made sleep an impossibility at Bendigo; Lillywhite was bilious at Ballarat. The wickets were poor, unsurprisingly, at Ararat, where only a wooden roller was in use, 10 feet in diameter. Lillywhite was bruised on the hand, Selby on the head. The English performances were sluggish. 'We were quite stale', admitted Southerton, 'done up by our recent hard work and travelling.'

But the same 'carelessness' which the Auckland *Weekly Times* had berated was in evidence. Armitage (his mind no doubt on solicitors' telegrams) missed the train to Bendigo and arrived on the ground at 4.00 p.m., just in time to bat at number 11. Emmett in turn missed the train to Ballarat and arrived to find All-England 90–7, whilst Armitage and Selby reached the Ararat ground an hour after play had started. Because of Pooley's confinement at Christchurch, the XI had no reserve to cover such embarrassments. Late nights, too, continued to take their toll. The 'young bloods' attended an all-night banquet and ball at Bendigo. Early mornings complemented late nights. On the final day's play at Bendigo the XI were taken off at 6.30am in wagonettes on a seven-mile drive to Sheep Wash, where the Emu Vineyard was to be found. The XI went right through the cellars, 'tasting' as they went. Their condition at the start of play at 12.30 is not known.

All three matches against the goldfield XXIIs were drawn. The older players emerged with the most credit, Lillywhite, Southerton and Shaw all doing well, Lillywhite taking 12 for 19 at Ararat,

and Shaw, opening the innings on a heavy mud wicket, scoring
88 runs, for which he was presented with a very handsome locket.
The team's outstanding opponent was Bendigo's Harry Boyle,
who, apart from being an accurate medium-pace bowler and the
credited inventor of silly mid-on, was also a tough miner.

After this week in the goldfields the team returned for its final
match at Melbourne, to be played over Easter. It had originally
been planned to play another game at Sydney over the public
holiday but the players were unwilling to endure yet another
unpleasant sea journey when they were so comfortable in Melbourne and Jim Lillywhite was forced to contact Sydney with the
bad news: 'Match off; players refuse to go; prefer Melbourne at
Easter.' The telegram says much about Lillywhite's unwillingness
to assert himself in the role of manager.

Melbourne was *en fête* over Easter. The whole city seemed on
the move, pleasure-bent, taking trips down the bay, heading for
the Kensington Park races, watching processions of the Ancient
Order of the Druids, going off to the volunteer encampment at
Sunbury and, of course, visiting the MCC ground to enjoy the
hastily-organized return fixture between All-England and the
Combination XI, the second Test.

Interest was particularly keen as F. R. Spofforth, the demon
fast bowler from Sydney, had arrived. The young Spofforth, then
a bank clerk earning £40 a year, had earlier caused much excitement when, playing for New South Wales, he had not only
destroyed a Victoria innings but had broken two stumps and three
bats in the process. Bowling off sixteen places, he generated great
pace. C. B. Fry reckoned he was the greatest swerver of a ball he
had ever seen, and suggested, somewhat boldly, that the swerve
was caused by his bowling from one yard behind the crease.
Spofforth was impressive physically: 'Very tall,' wrote a contemporary, 'spare, though not thin, big-boned, with muscles strong
and resilient as watch-spring steel, a great promontary of a nose,
a strong pushful chin, and an equally resilient mouth, covered by
a light brown moustache, and steady, well-opened dark grey
eyes, Mr Spofforth is the personification of almost fierce determination.' Stories about his nose were legion. Once, when he
was walking in Bendigo, where no one talked of anything else

but gold, two small boys recognized him. 'That's him, Jimmy', said one, 'that's the Demon. What do you think of him?' The other looked at the fast bowler long and hard. 'I'd like to have his nose full of gold dust.'

Big crowds attended the match. Lillywhite's men were particularly delighted, for this was to be the second of their benefit matches and of the massive sum of £1,200 taken at the gates they received £717, to be divided among them. Even so, Armitage's share would not be enough to pay his betting debt.

The second Combination match did much to restore the cricketing reputation of Lillywhite's team. On the first day they bowled out the Australians for 122. Allen Hill, at last proving penetrative and bowling out Bannerman, 'neck and heels by a rasper', was well supported by accurate spells from Shaw and Lillywhite. However, as the light faded towards the close of play at 5.00 p.m., with Spofforth bowling very fast, All-England lost both opening batsmen, Jupp and Shaw, cheaply. Blackham had stumped Shaw brilliantly off Spofforth, but the batsman, as was his wont, was most unhappy with the decision: 'The umpire must have been mistaken in the bad light as I did not move my feet, nor had I the least occasion to.' Nonetheless, throughout the second day All-England prospered, building up an eventual lead of 140. The third day was therefore crucial to the Australian cause and an all-night effort was made to produce as perfect a new wicket as possible. 'I assure you', wrote Southerton of this, 'in Australia they are not in any way behind in looking after their own interests.' On this fine wicket Dave Gregory and Nat Thompson made a strong opening stand, aided by some poor wicket-keeping from Harry Jupp (who had displaced the timorous Selby). The turning point of the innings came, at 88–1, with the appearance of Charles Bannerman. He started by driving Lilly-white firmly for 4, and was then dropped by Emmett at point; the crowd roared its delight and continued to do so as the remaining three balls of Hill's over were also driven to long-on for 4. He had just hit Lillywhite powerfully for 4 and 5, bringing his total to 30 in 13 minutes, when Ulyett was brought on. Lunging forward a little tentatively to the first ball, he was caught behind by Jupp, 'who was keeping wicket but standing back towards short slip'.

The confronting of Bannerman with Ulyett would seem to have been an excellent piece of captaincy, but overall Lillywhite seems to have been an uninspiring leader. He had not had much previous experience, for amateurs always captained Sussex and the Graces dominated the United South of England XI. Southerton's summing-up of Lillywhite's captaincy was typically cautious: 'As a captain he would probably be "highly commended" but an opinion is prevalent that he would not get the first prize.' Like many a bowler-captain, he tended not to bowl himself enough, often needing considerable persuasion before taking the ball. Stronger personalities usually got their own way. Tom Emmett would continually lecture Lillywhite about field-placings, until the latter's patience eventually evaporated, and even the generous Southerton became exasperated by the over-bowling of Shaw in the second Test. 'He was bowled too much and not for the first time in the opinion of many of our side.'

Nonetheless the departure of Bannerman, inspired by Jim Lillywhite, opened up the Australian innings, for the later batsmen, pushing across the line a little too much, got themselves out. By the fourth day the Australians had been dismissed for 259, leaving England 120 to win. There was initial alarm. Jupp and Selby both fell early. Ulyett, however, played responsibly and his 63 won the second Test for All-England, Hill hitting off the final runs in a narrow 4-wicket victory.

The second Combination match was the last serious cricket of the tour. The team enjoyed a few more days in Melbourne, making their last purchases, saying the final farewells. They were loath to leave the Old White Hart, where the food and liquors were much to their taste; their host, Mr Edwards, whom they praised for being 'a thorough Britisher in heart and appearance', presented each with a gold locket. Jim Lillywhite, in particular, had cause for celebration, for he had just learnt of the birth of his son John, born during the dismal match at Ararat. There was a bibulous leave-taking which they soon regretted on the *South Australian*, the two-day passage to Adelaide being as rough as ever. However, the players suffered in their bunks in fortitude, for at least they were now on the way home.

Rain spoilt their return match at Adelaide against the XXII of South Australia, a match significant mainly for the debut of George Giffen in important cricket. Rain also spoilt their final game, played for charity, against the XXX Muffs, or 'old duffers'. This was a light-hearted affair, much enlivened by the antics of Emmett and Ulyett. Jupp opened the bowling, Lillywhite kept wicket, Conway substituted for Selby (but failed to score). The Adelaide Oval looked odd with the thirty fielders, the novelty heightened by the sight of 'back-stop' wearing a greatcoat and 'long-field-off' operating from a carriage (where he was later joined by Bennett, one of the umpires). A bizarre occasion was enriched by the Norwood brass band. 'Their efforts collectively', wrote the *South Australian Register*, 'were certainly not productive of harmony. Before again making a public appearance they would be wise to practise a little more in private.'

It was just as well that the team had no serious cricket to play in Adelaide as the entertainment was again prodigious. It included trips to a number of vineyards, an evening of singing and imbibing at the Potato and Herring Club and visits to White's Rooms to see their friends the Royal Illusionists, fellow travellers from Melbourne, also staying at the Globe Hotel. It was at Adelaide too that a benefactor presented the team with scarves and quartered caps of black, red and white. Jim Lillywhite was much taken with these and thereupon resolved that his touring teams of the future should wear conspicuous colours.

At Adelaide, Selby organized an ambitious athletics programme, 'The Champion Athletics Sports', held on the Exhibition Grounds. In a full afternoon's racing – with events for boys, bicyclists, and walkers – the highlight was his own contest over 130 yards with Goodfellow, the champion of South Australia for £50 a side. Selby was in need of a profitable final venture after an upset when he had raced a Victorian champion called Hipe at the Melbourne Cricket Ground at the end of the second Test. It seems that a piece of trickery went wrong, for Selby, having lost a first race, for £50 a side, arranged a re-match at £100 a side, only for Hipe to withdraw at the last minute, forfeiting his deposit. He had probably been warned that he would find the Englishman considerably faster on the re-run. The final race, at Adelaide, did not go according to plan either. Selby, having trailed Goodfellow for most of the 130 yards, made a late effort, forcing his way through at the line to claim a dead-heat. Although his rival's supporters protested to the judges that Selby had jostled their man on the line, the result stood. Selby again tried hard for a re-match on the Oval the next day, that of the team's departure for England, but Goodfellow cautiously declined.

Before leaving Adelaide on the evening of 19 April, the team enjoyed one final farewell dinner. Presentations abounded. One of the South Australians' greatest benefactors, Dr Peel, presented all the players with a 'small trinket', and Conway on behalf of the XI presented him with an engraved locket. Jim Lillywhite then presented Conway with a locket 'for all the trouble he had taken in making and carrying out the arrangements of the trip'. J. H. Bennett, however, although present, received no recognition for his services, until some of the tourists, feeling sorry for him, bought him a gold pin. Conway had taken over the running of the tour's final phase and there was little love lost between the two men. 'They mutually blame one another for the mismanagement and consequent losses', wrote Southerton, 'but which is right we cannot say.' The losses were largely those made by Bennett in New Zealand, but Southerton seems to have found him more sympathetic than the assertive Conway.

At 9.30 in the evening, the dinner over, Lillywhite's men, surrounded by South Australian friends, journeyed down to Glenelg, to begin their voyage, eventually setting sail at 1.00 a.m. in the mail steamer *Bangalore*. They took three weeks to reach Ceylon, complaining that their fellow passengers were 'not very lively'. At Galle they saw English newspapers and were interested in three things only: the war with Turkey, the cricket fixtures for 1877 and the latest racing results. After a gay night at the Oriental Hotel, Galle, they changed ships for a two-week voyage on the *Indus* through the Red Sea to Suez. As before, they experienced many trials. One night, for example, the rough sea swept into all the cabins on the port side, washing out the occupants from their berths and soaking all their baggage and clothes. From Suez they travelled north by train to Alexandria, a tough journey upon which they embarked cheerily. As the train steamed slowly out of Suez station they noticed natives, standing like statues, holding long poles at the end of which were oil lamps in glass bowls. The cricketers were well stocked with oranges and their aim was good. The train left Suez amidst the sound of crashing glass and much consternation. Perhaps this was forced hilarity, for it was a dangerous and uncomfortable journey, the team travelling with pistols in their pockets. The 200 miles took twenty-two hours to cover. From Alexandria things improved. They sailed 'with the best table and attendance it has been our lot to participate in'. Typically, when they reached their destination, Brindisi, their only concern was to find out who had won the Derby, for somehow they had managed to put some money on it. A rail journey through Europe brought them, after several changes of train to Dieppe. Here they had a particularly good breakfast of mutton chops and potatoes, cold fish and asparagus, roast chicken and salad, sponge cakes and custard, a cup of coffee and a pint of champagne. A rough crossing of the channel made them regret this feast and they were only just recovering when they reached King's Cross.

It was early June. Their journey from Adelaide had taken nearly seven weeks and they had been together on tour for eight and a half months. Ted Pooley was to arrive by himself a few days later. They quickly went their different ways, Jim Lillywhite to Chichester, to see his son John, now nearly four months old, the Yorkshiremen northwards, Jupp to Godalming, Southerton to the Oval, Shaw and Selby to Prince's ground. All were playing for their counties within days; indeed Jupp and Southerton turned out the very next day at Guildford against a Young Players of Surrey XXII.

It is not certain how much profit was made from the tour. Losses in New Zealand and in the smaller Australian matches, like Ararat, were undoubtedly compensated for by big financial gains at Melbourne and Sydney. Jim Lillywhite kept accounts of his later tours in small pocket-books. Unfortunately that of 1876–77 does not survive. Legend has it that it never existed. Jim Lillywhite, so the story goes, happened to be walking down East

Street, Chichester shortly after his return when he came across Arthur Hobgen, who had put up the initial money. 'Jim! You're back! Excellent fellow! You must come over for dinner and settle accounts!' Later, so we are told, after an excellent meal with a few friends Hobgen suggested to Lillywhite that they move to another room to discuss the finances of the tour. Lillywhite told his friend that all bills were paid but he had no accounts as such. He then emptied his pockets of gold and notes. 'And that', he grinned, 'is what there is over.' The sum was said to have exceeded £4,000.

Jim Lillywhite's tour of 1876–77, therefore, ended as it had begun, a private expedition, supported in no way by the English cricketing establishment. Indeed his return in June, after the beginning of the English season, was greeted with downright hostility in some quarters. *The Sporting Gazette*, for example, berated the players for not being back with their counties. Sussex, without Lillywhite and Charlwood, had been 'left in the lurch' and no time for recuperation could be allowed to these disloyal professionals: 'The Australia trip was purely a private speculation with which "England" has nothing to do; so that, stale or not, members of county XIs who have taken part in it ought to come up smiling at the call of time for their main engagements at home.' History, however, would award the tour a greater importance than *The Sporting Gazette* and to Jim Lillywhite would go the long-lasting honour of having led 'England' in the very first Tests.

Postscript

FROM LILLYWHITE TO WARNER

Undeterred by his critics, Jim Lillywhite persisted in developing Anglo-Australian cricket links and over the next twelve years took out four more teams. Moreover, he encouraged Jack Conway to bring over, in 1878, the very first Australian team to England. A second visit followed two years later and on both occasions Lillywhite acted as agent and organized the fixtures.

Lillywhite was keen to make his next visit to Australia in the winter of 1878–79, but the Melbourne Club, wary, perhaps, of the antics of working-class professionals, opted for a team of amateurs and a more exalted social tone. Accordingly, the young Lord Harris took out 'The Gentlemen of England', but the gentlemen needed two professionals to do the bowling and so Tom Emmett and George Ulyett also toured (albeit travelling second-class and using less smart hotels). Lillywhite had declined a similar invitation. It was to be a difficult tour and included the famous crisis at Sydney when the Englishmen were attacked and a crowd invasion caused the abandonment of play. Tom Emmett and George Ulyett were said to have made things worse by addressing the invading mob as 'sons of convicts'. In the end, the Melbourne Cricket Club, which underwrote the tour, made a reputed loss of £6,000, a sum alleged to have been exceeded by the Gentlemen of England's wine bill.

Jim Lillywhite, meanwhile, became involved in the sports goods business started by his late cousin John at Euston Square, London, for which he now took full responsibility, whilst retaining a manager to run the shop. It catered for every possible sport, its warehouse said to house the biggest selection of sporting goods in the world. He also took on the running of the 'green Lillywhite', changing its title to include his own name. One of his first and saddest duties as proprietor was to commission an obituary notice of Jim Southerton, who died, whilst still employed at the Oval, only three years after returning from Australia.

In the early 1880s Jim Lillywhite's business success was at its peak. In 1881–82 he made his third visit to Australia, a joint management venture with Alf Shaw and Arthur Shrewsbury of Notts. Their underwriting of a tour, without financial guarantees from Melbourne or Sydney, was both enterprising and hazardous, but Lillywhite had just enjoyed a successful benefit match (Gentlemen v Players at Brighton) which made his initial contribution of £300 somewhat easier. With Shaw to captain the team, Lillywhite as player-manager and Shrewsbury to open the batting, only another nine players were needed. The itinerary included three matches in America. Mark Twain came to watch them but was unimpressed. 'I'm pleased to have seen your cricket, Master Lillywhite,' he said, 'but a haycock in the sun and a glass of wine and a pipe are more in my line.' He would have been impressed, however, with the outcome of the tour, for Lillywhite received at least £1,590 from his £300 investment.

Jim Lillywhite's own playing days were now coming to an end. During his absence in 1876–77 the Graces had taken over the organization of the United South of England XI and when Fred Grace, its leading light, died suddenly in 1880 the club died with him. By 1883, too, Lillywhite, at the age of 41, had played his last for Sussex. In one of his final matches, when Sussex were playing Gloucester, news came on to the field that his fourth son had just been born. 'Name him after me', implored W.G. So the child was christened William Gilbert Lillywhite.

In 1884 Lillywhite was off to Australia again (following a team of amateurs, captained by the Honourable Ivo Bligh, who had returned with a present of Ashes and Urn). Lillywhite was again joined in management by Shaw and Shrewsbury, the latter this time captaining the team. Shaw claimed in his memoirs that he was the manager and Lillywhite simply the umpire, but, in fact, it was Lillywhite who kept the team's accounts throughout and who still negotiated terms with the shipping companies. Lillywhite had, however, become one of Sussex's umpires, probably through love of the game and reluctance to leave, for there were few pecuniary advantages and it cannot have helped the management of his business. From this tour in 1884–85 Jim Lillywhite made another massive profit, more than £1300. His partners subsequently made a little more with the publication of a book about their experiences.

By the end of the tour, unfortunately, the Euston Square business was in trouble. Cash-flow problems are indicated by Jim Lillywhite's plaintive advertisements: 'James Lillywhite begs to inform colleges, schools, clubs, and the public in general that in compliance with the spirit of the age he will in future conduct his business on a READY-MONEY principle.' Ironically, his fiercest competition was coming from the purveyors of the 'red Lilly-white', Lillywhite & Frowd. Although James senior had died some time before, Frowd continued to use the Lillywhite name to the confusion of many, forcing the frustrated Jim to make this angry announcement in the green annual: 'James Lillywhite, who is the only Lillywhite now alive, and who played county cricket for twenty years without missing a match, begs to inform the public that he is the SOLE PROPRIETOR of the *Cricketers' Companion* and of the cricket business carried on at 10 Seymour St, Euston Square. He has NO CONNECTION WITH ANY OTHER FIRM EITHER IN LONDON OR THE PROVINCES.' The plea was not enough. Shortly afterwards the firm was taken over by Mr Frowd, who soon closed its premises and incorporated the 'green Lillywhite' in his own red volume.

Notwithstanding the demise of his company Jim Lillywhite optimistically set off for another Australian adventure in the winter of 1886–87, again with the same management team, and he returned £600 the wealthier. It was probably the continual success of their ventures which now led the partnership to over-reach itself, though the animosity between Shrewsbury and the Melbourne Club was a contributing factor. The latter, learning of the professionals' plans for a fourth tour, made expensive arrange-ments for another, rival English team to come. At the cost of £4,000 the Honourable Martin Bladen, the future Lord Hawke, raised an amateur team, whilst the three professionals, encouraged but not subsidized by Sydney, pressed on with their own arrange-ments. 'The least that can be said of the blunder', wrote Shaw of this tour, 'is that it was such stupendous folly that a similar mistake is never likely to occur again.' There must have been some misgivings when the two teams sailed to Australia in the same ship. Shaw himself did not travel but stayed behind to organize a new scheme, a tour of rugby footballers to Australia and New Zealand.

Low gate receipts on the tour of 1887–88 proved a disaster for Shrewsbury and Lillywhite. In desperation they took their team to New Zealand, but this did not help. The entries in Jim Lillywhite's account book, usually so neat and careful, got more and more hurried and untidy as the tour progressed. Across an ink-blotted final page, in large letters, he wrote: 'loss on cricket: £2,114 2s 1d.' For the first time in their experience Lillywhite and Shrewsbury were unable to pay their team what they had promised and they faced big debts on their arrival in England.

There was still the rugby tour! But this would seem to have been an ill-considered gamble. The idea was that the team would play Australian Rules in Victoria and English Rules elsewhere. Shrewsbury's letters home to the organizing Shaw are naive in the extreme: 'Jack Conway has promised to make me a diagram of a football field, which I will forward . . . Am told that there is no off side or on side play in the Victorian rules . . . .' He envisaged that a little practice on the voyage out would be enough for the players to adapt to the different game: 'They could use the football on board ship for the little kicks from one to another, which is practised to a great extent in the Victorian game, as the players are not allowed to use their hands to throw it to another player.' It proved very expensive to look after a team of twenty players, particularly as most of them, despite being amateurs, expected much more than expenses. A. E. Stoddart, for example, who was a rugby international as well as a cricketer, received £200 during the course of the tour. Low receipts in New Zealand decided the issue and a further loss of £800 was added to the cricket debts.

It was a chastened Lillywhite and Shrewsbury who arrived back in December 1888 after an absence of fifteen months. Shrewsbury, England's leading professional batsman, had missed an entire home cricket season. Instead of the expected profit, each of the three men had debts of £1,070. Jim Lillywhite, no longer receiving a business income, had no means of meeting this figure. Somehow, at great cost to their own sports business, Shaw and Shrewsbury paid off the entire debt. The latter was understandably bitter about Lillywhite's inability to pay his share of the losses: 'He went out', he later wrote, 'fully prepared to drag us down, if the trip was not successful.' It is unlikely that Lillywhite had any such low intention. He was an honest, cheerful, easygoing man. Success had always attended his touring ventures. He simply took a chance, not believing it possible that his lack of funds would find him out.

Bleak days followed. Jim Lillywhite had a wife to support and seven young children. A second benefit match, North v South at Chichester, was hurriedly arranged for him, but this gave only temporary help, for in 1891, as he approached the age of 50, he was said to have 'only the bare necessities of life'. Arthur Shrewsbury, writing to Shaw, had heard of Lillywhite's plight: 'I have been thinking that a fund could be raised in Australia on behalf of Jim. Lots of friends that knew him when he was better off would be glad to subscribe a £5 or £10. You could suggest it privately to Tommy Horan, Harry Headley and Jack Conway, whom I'm sure would do their utmost on his behalf . . . Jim was well known in Sydney and Melbourne . . . a fair sum should be obtained for him. . . .' It is not known what became of this initiative or indeed whether the fund would involve the repayment of debts to Shrewsbury and Shaw. But three years later things were sufficiently desperate for Ada Lillywhite to write to Shrewsbury for help for her husband. She received a chillingly cold reply: 'Where has all the money gone to from the various trips Mr L has taken to the Colonies?' It is clear that, six years on from the disaster, Shrewsbury's sense of outrage was as strong as ever.

In 1895 Jim Lillywhite followed the example of many contemporaries and became the licensee of a pub, the Wheatsheaf, in North Street, Chichester. His fortunes, which had recently reached their lowest ebb with the death of his eldest son John, tragically lost at sea, began to improve. Around the turn of the century there was a considerable change and he was able to live for the rest of his life off income derived from investments. It is unclear how this came about. It would be pleasing to think that perhaps some gold shares, bought speculatively years before in Ballarat or Bendigo, suddenly produced a rich dividend. Shrewsbury himself would not have been able to reclaim his dues, for in 1903, around the time that Plum Warner was chosen to lead a side to Australia, he shot himself, wrongly believing that he was incurably ill.

The 1890s, hard years for Lillywhite, had witnessed a huge increase in the popularity and skill of cricket, coincidental with the growth of leisure and literacy amongst the working-classes and the development of the popular press and public transport. Cricket's Golden Age was dominated by flamboyant amateurs, and it was therefore appropriate that three of them, Grace, Stoddart and MacLaren, should have led sides to Australia in this period. For all their amateur status, however, it was still the promise of the Golden Fleece which inspired their travels. Yet Australian cricket was now no sleeping dragon. Of the twenty Tests which preceded Warner's tour of 1903–04, England won only three and Australia eleven.

By the turn of the new century, most of Lillywhite's team were dead. Few lived beyond the age of 40. Of those who did, Ted Armitage was living in obscurity in America (still eluding his creditors) and Pooley in drunken poverty in London. Jim Lillywhite himself, however, was now in his 60s keeping himself fit quarrying stone, still living in his delightful cottage by Goodwood racecourse. He would, of course, have followed the events of Warner's tour with considerable interest. He may even have reflected that the new England captain had been born in 1873, the year when his own association with Australia began.

3

PLUM WARNER'S TOUR

1903–04

Pelham Francis Warner, captain of the MCC tour of 1903–04, enjoyed a more privileged background than Jim Lillywhite. As the eighteenth and last child of Trinidad's Attorney-General, he grew up in a civilized outpost of Queen Victoria's Empire, his early life cushioned by gracious surroundings, deferential servants and that indulgence frequently allowed to the youngest member of a family. Although after his father's death his family's finances deteriorated, it was still possible for Pelham to be sent to England at the age of thirteen for education at Rugby, where he acquired the nickname 'Plum', and later at Oriel College, Oxford, whence he emerged with a Blue, a favourite Harlequin cap and a third in Jurisprudence. Thus by birth and education he was equipped for leadership and, just as he had grown up to accept unquestioningly the Englishman's mission to govern the Colonies, so, all his life, he was to believe in the prescriptive right of amateurs to pre-eminence on and off the cricket field.

One of the greatest influences on the young Plum Warner was the professional at Rugby, Tom Emmett, Jim Lillywhite's erratic left-arm bowler, then in his early 50s. Warner had the benefit of Emmett's wisdom for five years and later wrote most affectionately about him, describing him as 'my headmaster' and evocatively recalling his erect, active figure, striding across the fields, head thrown back, an old Yorkshire cap crowning his grey locks. Emmett's most prominent feature, however, was his red nose, a source of much amusement to the boys. Plum Warner recalled a hot summer's day when everyone was finding the flies particularly troublesome. 'They doan't worry me', smiled Emmett, 'for they aall get burnt when't come near my nose.' Much of Warner's cheerful approach to the game must have had its origin in the tutelage of the jocular Tom.

After leaving Rugby, Warner, aided by a small allowance from his mother and what he could earn as a cricket journalist, established himself in the Middlesex XI and toured extensively overseas, thrice under the aegis of his mentor and friend Lord

Hawke. At the same time he qualified for the Bar and did some pupillage under the distinguished cricketer and barrister Alfred Lyttelton. By 1903, however, when Warner had reached the age of 30, he had given up the idea of a legal career and had become instead that contradiction-in-terms, an amateur who had adopted cricket as his profession. If he was making money out of the game, he was doing so discreetly, for he was the cynosure of the Lord's establishment, having powerful friends in Kent's President, Lord Harris, and the Middlesex captains, A. J. Webbe and Gregor MacGregor. It was not just because he wore the right ties that Warner attracted the self-perpetuating amateur oligarchy which was running cricket at the turn of the century. He was an articulate, shrewd young man who wrote lucidly about the game, for whose history he had developed a deep regard. Moreover, the influential patrons of country-house cricket found in him a convivial companion and an admirable dancing partner for their daughters. Plum Warner, despite limited funds, was socially acceptable.

In one respect only did he not conform to the Edwardian amateur 'beau ideal'. As a batsman he lacked the flamboyance of hard-driving contemporaries like Jessop, MacLaren and Jackson and the glitter of personalities like Fry and Ranjitsinhji. His virtues were more pedestrian: a straight bat, a sound defence and an iron resolve. It was possible, therefore, for contemporaries to underestimate his batting and to ignore the formidable technique which was to allow him to score sixty first-class centuries and to play county cricket to the age of 46.

When the MCC undertook its first tour to Australia in 1903–4, therefore, Plum Warner would have seemed an excellent choice as captain. Although he had not played any recognized Test matches, he had captained Lord Hawke's team briefly in Australia only the year before. He was widely travelled and had scored runs regularly for Middlesex, whose captaincy he now shared with MacGregor. The series of circumstances which led to his selection began when Archie MacLaren, England's last captain both in a home series against Australia and on his own private tour of 1901–02, was asked by the Melbourne Cricket Club to take out another team in 1903. When MacLaren temporized, Melbourne offered the tour to Warner, who happened to be in Australia with Hawke's XI. Warner must have been tempted by the proposition. More cautious, however, than Jim Lillywhite fifteen years earlier, Warner eschewed financial risk by suggesting that Melbourne ask the MCC to sponsor the tour. In making this suggestion Warner was prompted by Hawke, Harris and other friends at St John's Wood, who farsightedly regarded the Club's involvement as a logical step in the development of international cricket and, less altruistically, saw it as a means of removing the English captaincy from the volatile MacLaren. The MCC's first choice of captain was Stanley Jackson, but soldiering had prevented his acceptance. Warner was then offered the job and, after two week's hesitation, he accepted. This lengthy delay suggests that he must have realized some of the implications of acceptance. 'It seemed a duty that ought not to be shirked', he wrote ambiguously afterwards.

Many sections of the cricketing world greeted his appointment with great hostility, belabouring the MCC for 'jockeying Mac-Laren' out of the captaincy. Warner's lack of Test match experience was emphasized. All his good points were conveniently forgotten. Warner's resignation and MacLaren's reinstatement were widely and loudly demanded and there was vitriolic condemnation of the 'hole-in-the-corner petticoat ways of the Lord's party'. Merciless cartoons depicted Warner as a baby doing what his nanny, Mrs Marylebone, told him. 'Mr Warner', commented *Cricket* magazine, 'has taken the place of Mr Joseph Chamberlain as the man at whom it is thought convenient and even praiseworthy to throw as many stones as possible.'

Archie MacLaren, the centre of the controversy, was, at 32, two years senior to Plum Warner, and one of the outstanding classical batsmen of his generation. But his golden full-faced drives, such hallmarks of the age, were accompanied by metal of a baser nature – a moody, self-assertive personality. Thus, whilst his county, Lancashire, had agreed in 1902 to pay MacLaren £450 a year for his services over the next five years, it had also tried, albeit unsuccessfully, to remove him from the captaincy for which he was temperamentally ill-suited. The MCC, therefore, in appointing Warner, was not acting simply out of hostility to MacLaren.

The Warner-MacLaren debate raged on for many weeks, and as luck would have it, Middlesex visited Old Trafford where, in a conversation in the Lancashire amateurs' dressing room, Warner told MacLaren that he would be prepared to play under his captaincy, if the MCC so desired. MacLaren at once relayed this to the press, further embarrassing Warner and the MCC. The latter, having tried to keep aloof from the controversy, now responded decisively with an official statement: 'The MCC committee selected Mr Warner to be captain of the English team from the first and have in no way qualified that selection at any time since.' Thereafter the arguments gradually grew less heated and turned, instead, to the vexed question of team selection.

Much resentment had been caused by the MCC's refusal to publish the names of the invited players before their replies had been received and there was much derision of the club's 'underhand' methods. 'A wondrous atmosphere of mystery pervaded the MCC's action', commented *Baily's Magazine*. The committee's position was not helped by the reluctance of some senior professionals, such as Lilley and Tyldesley, to accept the terms, £300 plus expenses, the same sum which Shaw had negotiated from Lillywhite in 1876. In some anxiety MCC let it be known that expenses would include a bonus, 'if the tour is financially successful', and all washing bills, a statement which offered much scope to satirists. However, after the MCC had sent a reminder to the hesitating professionals and Warner had hinted publicly that others, just as good, were being considered, things were resolved and eleven professionals signed terms.

Non-availability of amateurs proved a bigger problem, and, in the end, only three travelled – Warner himself, B. J. T. Bosanquet of Middlesex and R. E. 'Tip' Foster of Worcestershire. The list of those who turned down invitations included Jackson, MacLaren (who rejected a belated invitation), C.B. Fry (who delayed for a long time in the hope of finding lucrative journalistic contracts, to pay for the trip), H. Martyn (the Somerset wicket-keeper), E. M. Dowson (the Cambridge University captain), Lionel Palairet and Gilbert Jessop. Ranjitsinhji did not receive an invitation, 'not being English', although he had already played fifteen times for England. Finally, only one week before departure, the young

Lancashire amateur, R. H. Spooner, declined a late invitation. For its inability to attract the best amateur talent the MCC was – quite unfairly – severely criticized; unpleasant innuendo suggested that Warner's captaincy was responsible for the 'unrepresentative' nature of the team.

The critics would have been nearer the mark had they pointed out that, with the MCC in charge, amateurs who in the past had received generous payments for touring could not now hope to do so. Shamateurism was a big issue at the turn of the century. 'I hope', thundered Lord Alverstone, MCC's President in 1903, 'that the MCC will never encourage the idea of the paid amateur and that those who go as amateurs really *will* be amateurs.' Alverstone's anxieties probably centred around the recent appointment of R. E. Foster to be the tour's financial manager, J. A. Murdoch acting as his assistant. Rumours at once circulated that Foster's appointment was purely to help with his expenses and that Murdoch would be managing all the finances. This seemed likely. The 25-year-old Foster had just started a career in the London Stock Market and probably needed financial help from the MCC to be able to tour. Murdoch, on the other hand, for the past 34 years the Assistant Secretary of the MCC, was a man of wide financial experience, who had seen the Club grow from a membership of 1,500 to over 4,000. A tall, imposing, elderly man with a straight white beard, Murdoch became the tourists' father figure and it was to him that the professionals turned on all financial matters.

However, it is clear that Tip Foster did take some interest in the tour's finances. In his diary he kept a record of each day's takings at the gate and on his arrival at Melbourne he and Warner negotiated with Ben Wardill, the MCC Secretary, over a number of items, in particular the possibility of guaranteed money at the smaller fixtures. 'Wardill says that we cannot get guarantees anywhere', noted Foster in his diary, adding with some determination, 'I mean to have the best terms too and we may have some trouble about it.' It seems likely, therefore, that Foster did indeed begin the tour as the financial manager, but that, overwhelmed by cricket commitments and illness, he allowed the capable Murdoch to take over as the tour progressed.

The whole subject of finances was viewed with suspicion by the critics. Dark rumours were abroad that the MCC was preparing to line the coffers of Lord's with the tour profits and eventually the Club issued a statement re-emphasizing its declared intention not to make money for itself. Rather, any profit made would go to English cricket generally. It may have been the baying of a hostile press which encouraged the Club into making extremely unfavourable financial terms with Melbourne. Although the expenses of the tour escalated to £14,000, the MCC had agreed to only a 50% share of gate receipts. The net result was an eventual loss of over £1,000.

No team could ever have been assembled in an atmosphere of greater hostility than Warner's, which, when it set out, was still being widely derided as being woefully inadequate. Ironically, it was, in fact, one of the most balanced teams ever to leave English shores; it contained in its eleven professionals a marvellous cross-section of Golden Age talent. There were three experienced batsmen – Tom Hayward of Surrey, Albert Knight of Leicestershire and Johnnie Tyldesley of Lancashire. There were two fine wicket-keepers in the 36-year-old Dick Lilley, still the automatic choice for England, and the 23-year-old Herbert Strudwick, who had only recently established himself in the Surrey XI. Above all, the team was especially strong in all-rounders: George Hirst and Wilfred Rhodes of Yorkshire, Len Braund of Somerset, Albert Relf of Sussex and Ted Arnold of Worcestershire. Kent's fast bowler Arthur Fielder was the only genuine tail-ender.

Warner's influence on the selection was crucial. With his experience of touring he knew that temperament was just as important as talent. Fine players, therefore, like Barnes and Lockwood were excluded, Warner preferring men of a sunny disposition. Thus, in Lilley, Hirst, Tyldesley and Hayward he had chosen senior professionals of proven integrity, men who were helping to give their profession a dignity it had previously not known, whilst Albert Knight was a devout Christian, gently chaffed by his fellows for his insistence on saying his prayers at the wicket. Of the young players, Strudwick, Rhodes and Braund would prove loyal and enthusiastic. Altogether, it was an admirable blend of experience and youth, ability and equanimity. There was a steadiness of temperament, which Jim Lillywhite's team so notably lacked, and it is no surprise to read Dick Lilley's comment that they were 'the nicest lot of fellows it has ever been my privilege to be associated with'.

The three amateurs provided the critics with easy targets. Bosanquet's invitation, it was said, was a clear case of favouritism. Bosanquet was a friend of Plum Warner, a fellow traveller on two tours, a member of the same Middlesex side; they had even attended the same Oxford college. Bosanquet once have might scored a century for Eton against Harrow but no one had seen a more ungainly batsman, and, as for his new-fangled googlies, it was said that the first one to take a wicket bounced four times! The critics were more circumspect with R. E. Foster. It had to be admitted that he possessed talent and that three years ago he had astonished the cricket world by scoring 171 in the University match and two hundreds in his first appearance for the Gentlemen against the Players. But since then he had played little first-class cricket and his inclusion, after such inactivity, seemed at best a gamble.

Yet Bosanquet and Foster were, in fact, inspired choices! They and their captain had much in common: public school, Oxford and an accent which the Australians would love to parody. (The *Sydney Mail* could not help noting that the weather which the Englishmen had left behind was 'demned demp'). They lived for games. Foster's father, chaplain at Malvern College, taught all his sons cricket and rackets as soon as they could walk. Bosanquet's father, an army officer and land-owner, was similarly careful over his son's education. The result was that from 1895 to 1900 there was not an Oxford cricket side without at least one of the three. Their most unifying quality, however, was their supreme self-belief, which at times, it must be said, verged on the arrogant.

Plum Warner himself possessed such cheerful individuality that, according to *Vanity Fair*, it led him to 'being called an Optimist and other bad names'. In the midst of that summer's furore Warner, far from being hurt or dismayed, 'revelled in the notoriety and gleefully commented that he was the most talked of man in town'. Warner was never short of a word and always keen to enter a verbal contest. 'Well', he would begin, 'as you know I am a barrister, briefless now perhaps, but I feel I would like to argue the point with you.'

R. E. Foster's close friends found him a delightful companion, but those who knew him less well found him conceited. Sporting success had come early to Foster, a much-lauded athlete since his early schooldays. By 1903 he had already played inside-left for the England football team (at a time when amateurs and professionals vied for places). He was a man of strong opinions, who voiced them forcibly, and yet he could also be quiet to the point of aloofness. On the cricket field this aloofness evidenced itself together with certain eccentric mannerisms, a strutting and posing, which seem to have been *fin-de-siècle* Oxford practice. An Australian Test cricketer, after watching Foster on tour, wrote: 'I know of no one who possesses such strong mannerisms while batting. This alone would never make him a popular player in this country.'

Bernard Bosanquet, was, like Foster, 25 years old and a similarly talented all-round games player. He had represented Oxford at ice-hockey and as a hammer thrower and billiards player, whilst at Eton he had excelled at the Wall Game. A member of an old Huguenot family, he could trace his ancestry back to the 16th century and possessed an inspiring family motto – 'Per damna, per caedes' – 'We may lose the first Test, but we'll slaughter them in the second.' Bernard Bosanquet's outstanding characteristic was his imperturbability. 'He is never flurried', wrote one observer, 'never worried, just as cheerful when getting pasted in all directions as when he is getting 6 for 64. His imperturbability is astounding'. Off the field he was so similarly lacking in anxiety that he was frequently late. 'He used to drive me crazy', remembered Warner over thirty years later, 'by always catching a train when the guard was waving his flag or blowing his whistle!' His air of lofty unconcern became proverbial. He would walk through busy hotels 'without noticing anyone in particular'; he made a point of getting his own way, very quietly but very firmly. Some people found him quite insufferable and even Plum Warner felt the need to defend his friend at the time of the tour: 'He never knows when he is beaten. He has that inestimable value of always thinking he is going to make runs.

Unkind people have called this attribute by a harder name before now, but confidence in one's own abilities is a very different thing from conceit . . .'

Warner, Foster and Bosanquet were the three who, as the amateurs, would set the tone throughout the tour, make the decisions and, indeed, in this way decide the outcome of the series. They fortunately possessed enough self-belief to ignore hurtful criticisms of 'the strange selection which has set the whole world a-laughing at the Marylebone club'. They probably even failed to appreciate the bizarre fate which had placed them in authority over eleven leading cricketers of the land. Warner had supreme confidence in himself and in his team, despite the pessimists who were predicting 'the addition of fresh ashes to the rapidly filling urn of English cricket'. He knew, as he packed his bags in mid-September, that 'the most abused man in cricket' might yet confound his critics. Surely no England captain ever left these shores for Australia in more determined vein.

Warner's team left England in two groups, the better sailors travelling from Tilbury, the less intrepid joining the ship at Marseilles, thus avoiding the Bay of Biscay. This, though only half the team assembled at St Pancras, on 25 September, a crowd of over 2,000 people had gathered to give them a big send-off. It was an auspiciously beautiful morning. Amidst the bustle of porters, billowing steam and shrill whistles, loud cheers were raised from the bowler-hatted and straw-boatered throng every time a cricketer was sighted – first, Strudwick and Relf, then Fielder and Knight, the popular Len Braund, finally Tip Foster and Plum Warner himself, both amateurs and professionals the epitome of sartorial elegance. In particular much admiration was expressed for their ties and hatbands in the new MCC touring colours of dark blue, red and yellow; and the team blazers and caps, with the new badge of St George and the Dragon worked in white silk, were displayed to great acclaim.

Amongst the well-wishers were many current cricketers, Tom Richardson and Sammy Woods towering among them, and there were many establishment figures, such as Lord Hawke, Lord Alverstone and Gregor MacGregor. 'When I arrived at the station', wrote Warner, 'I was simply amazed at the sight that greeted me. Every corner was occupied. Piles of luggage on the crowded platform. Porters everwhere.' 'It was wonderful', agreed the wide-eyed Herbert Strudwick, 'I never heard so much cheering or saw so many people on a railway platform before.' There was one late arrival. As the special boat-train noisily departed and the cheers began to fade, an immaculately tailored young man climbed out of a hansom cab to join the throng. It was Bernard Bosanquet, one of those travelling overland to Marseilles, arriving, as usual, just a little late and missing his friends' departure by exactly a minute.

At Tilbury the cricketers were suitably impressed by their first view of the P & O liner *Orontes*, floating massively alongside the quay. Launched only months before, she was to prove, in Warner's words, 'a veritable palace of comfort'. She was three times as heavy as the vessels of 1876, twice as capacious (accommodating 640 passengers), and, at 18 knots, nearly twice as fast. She would offer smooth sailing in all but the heaviest of seas and would transport Warner's team to Adelaide in 5½ weeks, taking two weeks less than the ships of Lillywhite's day.

Before departure a champagne reception, such as would have warmed the heart of George Ulyett, awaited the cricketers on the upper deck. Champagne was indeed a fitting drink for such an occasion, for it is said that the first Englishmen whom the Australians described as Poms were the cricketers of Lillywhite's era, so noted were they for their consumption of Pomerey champagne. Other passengers at the reception were the Countess of Darnley (whose husband, the Honourable Ivo Bligh, had won the Ashes on tour twenty years before) and a certain Miss Agnes Blyth.

Agnes Blyth was Plum Warner's fiancée. It had been a whirlwind romance. Only a few months before, in July, England's newly-appointed captain was still sending Agnes somewhat unromantic telegrams: 'Middlesex won; seven wickets; Warner'. But in August he was asking for her hand. The marriage, arranged to take place shortly after the tour's conclusion, had only been agreed two weeks before the team's departure. Agnes was rich and well-connected. She lived in Portland Place, London, with a family country house in Essex, and her engagement photograph appeared, as a matter of course, in *The Tatler*; her uncle, Sir James Blyth, and her late father were both directors of the gin distillers, Gilbey's. Sir James would seem to have been no match for his niece, a pretty, progressive 26-year-old, who was determined not to let the ever-increasing dossier of cricket statistics, which her fiancé sent her, spoil the course of true love. Agnes seems, at the least, to have pursued Plum Warner with zeal, and the P & O Chairman at the reception raised some smiles with his *double entendre* as he praised 'Miss Blyth's ability in the hunting field'.

Agnes brought with her a young friend, Josephine Starkey, to act as chaperone, and she had further female company, for Tip Foster was bringing his wife Diane with him. For the Fosters, in fact, the tour represented a glorious seven-month honeymoon, for they had only married that July. Although there were precedents for such a honeymoon (W. G. Grace having taken his new wife on the controversial tour of 1873–74), one may well wonder what the professionals thought of the presence of Agnes Blyth and Diane Foster. The young Wilfred Rhodes, for example, was leaving his wife and one-year-old daughter behind, whilst Bert Relf's wife was pregnant and already had a very young daughter to look after. However much professional cricketers of this period accepted such family deprivations as part of their job, they must, at the least, have muttered about the travels of Agnes and Diane, for in 1903 a woman's place was very much in the home. One can learn the contemporary view of womanhood from the strong comments of Monty Noble, the Australian captain at this time. Tourists, he believed, had a public duty to perform and ceased to be private citizens with private interests. Wives were potential trouble-makers: 'Women are more concerned with social standing than men. Take the case of four wives travelling with a team. It's a thousand to one they divide into two and two and the one pair immediately attempts to establish its superiority over the other pair.' A male chauvinist from his white boots to the peak of his green cap, Noble continued: 'Whilst every right-minded man appreciates women's society, a train compartment with a band of touring cricketers is hardly the place for women.' In short, as far as Noble was concerned, wives would be acceptable only if they travelled by different ships and stayed in different hotels! These were the views of the time. It was Diane Foster, therefore, and, especially, Agnes Blyth, who were challenging the conventions.

There was one overwhelming reason for the presence of Agnes and Diane on tour: they were paying most of the bills. Unlike the bachelor Bosanquet, who had ample private means, Warner and Foster were not well off. Diane Foster came from a wealthy Yorkshire family, her father being a successful Sheffield business-man. Her presence, therefore, would seem to have been a *sine qua non* of Tip Foster's participation. Similarly with Agnes: Plum Warner's 2-week delay in accepting the captaincy may well have been caused by long financial deliberations. His newspaper articles are unlikely to have earned him more than those of C. B. Fry, whose income from journalism did not allow him to tour. If Agnes was subsidising Warner's travels, she would probably have preferred to risk the loss of her reputation, by travelling, rather than the loss of her fiancé at the predatory hands of Australian womanhood. Her grip on the England captain on tour seems to have been very firm, and certainly the chaperone Miss Starkey spent most of her time with the Fosters and little of it with the Warners.

It would seem, however, that on the voyage, at least, Noble's worst fears were not realized, for all was harmony and peace on board the *Orontes* from the moment she slid slowly out into the Thames. She was a proud ship, a symbol of British superiority at sea at a period when Englishmen really did believe that Britannia ruled the waves. She was full of proud passengers. 'We did not forget', wrote Bishop Welldon (who befriended Warner on the journey and became the team's chaplain), 'that we were English-men and Englishwomen, representatives of the greatest Empire under heaven . . .' The tourists genuinely believed that they were playing their part in their Empire's story of benign expansion. 'International cricket matches', wrote the Bishop, 'promote a kindly feeling between nations . . . Strong patriotic feelings in the colonies have largely sprung from the interchange of courtesies and the fostering of mutual respect through international competitions.' There was, therefore, a unifying patriotism aboard the *Orontes*. When Lady Darnley invited the team to afternoon tea in the ship's saloon, no amusement was caused when the table was decorated with the MCC flag. The bright MCC colours were to be a symbol of King Edward's Empire, as revered in distant parts as the Union Jack itself.

Although during the course of the journey there were times of violently rough weather and much seasickness – and George Hirst, the team's worst sailor, was said to have felt well only when travelling slowly through the Suez Canal – it was generally a cheerful voyage, in which all passengers, cricketing and non-cricketing, were happily integrated. Deck games flourished and there were regular competitions in deck quoits, bucket quoits, peg quoits and ballboard. The athletic Bosanquet beat the *Orontes* First Officer in the final of a deck sparring competition (combatants fighting with cushions while sitting on a pole 4 ft from the ground). There were several amusing varieties of race; a 'cigarette race' proved popular and so too a 'hat trimming and whistling race'. A potato race caused excitement and Lady Darnley, who presided over many of these activities, took pity on Herbert Strudwick who had knocked over his bucket when about to win and awarded him a special prize. In an obstacle race, run in temperatures of 90° in the shade, the contestants had to squeeze under a low plank, roll over a high one, scramble under heavy netting and crawl through a 20-foot long airshoot, before finally jumping through a life belt suspended from the roof. 'Strudwick won the obstacle race', noted Bert Relf, 'and knocked himself about a bit doing it.'

On many afternoons there was a game of cricket, played under a disconcertingly low roof. Warner's XI had its first victory (over Archdeacon Samwell's team) and its first loss (against the ladies, the XI playing with the wrong hand). What with Wilfred Rhodes bowling constant right-arm wides and Agnes being allowed a 2nd innings by her fiancé when she was patently out skirt-before-wicket, the MCC never had much of a chance.

Two or three nights a week there were concerts, and in a famous fancy dress competition Plum Warner won 1st prize as

'The Rajah of Bhong' (a character from the musical comedy hit *The Country Girl*, all the rage at London's Daly's Theatre), Tip Foster coming second as a 'gondolier'. As Agnes won 2nd prize in the ladies' section, as 'a nurse', voting seems to have been tactfully in favour of the team's leadership. On other evenings there were outdoor dances and sing-songs. There were daily sweepstakes on the ship's run, much whist was played and there was ample time for the Edwardian crazes of filling autograph books and collecting and sending picture postcards.

Writing up diaries also helped to while away the time. Bert Relf, the Sussex all-rounder, regularly jotted down a few comments each day and through his eyes one can enjoy the various ports of call. Gibraltar was the much-appreciated first stop, where the team spent one extremely hot morning seeing as much as they could. 'Hired carriage for four', wrote Relf, 'and had a good drive round this magnificent fortified place; rather dusty; none of England's freshness about it; flowers were lovely colour. Bought picture postcards. Fruit very cheap, lovely baskets of mixed grapes, pears, pomegranites for sixpence.' The view of the Rock as the *Orontes* steamed away moved Relf to write: 'I shall never forget such grandeur.' Marseilles was 'a magnificent sight' as they steamed into its harbour with Notre Dame on the hill behind. 'Went ashore three hours. Had cab and drove round, visiting Hotel Metropole, where we were charged 1s 3d for bottle of ginger ale. Tree-lined streets, very cool and pretty, though not very clean.'

A day spent at Naples was a highlight, the *Orontes* approaching it on a glorious Sunday morning, Mount Vesuvius smoking in the distance. All day, as the *Orontes* lay at rest, groups of local musicians in small boats serenaded the liner's passengers with Neapolitan ballads. Relf and his friends meanwhile swiftly obtained a guide and hired two cabs. The city aroused mixed emotions: 'Naples has some magnificent buildings but the sanitary arrangements are awful. It's amusing to see cows and goats driven round to people's doors and milked as you want it. Excavations of the Roman remains of Pompeii and Herculaneum were in a comparatively early stage in 1903 but Relf was very impressed. The macabre nature of Pompeii's destruction had clearly interested him: 'Where the passages are chiselled out you can see the forms of bodies just as they were buried in the boiling lava.' Like many before him and since, Relf succumbed to the pressures of the souvenir-seeking tourist. 'Brought away a piece of marble from the wall', he confessed, 'also two pieces of mosaic.'

At Port Said the *Orontes* took on board 1,500 tons of coal ('put in by a swarm of coolies, poor beggars, how they have to work'), whilst Relf went round the town, making purchases: picture postcards (inevitably), a flyswish, fans, a seedfruit, and, for his wife, beads and a Maltese lace collarette. Relf, Strudwick and Arnold then took donkeys for a full ride round the town: 'A very poor place and not safe to go alone, but one can get cheap cigars and cigarettes.'

The final stop before Australia was Ceylon, where the team spent a very full day. Relf and his friends went round Colombo in rickshaws, admiring the silks and curios on sale, watching conjurors and fights between mongeese and cobras. The highlight of the day was the 7-mile drive to Mount Lavinia, 'a most beautiful ride amongst the magnificent foliage of coconut trees and palms'. The day ended with a dinner at the Galle Face Hotel in some style and by midnight the team were back in the *Orontes*, absolutely exhausted.

The stop at Colombo had not been without its tensions for Plum Warner, since negotiations had been going on for some time for a match to take place in Ceylon. Warner, however, before sailing, had intimated that the MCC would only be prepared to play a team of Europeans. Further negotiations led to the cancellation of the fixture. Warner later glossed over this incident, promulgating the official version that the team had too many injuries to make a match in Ceylon helpful.

A few weeks later all these previous ports of call were forgotten as the *Orontes* approached Australia. 'We were all delighted to get a glimpse of the coast', wrote Bosanquet, 'and even though we had another thousand miles to go, were very grateful for a few hours at Fremantle. All the shops were full of the most delightful fruit and flowers.' Most of the team went up by special train to Perth. The Great Australian Bight, which had sorely tried Jim Lillywhite on many journeys, proved kinder to Plum Warner and even the worst sailors began to appear regularly in the saloon for meals. By way of a good omen the Aurora Australis was sighted by the team one evening. 'It is very rare for this phenomenon to be seen so far north', noted Bosanquet, 'but we saw it plainly for about half an hour. Starting with peaks of light shooting up into the sky from the horizon, it developed into an arc of light in the sky, and faded slowly away.'

At last, on November 2nd, the *Orontes* approached Adelaide and Warner's much criticized team made preparations for disembarkation. It was a final time for exchanging autographs and addresses and the team assembled on the top deck to be photographed by about thirty of the passengers. 'It was a perfect morning', wrote one waiting Australian. 'I happened to be at Largs Bay in the early and beautiful morn and with a pair of glasses watched the faint speck of smoke on the horizon gradually develop into the whole ship. . . .' Launches set out, the leading one decked out in South Australian cricket club colours, their captain and leading batsman, Clem Hill, visible in its stern, together with his father John. Clem Hill had been born the day after the Combined Australian XI won the first Test against the All-England XI and his father had himself, as proprietor of a coaching firm, driven Lillywhite's men to Adelaide from disembarkation at Glenelg those twenty-seven years before.

There were mixed feelings as the team bade farewell to the *Orontes*. They were glad to be on land again, but sorry to have to part with their many new friends. 'One thing that did a great deal to mitigate our grief', wrote Bosanquet cheerfully, 'was the discovery that strawberries were ripe, and could be obtained (with cream) in considerable quantities. . . .'

Much had happened in Australia since 1876 when Jim Lillywhite's men first arrived there. Although the recent coronation of Edward VII had re-emphasized imperial ties, the rival Australian colonies had only recently accepted a federal constitution to become a single nation and in 1901 the Commonwealth of Australia had been founded. There were lively discussions, therefore, at the time of Warner's arrival, about proposals to build a new capital city, the future Canberra, symbolic of a new-felt national pride, a quality which now found supreme expression in the game of cricket. The previous year, when a party of Australians had visited England, there had been fervent rejoicing at their overwhelming success in the Test matches and the fact that the tourists had won twenty-six of their forty-five matches and lost only two. The arrival of the first MCC party, therefore, had been awaited with great anticipation, for it was readily expected that the Australian team, boasting such players as Monty Noble, Victor Trumper, Reggie Duff, Hugh Trumble, Clem Hill, Warwick Armstrong, Syd Gregory and Jim Kelly, would be more than enough to ensure further celebrations for the new nation.

Warner found cricket at Adelaide flourishing. Indeed the development of South Australian cricket in the years since Jim Lillywhite was typical of that of Australian cricket generally. The Adelaide Oval, on which Jim Southerton had laboured so hard and unsuccessfully, now had a splendid batting wicket and an improved, if still slightly rough, outfield. Jim Lillywhite had been commissioned by the South Australians, on his return in 1877, to find a suitable coach and encouraged the Sussex all-rounder Jesse Hide to go out to Adelaide. Hide's influence led to a rapid improvement in pitches and play, the Colony soon being able to compete with Victoria and New South Wales and producing fine players. Clem Hill, a left-handed batsman, twenty-six years old was now the pride of South Australia.

Whereas Jim Lillywhite enjoyed some extremely friendly private receptions, Plum Warner now experienced even more enthusiastic public ones. A special train conveyed the team the fifteen miles from Largs Bay to Adelaide Station where they were met, with speeches, and escorted to the South Australia Hotel, which was gaily decorated in their honour. After a pause in the afternoon, which allowed an hour's practice at the Oval, the Mayor welcomed the team at the Town Hall. 'We marshalled our forces in the Mayor's private room', wrote Warner, 'and as we marched in procession into the Hall we received a magnificent reception from fully 2,000 people, every seat in the building being occupied.' Flags hung everywhere, the red, yellow and black of the South Australians blending colourfully with the new MCC emblems. After four speeches from local dignitaries, the city

organist played 'The Soldiers' March' from Gounod's *Faust* and
then Plum Warner began the first of his many public speeches.

The speech was spirited and combative. Warner did not eschew
the controversy which had preceded his departure: 'It is a great
regret to me that Jackson, MacLaren and Fry could not come.
Contrary to opinion in some quarters MacLaren and I are great
friends. . . . There is no such thing as jealousy between him and
myself. . . .' Whilst acknowledging that he and Bosanquet were
not among the best amateurs in England, he vigorously defended
his right to captain the side: 'I have been captaining XIs since I
was 15-years-old and have travelled about 130,000 miles all over
the world playing cricket. I will not say that I am good or bad as
a captain, but those who have travelled with me have not found
any great fault with me. . . .' Writing of himself in the third
person (as Special Correspondent of *The Sportsman*) Warner
summed up: 'He had quite an ovation, many of the audience
rising and enthusiastically waving their hats. . . . His speech
evidently went down well.'

The night was not yet over. After retiring to a smaller room in
the Town Hall, for refreshments, there were further words: 'We
had two more speeches from his Worship', wrote Bosanquet (in
one of his reports for the *St James's Gazette*) 'and another, shorter
one from Plum, and one from a gentleman who had been too late
for the earlier speechifying.' Then from the Town Hall the team
was escorted to the fire station where the brigade gave a
demonstration.

There were four more free days before the first fixture with
South Australia. Most mornings the team practised in the nets,
with Agnes Blyth, Diane Foster and Josephine Starkey sitting
directly behind, observing all. On two evenings the tourists went
to the theatre (*Oh, What a Night!* and *Are you a Mason?*), and one
evening the team was taken for a carriage drive round the hills
('Rather a cold performance', noted Tip Foster in his diary).

Adelaide had grown much since Lillywhite's tour, the population, including suburbs, having risen from 60,000 to 160,000.
Strudwick found it 'pretty, clean, quiet and friendly' but A. E.
Knight, who was writing dispatches for the *Sheffield Daily Telegraph*, was less impressed, feeling that 'the extreme widths of the

streets is apt to dwarf the appearance of the notable buildings', though he approved of its Art Gallery 'with examples of Bougerau, Rossetti, Poynter and Waterhouse'. He enjoyed a moonlight drive to Glenelg, then a fashionable seaside suburb, and his historical curiosity was satisfied by the sight of the 'gum tree beneath which, in 1836, the Colony of South Australia was proclaimed'. He was, however, taken aback at the aridity of much of the countryside: 'Driving here is as dusty as motoring at home, nor can the scenery be said to approach that of the Motherland. By innumerable gum trees, with here and there the charred and stunted blocks that tell of previous bush fires, one looks at fields parched with heat and laden with dust. Well arranged fruit gardens are bright spots amid the dust, whilst the wild flowers are of rare and delicate hues, and the scanty bird life of brilliant plumage, but one was rather disappointed with a scene which had neither the smiling appearance of a grove of fruit or flower, nor the severer beauty which characterises our "dark and true and tender" North.'

These were feelings of alienation in a strange environment such as have been experienced by many in the first few days of a tour and it was probably with a great sense of relief that Warner's team eventually turned to more familiar territory, a game of cricket. But even here there were strange new factors. Warner noted 'the fierce light beating down on the brown, grassless pitch which renders it undoubtedly hard to watch the ball off the ground on first going in.' Herbert Strudwick was similarly struck by the strangeness of the wicket, 'shiny as a piece of glass and hard as a rock. There is not one blade of grass – all has been killed and scorched. It is mostly full of cracks and puts one in mind of a jigsaw puzzle. To the batsmen it is a paradise; to the bowler a nightmare.'

The Oval was gay with bunting and the hum of over 6,000 people when the first match of the tour was played. It began significantly. Warner, having won the toss, opened the batting with Tom Hayward and they both proceded to bat with a caution quite exceptional for the period. By lunch there were only 45 runs scored in ninety minutes. This was a deliberate tactic on Warner's part. A sound start was essential for team morale. Taking risks in the bright light might lead to a quick fall of wickets. So he forbade them. Thus Travers, the slowest left-arm bowler in Australia, sent down thirteen 6-ball overs for only 2 runs! After lunch, as the heat of the day intensified, Warner and Hayward began to play strokes. Warner jumped down the wicket off-driving to the boundary with some regularity, one ball going in the direction of Clem Hill so savagely that he 'drew back as the ball flew past him'. Warner's 65 and Hayward's 157 laid the foundations of an excellent first performance and only a century from Hill saved the South Australians from an innings defeat.

Following in Lillywhite's tracks, Warner now took his team to Melbourne, but whereas Lillywhite's men endured a rough sea passage of fifty hours, Warner's travelled overland by railway, the 500-mile overnight journey taking only eighteen hours. However, though the train contained two-berth 'boudoir cars', the journey itself was endured rather than appreciated. The train swayed and jolted and as it crossed great stretches of desert, dust choked the corridors and it was possible for the players to write their autographs half-an-inch thick on the windows. Moreover, dining cars had not yet been introduced and so meals were taken hastily in station dining-rooms. They eventually arrived at Melbourne Station 'tired and uncomfortable', to be revived by an auspiciously enthusiastic reception.

The team's first stay in Melbourne was a success. The Victoria XI which they met was a fair one, but it was soundly beaten by an innings. Respect for the tourists was starting to grow. The *Sydney Mail* noted: 'People are beginning to say that Rhodes is not the simple bowler some would have them believe on Australian wickets. Further it is noticed that Rhodes, a man who got 1,100 runs last English season, is sent in tenth. . . .'

The English players were duly impressed by the Melbourne ground, with its magnificent scoreboard, huge stands, lovely turf and fine wicket. 'Far superior to anything we have at home', wrote Warner. He was also pleased that, unlike Adelaide and Sydney, it did not have a cycle track round its perimeter. With his keen sense of history, Warner was delighted with the portraits of famous players and grounds in the Members' pavilion. He was less impressed by the Melbourne crowds which (as at Adelaide) actively supported the home side but gave little applause to the visitors. Barracking too was frequent. When Strudwick missed a stumping, there were cries of 'Send out Lilley! We want Lilley! Give him his return ticket and send him home.'

The Englishmen were upset as much by the umpiring as the barracking. Tip Foster confided to his diary: 'I hit one to mid-off which hit the ground quite three inches in front of the fielder – Collins. He sort of rolled over and the umpire, Barras, to my and everyone's astonishment, put his hand up without anyone appealing. Neither Laver the bowler nor I saw this, and the former prepared to bowl another ball when the umpire said he had given me out. So I had to go – but it was a disgraceful bit of umpiring and if Barras did it on purpose he ought never to umpire again, as it was deliberate cheating – all the Victorians say I was nowhere near out.' Foster had been similarly upset at his dismissal in his innings at Adelaide: 'Tom Hayward ran me out having hit the ball to cover – I thought I was in and so did everyone including Clem Hill and some of their side. . . .'

These upsets were mitigated by most hospitable entertainment and the pleasures of life in a cosmopolitan city. The first stay in Melbourne included a dinner reception at Menzies Hotel and tea at Government House (where the amateurs stayed on to dine with the Governor-General). Melbourne had more than doubled since Lillywhite's time to nearly half a million people, and most of the players agreed that it was little inferior to London. The devout Knight was particularly taken with the Roman Catholic Cathedral, recently completed in blue stone, 'the most sacred building in the Colonies, replete with some of the rarest offerings which art can give to worship. . . .'

Leaving Melbourne, the team continued on its leisurely and successful way. At Sydney, before enormous crowds, the MCC beat a strong New South Wales XI by an innings, and at Brisbane equally large crowds watched another MCC victory. In matches against the odds the MCC drew with Newcastle's XV and Maitland's XVIII.

The game at Maitland went very wrong. The weather was dreadfully hot, the telegraph service inoperative, a concert in the Town Hall embarrassingly poor and the hotel unsatisfactory. All this offended Tip Foster, who was captaining in Warner's absence, and he then gave offence to the Hunter Valley Cricket Association by insisting that there should be no toasts at luncheon. Aggravation off the field led to trouble on it. The Maitlanders bowled and fielded quite atrociously, several members of their XVIII treating the match as a joke. Tip Foster grew more and more irritable and at the end of the first day's play told the Maitland captain, and anybody else who cared to listen, that the home team were 'rubbish' and 'there was no use going on with it'. 'His remarks', said the *Maitland Daily Mercury* 'were in very bad taste.' Stumps were drawn early on the second day by mutual agreement and the MCC were relieved to turn their thoughts to Sydney and the imminent first Test.

Sydney, though still but a fraction of today's cosmopolitan city of 3½ million people, had quadrupled since Lillywhite's visit. Despite its sudden growth it had little of the artificiality of Adelaide or Melbourne about it, for its roads were less mathematically precise. Albert Knight, guide book no doubt in hand, noted that the streets wound in and out 'like the bullock car tracks from which they have developed'. A first-time tourist, whose horizons had hitherto been limited to the county cricket grounds of England, Knight was awestruck by the majesty of Sydney harbour, writing simply: 'It is almost like a visit to fairyland to sail down it on a bright and sunny day'.

The Sydney Cricket Ground also impressed the tourists. The old Albert ground, where Lillywhite had first played, had long since been built upon and Sydney's old Garrison ground had been developed instead into a remarkable stadium. The finely proportioned Members' stands, with their delicate iron tracery and graceful columns now dominated the ring and, together with the vast expanses of the Hill, adjacent to the new giant scoreboard, provoked much comment from the Englishmen. Standing in the centre of the empty amphitheatre for the first time, they gazed around incredulously. 'Do you ever have these great buildings filled?' asked one. Agnes Blyth and Diane Foster were likewise full of approval for the smart new ladies stand and a second pavilion where ladies were allowed to mingle with the opposite sex.

The tourists now had no less than five free days before the Tests, and the team split up, enjoying varied kinds of Sydney hospitality. The Fosters, for example, had a quiet time staying with wealthy friends just outside Sydney. Bert Relf and Dick Lilley spent two days at Sandringham, where they fished, rowed, ate oysters and shot seagulls, plover, kingfishers and 'anything that came their way'. Other professionals were taken on a two-day excursion to see the stalactites and stalagmites of the Jenolan caves. This trip had the added excitement of travel by new-fangled motor car, but horses had to be used to pull the cars up the steeper slopes in the Blue Mountains and, on the return, one motor expired. An old-fashioned post-chaise rescued the stranded players. There were also trips up Sydney harbour in special launches, delightful occasions with lunch taken up one of the many rivers, followed by a leisurely horse-drawn drive home, with tea en route. A shooting party to Botany Bay caused some drama. Ted Arnold had thrown up a bottle for Herbert Strudwick to shoot at, by way of practice, but the Surrey wicket-keeper narrowly missed the Worcestershire bowler and was not allowed to shoot again. Instead, he waded into the water, which looked ideal for swimming. 'Hey, Struddy!', yelled some anxious friends, 'The river's full of sharks!'

As the Test approached, the Sydney public discussed excitedly their team's selection. Apart from the exclusion of Hugh Trumble (whose banking commitments had forced his retirement), there were few surprises. The attack lacked fast bowlers and relied on the off-breaks of Noble, Saunders's left-arm spin and the medium pace of bee-farmer Bill Howell. But the batting looked very strong. The new captain, Monty Noble, a Sydney dentist, was a batsman of great tenacity and fine temperament, whilst Reggie Duff and Victor Trumper formed an opening partnership of devastating potential. The shy, idolised Trumper was now, at 26, at the height of his powers, his eleven centuries on the 1902 tour of England having been recently marked by an hysterical public reception in Sydney Town Hall. Jim Lillywhite had watched him

from the umpire's vantage point and rated him the best batsman
he had ever seen: 'I saw Grace play some fine innings and later I
saw Ranji, Fry, MacLaren, Abel and Hayward hit some brilliant
centuries. To me, however, it was a greater joy to watch Trumper
even than Ranji. The ease and polish with which the Australian
sent the ball to the boundary, like a shot from a rifle, are things
one cannot forget.'

Trumper, as it happened, had been born in 1877, the year of
the first Test, and there were further links with Lillywhite's tour:
as a youth, Trumper had learned much of his cricket in club
matches under the captaincy of Charlie Bannerman, whilst one of
his early jobs was in a Sydney probate office under another
member of the first Australian Test team, Tom Garrett. There
were other connections between the two series: Bill Howell was a
nephew of Edwin Evans, New South Wales's hero in the first
victory over Lillywhite's men, and Syd Gregory, now a stalwart
member of Australia's middle order, was a nephew of Dave
Gregory, Australia's first Test captain.

Two days before the match Warner's men met up at the
Australia Hotel. Bert Relf's account of these last two days reveals
a healthy respect for quiet living which the professionals of Jim
Lillywhite's team would simply not have understood: 'Wednesday. Went down to the ground for a good practice, lunched there
and had another good turn in the afternoon. Mr Warner asked me
to play in the Test and I feel rather pleased. Spent a quiet evening
at Tattersall's Club. Everybody looking forward to Friday. I hope
we get some luck. If fine, we have a hard nut to crack. Bought
new cigarette holder.

'Thursday: a fine day. Went down and practised. 'Got back to
lunch after which Lilley and I went to the club, then had a good
walk round the town, making lots of calls on customers of Dick's.
Had a 100 cigarettes and a box of chocolates given us. Back for
tea, then we went for a little trip in the harbour, over to Mosman's
Bay; lovely. Back to dinner. Hotel crowded with visitors for the
Test. Went to the Tivoli in the evening; enjoyed it; got home to
bed early.'

It was not only Bert Relf's first Test, but that of Warner,
Foster, Bosanquet and Arnold. Yet although the England team

lacked experience, it still looked formidable. Its depth of batting was notable and there was also great variety in its six bowlers. Fastest were Ted Arnold, delivering lively off-cutters in unpretentious style, and Yorkshire's George Hirst, whose left-arm swing bowling was hampered by the dry Australian air. Somerset's Len Braund bowled leg-breaks with a generous amount of flight, often to a packed leg-side field. Bosanquet varied leg-breaks with googlies, off-breaks with a leg-break action, his own invention, later to be known in Australia as Bosies. Wilfred Rhodes bowled classic left-arm spin and Relf medium-paced off-cutters and away-swingers with a less than orthodox action. No captain could have asked for greater variety at his command.

The sixty-eighth Test match proved a memorable occasion. There was already a crowd of 10,000 on the ground as the two captains came out to toss, crossing the banked cycle track of bright concrete which enclosed the playing area (a constant reminder of the popularity of this new Edwardian sport). Noble stood tall and handsome in his green blazer and cap, a *Boys' Own* hero, fair-haired and broad-limbed. By contrast Warner, in white shirt and flannels, looked slight and studious, despite the MCC cap hiding the bald dome. Noble tossed the coin in front of the pavilion, half-a-dozen eager photographers capturing the moment. When Warner called wrongly and the Australians elected to bat, there were some who thought that the match was as good as over, for rain was forecast later which would affect the uncovered pitch, whereas, for the time being, it looked full of runs. 'It had a brown glazed look', wrote Warner, 'as if a hot iron had passed over it and scorched the grass.'

Duff and Trumper opened for Australia much to the pleasure of the Sydney crowd, already swollen to 17,000. They approached the wicket expectantly, an impressive looking pair in their slatted pads and floppy sun-hats, Duff short and strong, with a trim moustache. No one would have guessed that both men, apparently exuding such youth and vitality, would not outlive their 30s. George Hirst opened the bowling, Trumper and Duff both taking a single off him. Ted Arnold was given the other end. As usual he was attacking the off-stump with eight men on the off-side, only Warner, at mid-on, on the leg. Arnold came in easily off his economical run, Trumper waiting poised, right knee bending in characteristically, the bat held at the very top of its rubberless handle. Trumper observed the ball pitch, just short of a length, outside the off-stump, rising high, and disdaining caution made to cut it fiercely backward of point. From off the upper edge the ball flew well to the left of Foster, at second slip, about knee height. Foster dived, catching the ball left-handed as he fell. Ted Arnold had removed Victor Trumper with his very first ball in Test cricket! 'The best I ever caught', wrote Tip Foster later that evening. There was further drama in Arnold's second over, when Duff, essaying a similar cut was caught by Lilley and, shortly afterwards, amidst horrified silence, Clem Hill snicked Hirst to Lilley and the Australians were 12-3. The young Warwick Armstrong came out to join his captain, Noble. Armstrong at 24 was tall, angular and supremely self-confident; he was still slim – not at all the gargantuan figure of the 1920s. He faced up to George Hirst, who was now 'swerving in his best style', and was all but bowled first ball.

Later, Armstrong and Noble effected a considerable recovery, prospering until well on into the afternoon. Braund had come on first change with his leg-breaks, Bosanquet second change with his googlies. This was, after all, the Golden Age, when the subtlety of wrist spin was highly prized. Eventually, in late afternoon, a googly deceived Armstrong and knocked out his middle-stump. Later, Bosanquet also bowled Gregory with a ball which pitched off-stump and hit the top of the middle and leg, but by the evening Australia had recovered to 259 for 6, with Noble 131 not out. The Sydney crowd gave him a magnificent reception. 'Never a risk and hardly a faulty stroke', commented Bosanquet. 'It was the first great innings of the match.'

Monty Noble, like the non-smoking, teetotal Trumper, was typical of the new breed of Australian players, so different in outlook from the epicurean Charlie Bannermans of earlier days. Noble believed in going to bed early before a match and not drinking before batting: he also believed in the philosophy of 'clean' cricket, so prevalent, but not always evident, in the Golden Age. 'Cricket teaches you to be clean', he wrote. 'The exercise and the environment promote clean thoughts. It discountenances boastfulness, shady tricks and unhealthy practices and sets high value on quiet demeanour, gentlemanly conduct and modesty. . . .'

The rain forecast for Friday duly came during the night and a damp wicket made batting precarious on Saturday morning. Wilfred Rhodes made the ball turn 'almost at right angles' and Australia were soon bowled out for 285. Despite a strong drying wind, the wicket was still difficult as the England innings began and, when Warner was out for 0, an England collapse looked likely. However Johnnie Tyldesley, the Lancashire professional who outdid the greatest of Golden Age amateurs in his uninhibited stroke-play, attacked the spinners from the start, at one moment running out to off-drive, the next staying back and pulling savagely to leg. Tyldesley hated defence so much that if ever he played a maiden he would gnaw on his glove in frustration. There was to be no glove-gnawing at Sydney. His 53 was a turning-point in the game, for, had he failed, half the side might have been out in the first hour. After lunch, with 33,000 on the ground and many more streaming in, the wicket eased and, by tea time, it was playing perfectly. The second day ended with a good unbroken stand by Tip Foster and Len Braund which brought England to 243 for 4, only 42 runs behind.

A rest day now ensued, for no cricket, of course, was played on Sundays. As usual the team dispersed. Most of the professionals went for a picnic in the National Park. The three inseparables, Lilley, Arnold and Relf, were invited by a racehorse owner to his stud, Lilley trying out a thoroughbred which had been named after him. For the amateurs Sunday was more formal. After church on Garden Island they lunched separately with friends (the Fosters as the guests of the commander of one of His Majesty's warships in the harbour). For tea the Fosters and Warners called on Walter Allen, whose house on Bellevue Hill enjoyed spectacular views of the harbour. Allen, a contemporary of Warner's, had wide sporting connections in England. More significantly he had a one-year-old son called George, who would one day be known across the cricketing world as Gubby.

Monday 14 December 1903 dawned bright and hot, a good day for batting. Foster (73 not out overnight) and Braund continued to prosper, the former reaching his century first with a fine late cut, his favourite shot. It was, claimed Warner, 'about the finest stroke of the whole tour, the batsman dabbing down an off ball with lightning wrists'. Braund, however, was soon out after his century and further wickets quickly fell, eroding England's good position. Foster, a highly competitive if slightly humourless character, was furious with Bosanquet and Lilley for throwing away their wickets. Bosanquet, he wrote, was out to 'a rotten shot', whilst Lilley 'played the fool and was caught off a wild blow to the country'.

It was Tip Foster's partnerships with Relf (30) and Rhodes (40 not out) which finally turned the match England's way, by raising the score from 332–8 to 577 all out. Foster dominated both these stands, scoring his last 130 runs in under two hours. His diary records these happenings tersely and modestly, whilst nonetheless revealing something of the grim resolve which underpinned his elegant play: 'Lilley's departure left us 47 runs on – which was chucking our position away. However, Relf came in and he and I sat down and played steadily and began to collar them, and Relf played beautifully till he was caught at short slip off Saunders – a ball I thought he distinctly threw. Anyhow it turned about eight inches, a difficult thing to do on a plumb wicket. Meanwhile I had got to 203 and so had beaten Gregory's highest score in a Test match in Australia. Here we stopped for tea and Rhodes and I went on – we did not give anything away at first and then got our eyes in and began to paste them properly and in an hour and ten minutes put on 130 for the last wicket before I was caught at cover, my 287 beating Murdoch's 211' (as the highest ever Test score).

It was a remarkable innings. On the Saturday the crowd had barracked Foster unmercifully, disliking his poses and mannerisms and mocking his irritation with troublesome flies. On the Monday, however, they applauded him enthusiastically, warming to the way he shielded Relf and Rhodes whilst raising the tempo of his own play. Running down the wicket he bombarded the valiant Duff at mid-off (a key fielding position in the Golden Age); constant forcing shots between cover and extra-cover were likewise made with astonishing power. But he played strokes all round the wicket, more and more furiously, until exhaustion at last cost him his wicket.

Warner, usually so detached in his newspaper reports, was exultant. Never before in his life, he said, had he seen cricket such as Foster's. He could not resist a reference to his amateur rivals at home: 'Foster's off-driving and cutting have never been equalled, while he drove straight, pulled and forced the ball away in a manner that MacLaren, Fry, Ranjitsinhji and Jackson may have equalled but certainly never excelled.' Warner's book of the tour, *How We Recovered The Ashes*, contains an interesting photograph of Foster at his stance. Like Trumper he is holding the bat at the top end, but there comparisons end, for Foster's stance is all right shoulder and right leg, completely two-eyed, a purist's nightmare, opened up ready for an on-drive but impossibly positioned for the cover-drive. Foster rarely looks impressive in photographs, yet all accounts agree that he was a natural, wristy, classically-correct batsman. It would seem, therefore, that the presence of a camera elicited from him a self-conscious, unnatural pose.

December 14th had been a day of records, no less than nine being broken. In addition to making the highest ever Test score, Tip Foster had eclipsed the previous highest score made by an England Test player (Grace's 170) or by someone playing for an England team (Ranji's 175). He also beat a record which had stood for twenty-six years – the 165 which Charlie Bannerman had made against Lillywhite, the highest score of a Test debutant. The days of records ended with Australia, nearly 300 runs behind, sending in two night watchmen to play out time. It had been one of England's greatest days in Australia and one which Warner and Foster would never forget. When, ten years later, Tip Foster died of diabetes at the age of 36, Warner sent a laurel wreath to the funeral with a ribbon in the MCC touring colours and the simple valediction: 'Tip from Plum – Sydney December 14, 1903.'.

The remarkable match was far from over. It had been agreed that the Tests should all be played to a finish and this one was only half through. The Tuesday and a rain-affected Wednesday belonged to Victor Trumper, who scored 185 not out, well supported by Duff (84) and Clem Hill (51). Though Trumper's poor health was cause of Australian concern all summer, in this innings he outshone even Foster and Tyldesley. There was no one quite like him in 1903. 'Trumper stands alone', commented Warner. In the hour and forty minutes before the close on Tuesday, he scored 112, quite without chance. Wilfred Rhodes bowled beautifully throughout, confounding those critics who believed he would not be effective on hard Australian wickets, but Trumper transcended the Yorkshireman's art. Like Foster, he used his feet to attack the slower bowlers. However hard he hit, his sweet timing lent an air of delightful ease to the shots. Len Braund was given particularly harsh treatment and in vain he adopted his containing leg theory. Trumper stepped swiftly to leg and cut him mercilessly to the fence. 'It didn't matter where I pitched the ball', said Braund afterwards, 'Trumper could hit it in three different places in the field'. One of Trumper's most telling shots was all his own and was guaranteed to distress hard-working bowlers: 'He goes right back almost on his wicket', noted Warner, 'and forces a ball of just about a good length away past mid-on or between the offside fielders.' But even the perspiring English bowlers had to admire Trumper's innings: 'It was', said Bosanquet, 'the most beautiful and perfect cricket of the match'.

There was, however, in Australia's second innings an ugly incident which marred the match and even, briefly, threatened the series. It occurred during the magnificent rearguard stand put up by Trumper and Hill. Braund was bowling to Trumper, who savagely cut his first two balls to the Members' pavilion. Braund responded by bowling a quicker ball, which went for 4 byes. The next Trumper drove imperiously past extra cover for 4. 16 runs off 4 balls! The crowd was exultant. The last ball of the over again brought them to their feet, for Trumper drove Braund hard past mid-off and George Hirst only just managed to stop it on the boundary. Hirst returned the ball to Braund, backing up, and the bowler, seeing Hill out of his ground as he completed the fourth run, hurled the ball at the wicket and missed and, to the crowd's delight, it went hurtling to the boundary, where Relf fielded it. Clem Hill, however, had over-run the wicket by ten to fifteen yards in completing the fourth run and, when Trumper called him for a fifth, he was struggling. If Bert Relf had fielded badly that day he might well have been forgiven, for his thoughts must surely have been in England with his one-day old daughter. Instead, his throw came hard and low, first bounce to Lilley, and Hill was run out, Lilley reckoning that the South Australian was a foot out of his ground. Most eyewitnesses, including Noble, agreed that he was out, the distance varying between a foot and a yard. 'Hill was out quite easily', Braund told the readers of the *Daily Express*. 'When told he was out, he tossed his head in the air and looked disgustedly sick at the decision. When asked by members in the pavilion, he said it was a bad decision. Then the trouble commenced.' Clem Hill was a pugnacious character, hot-tempered enough to land a punch on a fellow Australian team-selector. Now, in the heat of his disappointment, his loss of composure caused much bitterness. Tip Foster, like most of the tourists, was incensed by Hill's reaction: 'I was standing at short-leg with umpire Crockett at the time and could see. But Hill appeared dissatisfied and stupidly showed it in walking to the pavilion and the members started hooting and hissing, which of course was taken up by the rest of the ground and the most disgraceful scenes ensued. For some time we could not go on and for the rest of the day every shot was hooted and Crockett was barracked very badly. It was disgraceful the members starting it and, though many tried to excuse it, nothing could make up for the scene. The crowd shouted so much that they must have frightened the other umpire as Armstrong and Hopkins were dead lbw and he gave them in. . . .'

Umpire Crocket was subjected to barracking for the rest of the day. As Rhodes ran up to bowl, with each of his first four steps there was a shout of 'Crock! Crock! Crock! Crock!' As he released the ball, on his fifth step, there was a mighty roar of 'Crockett!' There was also a barrage of random shouts from all round the ground: 'How much did you pay Crockett, Warner?' 'Have your coffin ready, Crockett.' The umpire was hooted off the field and a number of 'roughs' waited for him outside the ground, but he was smuggled out of a side gate by two detectives.

English outrage at 'the unsportsmanlike manner in which the

members behaved' seems excessive and Warner's actions provocative rather than conciliatory. He knew, like Lillywhite, that the Sydney crowd was highly volatile and yet, hot-headedly, he walked up to the Members' pavilion and tried to remonstrate with them. Shortly afterwards he had to be restrained by Noble from the inflammatory gesture of leading his team off the pitch. Moreover, his comments in his cable to *The Sportsman* reflect a surprising lack of restraint: 'If the members of a great cricket club cannot behave themselves as they ought to, then the sooner visits of England teams to Australia are discontinued the better!'

Fortunately the tense situation of the match at the beginning of its sixth and final day helped everyone forget the high emotions of the day before. England needed 194 to win on a wicket which was beginning to wear badly. Warner again failed with the bat, Tyldesley and Foster could not recapture their form of the first innings and, when Braund was out second ball, England had slumped to 81 for 4 and were struggling. Then came a key moment. George Hirst hit his first ball from Howell straight to Frank Laver at square-leg, just behind the umpire. There was an anticipatory roar from the crowd but Laver, the most reliable of fielders, put the catch down. At 81 for 5 the match might well have been lost. As it was, Tom Hayward and Hirst took England steadily towards safety and an eventual 5-wickets victory.

Great was the rejoicing in the English camp. Warner was delighted and old wounds showed through. 'We have', he wrote, 'wiped out the criticism of a certain Northern newspaper that "we were the laughing stock of cricketing England".' In his speech after the match Warner, showing a singular lack of magnanimity, renewed his complaints about the previous day: 'It seems to me that the first rule of cricket is to obey the umpire implicitly, and especially an umpire of the ability and integrity of Crockett. . . . When he was booed like that, it was an insult to the game of cricket. Whether the batsman was out or not does not affect the question; but members in the pavilion who took part in the demonstration were not in a position to say. However, now that the match is over, we have forgotten the incident. . . .' Monty Noble's reply seemed bland to some, ironic to others: 'We had a most pleasant game', he remarked. 'I am sure I echo the sentiments of the others of the team when I say that the game was played out in true British style.'

Despite the controversy it had been a magnificent match, avidly followed. Gate receipts of £4,250 were a record for any Test match. It was, in Bosanquet's words, 'the game of a lifetime'.

After the first Test the team moved back to Melbourne for a week, where they enjoyed a two-day victory over XVIII Victorian Colts and celebrated Christmas. Christmas Day itself was one of the hottest the tourists had yet experienced: 100° in the shade. Some, like the Fosters, visited the Cathedral for the midnight service and matins; others, like Bert Relf, spent the morning visiting a few hostelries, 'having a drink or two to the old folks at home'. All met up at their hotel, the Menzies, for Christmas lunch. It was an odd occasion. No holly, no ivy. The only logs in the hearth were those of the hotel gas fire. Iced drinks and tropical fruit strangely complemented the turkey and plum pudding. But spirits were high and afterwards in the drawing-room the party made merry, Plum and Agnes leading the dancing, Len Braund and Johnny Tyldesley the singing of seasonal ballads.

Later that Christmas afternoon they caught a train for the five-hour journey to Bendigo. As four of the fourteen tourists were incapacitated, the MCC included, in their team, a friend of Bosanquet's from his Eton days, George Whitfield. Whitfield was one of several wealthy young men who came out to join Bosanquet on tour, the latter no doubt deciding that he needed extra company, as the only other two amateurs were preoccupied off the field with the opposite sex.

They found Bendigo a prosperous city of some 30,000 people. Albert Knight saw much to admire in the town's buildings and was quick to pass on some more culture to the readers of the *Sheffield Daily Telegraph*: 'The city possesses a neat little art gallery, the *chef d'oeuvre* of which is a specimen of that melodramatic artist Herbert Schmaltz, and a noble statue to Queen Victoria, labelled 'To the Queen of the Earthly Queens'. The cricket gave

Knight rather less outlet for his lyricism. It was oppressively hot on Boxing Day, 96° in the shade and 152° in the sun, and the perspiring tourists were irritated to discover a bumpy ground and poor wicket. Although Arthur Fielder seized the opportunity of taking 11 Bendigo wickets cheaply, generally the match was endured rather than enjoyed. It was a strange contrast, after the packed Sydney Test ground, to be playing before 500 spectators at the Bendigo Upper Reserve. Boxing Day ended with the players lounging about their hotel, unable to sleep because of the intense heat and the flies. Warner's patience was strained. There had been many English visits to Bendigo, both before and after Jim Lillywhite, but Plum Warner regretted the fixture. 'It is very much a question of whether these matches against the odds do any good, for the Test matches and State games give quite hard enough work and the constant travelling about in trains is not conducive to that absolute physical fitness which the highest class of cricket demands.'

No visit to Bendigo was complete without a descent down a mine and one morning a motley party of eight tourists, including the Fosters, Bert Relf and Josephine Starkey, visited the Great Northern goldmine. This experience unsurprisingly elicited a full response from Albert Knight's expansive pen: 'With some little perturbation we descended a slimy, wet, oblong shaft in a cage four feet by two feet. Advised to keep shoulders and toes "well inside", there was something almost lover-like in the embrace of the men who faced one another in that narrow cage. The candle for a time permitted a view of the wet and greasy sides, but the drip which saturated one's neck and head soon put the faint glimmer out and the remainder of the descent of 2,000 feet was accomplished in darkness. Then, with one eye mindful of the timbering above and the other intent on the pitfalls beneath, we walked and crawled and wormed our way beneath these quartz tunnels, up and down ladders of questionable safety, in a vain search for gold. Our guides pecked and pecked away but no auriferous quartz could they show us.'

The impending second Test provoked great excitement, not least because Hugh Trumble had been persuaded out of retirement, and at every station between Bendigo and Melbourne crowds peered in at the MCC's carriage and shouted, 'Wait till you meet Trumble!' But not even Trumble could alter the luck of the toss which decided the match. England batted first and scored 221 for 2 on a perfect wicket, after which the rains came down and Wilfred Rhodes, without bowling particularly well, took 15 wickets to clinch victory. 'It was our first experience of a Melbourne sticky wicket', wrote Warner. 'In England, when a wicket is sticky, the ball turns quickly enough but it does not get up straight in your face as is its habit in Melbourne.' The match was distinguished by memorable batting by Trumper and Tyldesley. The former used his feet to minimize the turning ball, often cutting short ones off the back foot, Compton-like, from well down the wicket. Tyldesley's 62, out of England's second innings total of 103, was a remarkable performance, again the result of lightning footwork. Even Trumble, bowling his slow-medium off-breaks to a packed leg-side field, did not trouble him. His hitting was magnificent and one drive nearly went over the entrance gate. But few other Englishmen played well. Many catches were put down; bowlers lost line and length. 'We did our best to lose', wrote Bosanquet, 'but the rain won the match for us in spite of our efforts.' Poor Tip Foster, 49 not out on the first day, took no further part in the match. 'I felt very seedy in the evening with a headache and pains in the back.' He was to spend over a week in bed, his illness worsened by his exertions in the first Test.

Leaving Foster to recuperate in Melbourne, the party left for Ballarat, where another friend of Bosanquet's, George Drummond, recently of Harrow School, played alongside George Whitfield in the depleted MCC ranks. Ballarat was to the tourists the most beautiful of all the cities they visited. Knight compared its broad streets to the boulevards of Paris and, on discovering that the whole population turned out of doors in the evenings, fancied himself in the French capital. Less chic, however, were the hills of the famous goldmines, overlooking the city, pitted and mounded, like lunar landscapes. Inspired, perhaps, by the opportunity to study much religious statuary, Albert Knight celebrated his time in Ballarat with a century. Len Braund, too, at last found form with his leg-breaks, accounting for ten of the eighteeen local players. But Warner, despite the rare capture of a wicket (off a long hop), continued to dislike such games against the odds.

At Adelaide the MCC lost the third Test, their first defeat of the tour. The Australians won by dint of superior batting, Trumper, Hill, Gregory, Duff and Noble all doing well. Tip Foster probably should not have played. He travelled to Adelaide just before the match 'still feeling very groggy' and only two days before the game 'felt rather shaky'. He did not make many runs but believed he had had bad luck. In the first innings he was caught in the slips 'feeling for one of Noble's I could not see. The sight boards were very bad and Noble was right outside them and almost impossible to see.' In the second innings he played a ball which hit his feet and then 'just went into the wicket and knocked the bail off'. For his team-mates, however, Foster felt little generosity. 'The others got themselves out', he wrote simply. Plum Warner did his best to smile away the defeat – 'I slept in a room numbered 13' – but excessive Australian jubilation undoubt-edly smarted. Herbert Strudwick many years later remembered the orchestra at the hotel where both teams were staying striking up 'See the Conquering Hero Comes' which led to a little ill-feeling. There were also members of the Australian team willing to lay odds that England would not win another Test. 'The victory was deserved', wrote Strudwick, 'but we resented the rubbing-in part.'

The Australian victory intensified home interest in the series and increased anticipation for the MCC's return to Sydney a month later for the fourth Test. In the meantime there were two weeks of relaxation in Tasmania.

In the twenty-four hour crossing of the Bass Strait Warner's men experienced something of what Lillywhite's had often endured. They were sitting down to dinner when the rough seas started. Crockery and food slid across the tables and onto their laps. 'I thought the boat was going down', said Strudwick. Cabins offered little respite. One shared by six professionals was of miniscule proportions, terribly smelly and situated over the screw. Bosanquet, sharing with his friends Drummond and Whitfield, fared little better: the lower bunks had six inches of headroom. 'Our boat was the *Burrumbeet*', wrote Bosanquet, 'and it was bound to be a bad sailor with a name like that'.

Safely landed, the players admired the beauty of Hobart and Mount Wellington and were reminded of England as they looked at hawthorn hedges, gorse and brier. Albert Knight, ever in quest of a bold simile, likened the mountain to 'a great prison house', whilst Bosanquet saw it, more romantically, as 'the guardian-spirit of the place, seeming to threaten all who would approach in hostile guise.'

The team was generously entertained. There were visits to the racecourse and an old convict settlement, concerts in the Town Hall, trips in river tugs, drives to Longford and Mount Welling-ton, shooting, fishing, a tour round a British warship. 'We were rowed out', noted Knight, 'by jack tars who plied their oars with skill and beauty'.

There was also a little cricket. Two-day matches were arranged with Tasmanian XIs at Hobart and Launceston, in which there was much interest, for no English team had visited since Stod-dart's ten years before. The first match was enlivened by Bosan-quet's uninhibited hitting, his unbeaten 124 containing four 5s and eighteen 4s. One of his straight drives cleared the pavilion, another landed at the entrance gates. The second game was notable for the fact that all eleven players got a bowl, including George Drummond (who was playing because Foster and Bosan-quet had gone off fishing). Both matches were drawn.

Refreshed by their sojourn in Tasmania, the MCC defeated Victoria for a second time, bowling them out for a humiliating 15 runs (still the lowest total in first-class Australian cricket), Rhodes taking 10 for 19 after the rains came. New South Wales were also beaten for a second time at Sydney, Bosanquet, the matchwinner, scoring 114 in ninety minutes and taking 6 for 45. But the Australian selectors were cheered by a promising newcomer to the State side, the 20-year-old 'Tibby' Cotter – an excitingly fast bowler, who had recently sprung to notice as a rugby footballer. Strongly built, though not tall and with a low arm action, Cotter disconcerted the tourists by pitching very short and bouncing the ball around their heads.

After these successes the tourists crossed the Blue Mountains to play a Bathurst XV, the locals augmented by several Sydney men, including the Aboriginal fast bowler, Marsh. Warner, who quickly lost his middle stump to Marsh, reckoned he threw three balls per over. Foster agreed. 'I have never seen anyone throw so deliberately. It was a good wicket and he was turning the ball up to a yard at times.' Warner let the Australians know that any hopes they might have entertained of playing Marsh in the remaining Tests would be strongly resisted. Warner, not to be trifled with in negotiations at any time, was always in belligerent mood when playing second-class matches. To him each rabbit which burrowed ostentatiously on the Bathurst outfield was an insult, as was each dog which gave joyful, noisy pursuit. He had little time for the leafy, idyllic setting, the ring enclosed by a cluster of rustics and vehicles of every quaint description.

A further week's rest followed! The Fosters took off again, staying with friends at Blair Atholl and Darling Point. Whilst an unpleasant damp heat prevailed at Sydney and rain prevented the team practising, Tip Foster was still able to shoot some rabbits and play some vigorous croquet on the eve of the fourth Test. Plum Warner, meanwhile, was engaged in one of his off-field battles. He was determined to have for the Test the two best umpires, in his view Crockett and Argall, and he refused to accept the nominees of the New South Wales Cricket Association, one of whom, Giltinan, the tourists considered quite appalling. Warner's moral position was strengthened when a private letter of his to the Association, alleging Giltinan's incompetence, was ill-advisedly leaked to the press. Although, in fact, he was arguing a weak case (for before the team sailed the MCC had conceded that the Australians should appoint the umpires), Warner was implacable, pointing out that it had been the habit in the past for the two captains to make the choice. Eventually, the Australians were told that the MCC would withdraw from the fourth Test, unless Crockett and Argall umpired. Warner duly won his point!

Enormous, partisan crowds again packed the Sydney Cricket Ground for the fourth Test. England began slowly, Albert Knight occupying the crease for much of the first day, strokeless except for the occasional flashing square cut. He was an unlikely hero. Slightly built, with a light moustache, Knight was a man of proverbial meekness and courtesy, who always addressed his fellow professionals and umpires as 'Mr'. 'Oh, do come, Mr Tyldesley', he would call down the wicket. For once on the tour he mastered his excitability and erratic running, his unbeaten 70 allowing England to reach 249. Two days of rain cut short Australia's reply at 114–5. A terrible struggle for runs then ensued, Australia losing the last 5 wickets cheaply but Hayward holding the second English innings together with a skilful 52, much to Warner's delight. Here was another chance for Warner to retaliate at the critics: 'I have read that C. B. Fry considers that Hayward at his best is never worth more than 13 runs on a bad wicket. Mr Fry really should not make these statements!' At the end of the fourth day's play England were 155–9, leading by 273 runs.

At this crucial stage another off-field confrontation occurred. The Sydney authorities intended to roll the wicket that evening, but Warner, worried that this might help the Australian batsmen, argued that English practice forbade a roller in the evening. There were heated exchanges, during which Warner ordered his junior professional, Herbert Strudwick, to mount guard at the wicket and resist all rollers. In the end Noble capitulated and Strudwick was able to return to his hotel bed. On the final day the Australians were set a target of 329 to square the series. They were a strong batting side and there was much Australian optimism and English anxiety, but a match-winning performance by Bernard Bosanquet upset all calculations (except possibly his own). By taking 6 for 51 with his big-spinning leg-breaks and occasional googlies, he destroyed the Australian innings and won the Ashes. With this feat he vindicated the judgement of Charlie Bannerman, who two years before, after watching Bosanquet from an umpire's vantage point, had told Warner, 'Son, that off-breaking leg-break of his might one day win a Test match'.

For Bosanquet the fourth Test at Sydney was the climax of years of trial and error. It is said that he first conceived the googly as a boy when he was flicking a tennis ball over the bare slates of an old family billiard-table. He continued his experiments in games played with his brother involving a hard rubber ball and a broomstick. At Eton he kept quiet about his invention and at Oxford for much of his time he played as a conventional fast bowler. But now, at last, the googly was respected internationally and would enjoy a long period of respectability – some of its best practitioners, like Mailey and O'Reilly, being Australians.

Any wrist spinner depends much on his wicket-keeper and in this Bosanquet was most fortunate. Dick Lilley, who had never kept to him before the tour, anxiously studied him from behind the nets at Adelaide as soon as they landed. He quickly realized that it was impossible to detect from Bosanquet's action what the ball was going to do, but he resisted the temptation to ask the bowler to keep to a set procedure, which would have been inhibiting for him, and instead learned to take him intuitively. It was a happy collaboration, exemplified by his catch and three stumpings in the final innings of this fourth Test. The delighted Lilley rescued the ball at the end of the game and presented it to Bosanquet, suitably inscribed and mounted.

Back in England the news of the recovery of the Ashes was greeted with delight, some critics rapidly forgetting that they had ever forecast anything but success. Others, by failing to agree with the prevailing sentiment that Plum Warner was one of the greatest Englishmen living, sounded somewhat sour. Thus C. B. Fry, writing an open letter to Warner in the *Daily Express*, began: 'It cannot be denied that you have on the whole been a lucky captain. The great big public, however, my dear Plum, is inclined to attribute success not to good luck but good management. . . .' Warner did not agree: 'We won the rubber fairly and squarely', he tersely asserted, 'by superior cricket and our victory could be attributed in no way to fluke or chance.'

Warner's own contribution as a player was limited. He had not been particularly successful either as a batsman or a fielder. His captaincy also seems to have been lacking in imagination and authority. From time to time Tip Foster would confide to his diary his frustrations on this subject. At Brisbane, early on, he wrote: 'So far Warner has captained quite well, though things have gone our way and there has been no difficulty – but in this match he has captained very badly – he had no idea how to get

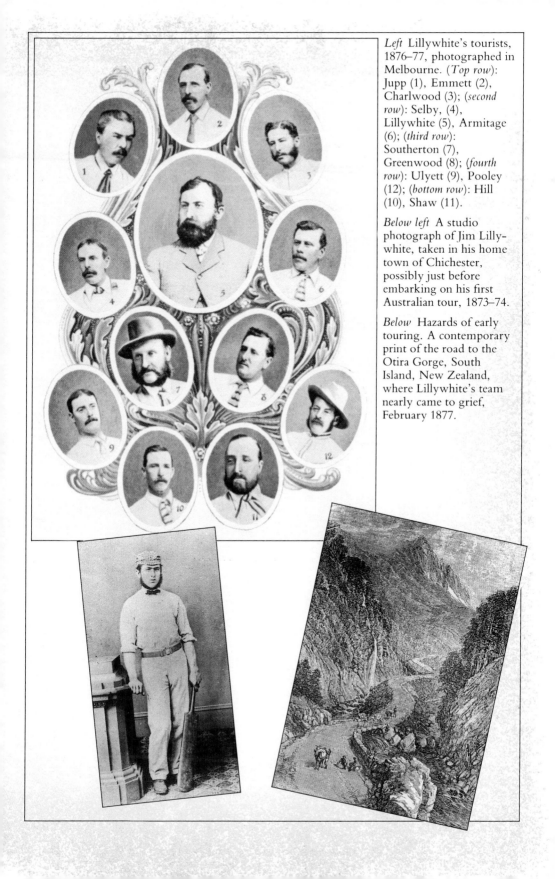

Left Lillywhite's tourists, 1876–77, photographed in Melbourne. (*Top row*): Jupp (1), Emmett (2), Charlwood (3); (*second row*): Selby, (4), Lillywhite (5), Armitage (6); (*third row*): Southerton (7), Greenwood (8); (*fourth row*): Ulyett (9), Pooley (12); (*bottom row*): Hill (10), Shaw (11).

Below left A studio photograph of Jim Lillywhite, taken in his home town of Chichester, possibly just before embarking on his first Australian tour, 1873–74.

Below Hazards of early touring. A contemporary print of the road to the Otira Gorge, South Island, New Zealand, where Lillywhite's team nearly came to grief, February 1877.

Above All-England in the field at Melbourne, 1876–77. The match is probably that against XV of Victoria in December 1876. Shaw is bowling and Pooley would seem to be keeping wicket while the bearded Lillywhite hovers in the slips. The new grandstand is well patronised.

Below Plum Warner (*centre*) at the Sydney Cricket Ground and his two amateur companions on the tour – B J T Bosanquet (Oxford Blue, 1898–1900) and R E Foster (Oxford Blue, 1897–1900).

THE AUSTRALIAN EXCURSION.

POINTS OF VIEW
A.C. MacLaren and P.F. Warner as they appear
to the "man in the street".

THE AUSTRALIAN EXCURSION.

Master "PLUM" WARNER:-"Oh, Mr. Fry please do come with me
across the seas, and shed a little lustre on our Mary-le-bones."

Two of the many
cartoons in the national
newspapers, deriding
Warner and his team
before their departure.

Top left On board the *Orontes*: the professional tourists of 1903–04. (*Back row, left to right*): Braund, Relf, Arnold, Rhodes, Hayward, Lilley; (*middle row, left to right*): Fielder, Hirst, Strudwick; (*front row, left to right*): Tyldesley, Knight.

Top right On board the *Orontes*: (*left to right*) Miss Starkey, Miss Blyth, Foster, Warner, Mrs Foster.

Centre The third Test match at Adelaide, January 1904. Warner is well caught right-handed by McLeod at mid-on for 48, 'the sort of catch that comes off once in twenty times', wrote PFW. Hugh Trumble is the bowler; Foster, the other batsman, looks not to have backed up very far.

Bottom The MCC party at Adelaide, January 1904, where they lost the third Test: (*back row, left to right*) Strudwick, Murdoch, Relf, Foster, Knight, Arnold, Fielder, Rhodes, Braund, Tyldesley; (*front row, left to right*) Hayward, Bosanquet, Warner, Hirst, Lilley. Foster is looking distinctly unwell and has chosen not to practise with the team.

Above The departure of the MCC's boat-train, bound for Australia, from a crowded Waterloo platform, September 1936.

Left MCC's arrival at Fremantle, October 1936. *Top row, left to right*: Ken Farnes reading a newspaper; Voce, Worthington and Fagg; Verity; Ames and Hammond, smoking; *centre row*: Howard (left), Wyatt and Allen (seated), Voce, Duckworth, Worthington and Copson (standing); Copson and Barnett; *bottom row*: Hardstaff, Leyland, Sims and Fishlock; Verity, Voce and Farnes disembark.

Two cartoons at the time of the 1936–37 tour. At the top Tom Webster illustrates the English reaction to Bradman's high scoring; at the bottom is the opposite Australian view.

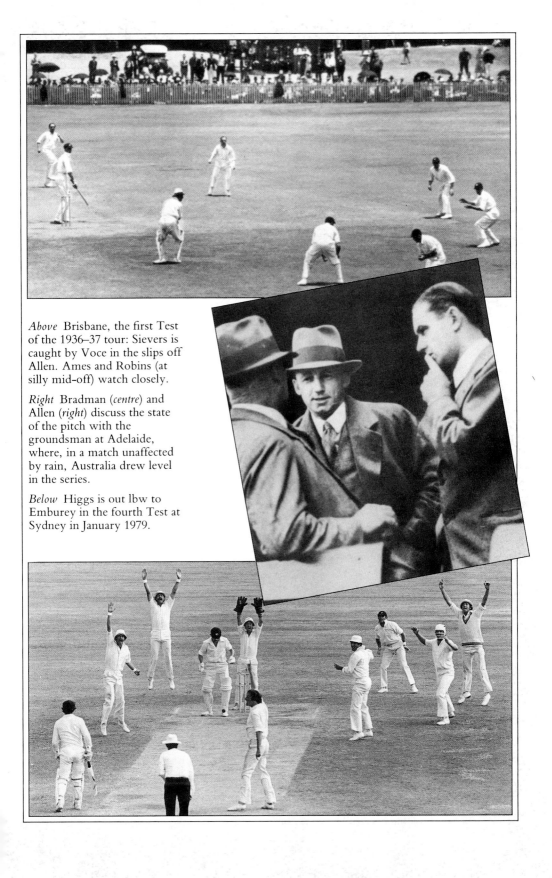

Above Brisbane, the first Test of the 1936–37 tour: Sievers is caught by Voce in the slips off Allen. Ames and Robins (at silly mid-off) watch closely.

Right Bradman (*centre*) and Allen (*right*) discuss the state of the pitch with the groundsman at Adelaide, where, in a match unaffected by rain, Australia drew level in the series.

Below Higgs is out lbw to Emburey in the fourth Test at Sydney in January 1979.

Above Gooch is given out lbw to Hogg for 40 in the third Test at Melbourne in December 1978.

Centre Randall is beaten but not out during his great innings of 150 in the fourth Test at Sydney in January 1979.

Below Ian Botham hits out at Yardley, only to be caught by Wood in the second Test at Perth in December 1978.

Evans out. . . .' After losing the third Test, Foster wrote: 'The captaincy of our side was very bad and has been all through except the first match – Warner dashes about the field and seems to lose his head.' Later, during a match with Victoria, he returned to the same theme: 'I have never seen a side captained worse than we were. Unless some keenness is got into the team they won't be able to pull themselves together for the Test matches.'

Nonetheless it was Warner who ultimately made the decisive contribution. Urbane, sensitive and charming he certainly was, but he had another side to his character, a ruthlessness and single-mindedness, which, in 1903–04, bordered on the fanatical. From the moment he arrived in Australia he was going to let nothing get in the way of success. When some reporters boarded the *Orontes* at Adelaide for an interview, he refused to speak to them. It did not fit in with his plans. When small boys at Ballarat barracked the team, he coldly remarked, 'These youths should be put down with a rod of good birch'. His speeches were often blunt to the point of tactlessness. At a Bendigo luncheon the local dignitaries were quickly put in their place: 'Thank you for your kind welcome. I must regret that the wicket provided is not a very good one. This is unfortunate and I am sure the local team would have done much better on a good wicket. I understand that the last English team had a splendid one to play on. A good wicket is essential for the making of good cricketers. It gives me great pleasure in proposing the health of the Mayor.'

As he progressed through Australia Warner seems to have seen himself more and more as the messianic representative of the MCC before whom all must show obeisance. He was always quick, in his off-the-field disputes, to invoke the name of cricket's governing body and from the first match of the tour, where he was embroiled in an argument about the follow-on rule, he seems to have been intent to convert the heathen to the Laws of the godly. In the subtle psychological battle he waged with his hosts, Warner was helped hugely by the poor behaviour of some of the Australian crowds, which must have been a great embarrassment to men like Noble with their high, Golden Age ideals. With the Australians very much on the defensive over this, it was all the easier for Warner, the representative of British fair play, to impose his will in other matters, so he took every opportunity to belabour Australian lack of sportsmanship. Thus, in the fourth Test, when umpire Crockett was slow in coming out after rain and some bottles were thrown, Warner was quick to criticize. It mattered not that there were less than fifty trouble-makers out of a crowd of 35,000; the incident stemmed from his own insistence that Crockett should umpire again at Sydney. Warner's intention was at all times to strengthen his position of moral superiority. It may not, in itself, have won any matches, but it certainly helped.

Warner was also successful in the way he was able to impose himself on his professionals. They seem to have liked him and respected his authority. It was easier for him than it had been for Jim Lillywhite to maintain discipline, for they knew that any wild off-the-field behaviour could lead to trouble back home, where the influence of Warner and the MCC was all-pervasive. Thus Plum could write with some confidence: 'One needs a team who are loyal and true, who will put cricket first, keeping out of the way of the many temptations of a great Australian city.'

In all the circumstances, therefore, it was not surprising that the winning of the Ashes filled Plum Warner with such pride. 'As long as I live, whatever lies ahead,' he wrote, 'I shall look back to the evening of March 3rd, 1904 as the golden evening of my cricket career, an evening of memories never to be repeated, but never to be swept away.'

The final Test was at Melbourne, where Australia won and so lost the series 2–3. The final match was at Adelaide, where the MCC beat South Australia, thus completing victories over all the States. There was a farewell banquet at Adelaide before the team travelled down to Largs Bay for the homeward voyage. There were some hurried final presentations. Wilfred Rhodes was awarded the ball, suitably engraved, with which he had taken his first wicket of the tour with his first delivery in Australia. Plum Warner was less flattered to be given a pickle bottle containing some burnt remains. 'Ashes of Australian cricket', read the label. 'Won by Captain Weather, assisted by Captain Warner.' The recipient somehow managed a smile. As the launch took the tourists out to the *Orontes*, colours were dipped three times. Three cheers for Warner's team rang out from the Australians on the jetty and these were quickly reciprocated. The launch sped into the bay and Warner quietly tossed his pickle jar overboard.

It was six months since the team had last been in England and it would take them more than five weeks to return. But they could reflect, as they began the 12,000-mile journey, on time well spent. Of their twenty matches, they had won ten, drawn eight and lost only two. How foolish now looked all the hysterical criticism when Warner was picked as captain instead of MacLaren.

They had been aided by the leisurely nature of the tour. Of their 130 days on Australian soil, only sixty-two had been spent playing cricket. Twelve of the twenty matches had been played at the three big centres, Melbourne, Sydney and Adelaide. This had allowed the players to develop roots and acclimatize themselves to local conditions. It compared very favourably with Jim Lilly-white's hectic schedule.

The development of railways in Australia had also been a great boon. Of course, travel in Edwardian steam trains was not always an unmitigated pleasure and the same journey could provoke different reactions from different people. The eighteen-hour jour-ney from Sydney to Brisbane, for example, was perfectly tolerable to Relf and Knight. Relf slept well overnight and enjoyed the scenery and refreshments; Knight noted that on the Queensland border they changed to 'a very comfortble saloon, which quite belied the reputation of narrow gauge for uneasy running' and he enjoyed the perpetual zig-zags on the single track across the Toowoomba range. Foster, by contrast, found the journey too long and too hot. Their arrival at Brisbane, in Relf's view, was quite triumphant: 'band playing and a great crowd to meet us'. Foster saw it differently: 'Received by a howling mob and band' and Warner sympathized: 'We might have been a collection of monkeys on the way to the zoo'. Foster and Warner increasingly hated the eighteen-hour trek from Adelaide to Melbourne. To Relf, however, this was a 'nice journey', the night spent in 'a nice sleeping-car'.

In addition to easier travel, Warner's team also enjoyed better hotels than those experienced by Lillywhite. They did not approve of the hotels at Maitland and Hobart, but those in the big cities were first-class. 'There are the usual smoking-rooms', wrote Lilley, 'bars, billiards-rooms, as in England, and nothing to suggest that in this particular Australia has departed from ideas of the homeland.' He believed the Australia Hotel at Sydney was the best hotel in the country and he was full of praise for the South Australia Hotel in Adelaide and the Menzies Hotel in Melbourne.

Overall the tourists loved the country and its people. Strudwick described it as a land of sunshine and freedom, the people 'good, clean, lovable and very social.' Few would have argued with this. Each had his own favourite city. Strudwick preferred Sydney, where the winding, narrow roads and 'many business houses' reminded him of London. Lilley praised Sydney's 'many fine suburban districts' but preferred the wide streets and splendid shops of Adelaide and Melbourne. Bert Relf was quite shocked when shown the latter's Chinese quarter with the many opium dens around Little Bourke Street, and was unimpressed by Brisbane (where he had expected there would be opals 'knocking about cheap'). He was very taken with Bendigo (with its fine buildings and trams). No one seemed to have liked Maitland.

As a team they had been as united as Warner had hoped. The shared experience of the voyage out was helpful to team morale. 'I'm sure this went a long way', commented Bosanquet, 'towards helping us all to pull together and further our better acquaintances and in engendering that feeling of good comradeship without which it is impossible for any side to do well.' There was, nonetheless, a very clear social divide between the amateurs and professionals. Warner might claim, with truth, that for the first time ever amateurs and professionals were staying at the same hotels 'and it was a great success' and they also shared the same dressing-room, whereas in England there was strict segregation. But these measures were more a sop to Australian public opinion than a token of any deep social awakening on the part of MCC; and the strict Edwardian class system dictated a dichotomy of off-field activities. On their first Sunday at Sydney, for example, whilst the professionals were out enjoying glorious sunshine with picnics around the harbour, the Fosters spent a much more formal day, going to church in the morning, lunching at Admiralty House and taking tea with friends. Arrangements at Hobart were interestingly varied. Whilst the professionals were booked late into poor hotels, Warner and Bosanquet were met at the railway station by the ADC to his Excellency the Governor, and were escorted to Government House where they stayed for the fortnight. (It may have been the strict protocol of Government House which forced Plum to leave Agnes behind in Melbourne.) The Fosters meanwhile found accommodation with a Vice-Admiral. Here Tip was able to relax in the social manner to which he was accustomed. For sport there was tennis and croquet and, in his honour, a cricket match was arranged with the Vice-Admiral's grooms. The amateurs and professionals, therefore, tended to go their separate ways off the field of play and close familiarity between the classes was not acceptable. Relf, the working-class professional, would address his amateur captain as 'Mr Warner' and would even write of him as such in his diary: 'Mr Warner gave me a bat . . . Mr Warner introduced me to Lady Darnley . . . Mr Warner is pleased with us . . . Mr Warner continues to get anonymous letters about some of us. . . .' Likewise, when Mr Foster chatted to him on the train coming down from Brisbane, it was an event worth chronicling.

Perhaps the most unifying factor for any touring team is a shared sense of outrage that the home officials are always favouring their own side. Warner's team was soon regretting the fact that the MCC had given up its original plan to send out an English umpire, for the home players certainly seemed to be exerting an undue influence over the local officials. 'It is not good', wrote Warner sternly during the second Test, 'to see a bowler shouting wildly when the ball hits the batsman in the waist, especially when that ball has turned so much it would not even hit six stumps, supposing they were high enough.' Foster's progress through Australia had been one long, gloomy catalogue of umpiring ineptitude. 'I was given out lbw'; he wrote of Sydney, 'but I hit my pad with my bat and the ball never touched it.' The umpires, however, seemed less trigger-happy when the Australians were batting: 'Trumper was given in lbw to Arnold', he wrote of the third Test, 'to what looked dead out.' The professionals were equally scathing. 'An appeal for lbw always makes an Englishman shiver', wrote Albert Knight feelingly, and Relf wrote of his dismissal at Newcastle: 'Worst decision I ever saw. Played the ball in the middle of my bat and someone shouted and I had to go.'

It was a party, therefore, united by shared experience and flushed with triumph which left the *Orontes* in mid-April and travelled up by train from Marseilles. At Paris they bade farewell to Tip and Diane Foster, who had decided to spend a few days by the Seine, and soon, at Dover, they met their first posse of reporters anxious to pepper them with questions. Plum Warner, perversely sporting a boater with Lord Hawke's touring colours, gave the first of many interviews, whilst Albert Knight blinked anxiously at the gathering crowd and wondered what would happen at Victoria. 'I was accused in certain quarters', said Warner expansively, 'of being a quick change bowling artiste but I knew my men and it paid. That was the great thing. Fregoli was a quick change artiste, and a success, and I followed his example. Take, for instance, the fourth and deciding match at Sydney. Here Arnold captured 2 wickets for 19 runs, but I substituted Bosanquet, and what did he do?. . . .' George Hirst pulled at his watch-chain surreptitiously. It was a long way from Dover to Kirkheaton . . . and the skipper seemed to be in alarmingly loquacious mood.

Attempts had been made to keep the arrival of the team in the Dover boat train a secret, but there were a thousand supporters waiting at Victoria in the early evening, crowding platform 3. Another thousand were waiting, less fruitfully, at Charing Cross. As the train pulled up, there was a general rush for the carriage doors and such great pressure against them that they would not open. For five minutes the team were penned in their compartments, while the crowd cheered and pushed and stayed exactly where it was. Then Southern Railway officials unlocked the doors on the far side of the train and the team began a dash along the unoccupied platform, whilst porters, entering the carriages, prevented the crowd from climbing through. In the general confusion afterwards one of the first spotted was Len Braund, wearing an Alpine hat, his face tanned a deep brick red. Plum Warner and

Bosanquet, escaping together, at first went unnoticed as they searched for family, friends and cabs, but then a cry went up, 'Here's Warner!' and the chase was on. Tom Hayward was discovered 'looking even redder than usual' and was swept away in honour. The northern trio, Rhodes, Hirst and Tyldesley caused a big diversion, running for a large four-wheeler. As the driver stirred his horses, the reporters pounced, only to meet with Yorkshire obduracy. 'I've nowt t' say', muttered Wilfred Rhodes. 'I'm tired and want to go home. We've train t' catch at Euston.' Herbert Strudwick, similarly trapped, was more forthcoming. 'It was a very happy time from start to finish.' Crowds surged around. 'Why did you win?', one asked. Fifty heads craned forward, eager to hear words of wisdom. 'We won', replied Strudwick, 'because every member of the team was a trier.'

The final act of the tour of 1903–04 was played out at the Trocadero, London, when a celebration banquet was held several days after the team's return. It was a magnificent occasion, the dining-room full of the most distinguished cricketing celebrities (with a few notable absentees such as MacLaren and Fry). Plum Warner sat at the right hand of Lord Alverstone, Lord Chief Justice of England and President of MCC. It was an opportunity for the club to celebrate formally its victory over its critics and to salute its hero. Plum Warner's hold on the reins of power at St John's Wood would never loosen over the next sixty years. He was in his element, fêted by friends, admired by all, his every decision vindicated. When at last he rose to speak, his eyes were twinkling. 'Lord Alverstone, my lords and gentlemen. A few weeks ago I saw a cartoon in *Punch*, where I was depicted as a lion to whom the kangeroo was handing over the Ashes.' Warner ran his hand over his bald dome, reflectively. 'I am afraid I am a lion without a mane. As Lord Alverstone will tell you, in the law one usually begins by denying everything, but I do not see how, standing before you here, I can well say that I am anything but maneless. . . .' Plum Warner continued to weave his spell on the distinguished gathering, deftly recounting the winter's glorious deeds, whilst the air grew thicker with the pall of expensive cigars. 'Is it quite the same Plum that left us last September?' queried Lord Hawke in some anxiety.

Postscript

FROM WARNER TO ALLEN

The wedding of Agnes Blyth and Plum Warner duly took place only a few weeks after the team's return. The successful recovery of the Ashes had made the bridegroom a figure of national interest and the wedding, with Lord Hawke best man and Lord Roberts and Henry Irving among the guests, caused great public excitement. Plum failed to keep the English captaincy for the next home series, but he soon became a Test selector and he led further MCC sides abroad, to South Africa in 1905, and to Australia again in 1911 (when he was accompanied by Agnes and their two young children). His captaincy of Middlesex stretched beyond the First World War, from 1908 to his retirement in 1920, when he began an even fuller involvement in journalism. Plum Warner's influence in the media was balanced by that at Lord's, where he was ever close to the heart of things.

The MCC, in sending three teams to Australia before the War, had established a four-yearly cycle, and this pattern was observed in the the 1920s and 1930s. The inter-war period was a time of great expansion of Test cricket. Four MCC sides played Tests in South Africa, two in the West Indies and one in India. The traditional foe still dominated, however. Five teams were sent to Australia in this period and Anglo-Australian cricket remained of paramount importance, watched by densely-packed, knowledge-able crowds and followed by millions on the radio.

One player, of course, was supreme in the inter-war period – Don Bradman. Born in 1908, the heyday of Victor Trumper and Clem Hill, Bradman was to become the most successful batsman of all time. In his long first-class career he averaged over 95 runs per innings, his Test average being just a fraction under 100. Bradman's apparent infallibility led, of course, to Douglas Jardine's body-line campaign of 1932–33, the most remembered tour of all, when Australian outrage at English tactics nearly severed a chain of Tests which stretched back over fifty years to Lillywhite.

Plum Warner was heavily involved with Jardine's team, both as chairman of the selectors and as manager. He is usually portrayed as an anxious onlooker, unhappy about body-line but unable to do anything about it – a very different Warner indeed from that of 1903–04, whose tenacity of purpose and toughness in negotiation were so much in evidence. It is difficult to believe that a man could alter so radically. Arthur Mailey, in 1932, saw Warner as an 'autocrat' and 'dictator'. Such a manager, with all the weight of the cricket establishment behind him, could surely have prevailed upon a captain, thirty years his junior? But surprisingly he didn't. He regretted the controversy, indeed was embarrassed by it, but, despite private misgivings, tolerated the tactics which were winning back the Ashes for England.

Later, however, in England, all ambivalence was cast aside and Warner spoke out against body-line, beginning the long process of convincing everyone that body-line was wrong. The change of viewpoint was politically inspired. Warner, seen by both Australian and British politicians as the man who mattered most at Lord's, had been firmly told that, for political and cricketing peace, body-line must be deplored and Jardine, as captain of England, discarded. Excuses and pretexts were the order of the day. By the time the Australians came to tour England in 1934 Larwood and Voce were no longer under consideration as England players and Jardine had abruptly terminated his first-class cricket career.

The politicians were similarly active when the next tour, that of Gubby Allen in 1936–37, began to be discussed. Appeasement was in the air. Just as fear of war led to the condoning of Hitler's and Mussolini's acts of aggression, so, too, fear of damage to the British Empire lurked at Lord's. Thus Larwood continued to be ignored, his old toe injury providing a convenient excuse. Neville Cardus might talk sadly of him 'compelled to use the canter of compromise instead of his old lovely gallop', but Larwood, at 31, was still one of the very best fast bowlers in England that summer, top of the averages with over 100 wickets. Yet, while MCC toured, Larwood coached in India. Never before had politics and cricket become so intertwined.

4

GUBBY ALLEN'S TOUR

1936-37

The tour of 1936–37 was a public relations exercise, inspired by Hawke and Warner. The latter frequently remarked that all tours were made primarily 'to cement the bonds of Empire' and 'cementing' became the catch-word of this tour. Kenneth Farnes, a team member, wrote in his autobiography that a new spirit of sportsmanship was to be engendered. The tour's sole purpose, he said, was 'that the implications of the word "cricket" might persist'. The players listened to 'sonorous speeches of exhortation' before departure. Quoting Warner verbatim, Farnes continued: 'There was to be constant cementing of the sacred bonds of Empire.'

Plum Warner believed that Gubby Allen was the ideal man to be captain. Allen, as the one fast bowler in 1932–33 who had refused to bowl body-line, was especially acceptable to the Australian Board of Control. In addition, he had been born in Sydney and, even though he had moved to England at the age of six and had been educated at Eton and Cambridge, he was a fourth-generation Australian, with many Australian relatives (including an uncle who had played for Australia in the 1880s).

Gubby Allen was equally acceptable to the MCC. Indeed he was that body's favourite son and Plum Warner's special protégé. The Allen and Warner families both lived at Datchet, near Eton, in the 1920s and Gubby Allen's mother was very friendly with Agnes Warner. Pearl Allen was a most attractive lady, and, according to Allen's biographer, E. W. Swanton, 'she kept at a discreet distance a string of admirers of whom Plum was not least'. It was not surprising, then, that Warner, when captain of Middlesex, kept a close eye on the promising Etonian, twenty-nine years his junior.

The strands of cricket's past are stubbornly interwoven with its present. Just as Tom Emmett had coached the young Plum Warner at Rugby, so the young Gubby Allen had been helped not just by Warner but, as a boy, by Albert Knight and, in his final year at Eton, by George Hirst. Allen did well at Eton but he was not deemed suitable material for captaincy, being of too strong-willed a nature, nor at Cambridge (where lack of academic success ended his career after only two years). Thereafter the need to earn a living, at first with the Royal Exchange Assurance and later at Debenham's, impeded regular county cricket. However, Warner's continued patronage, and Allen's own outstanding talents as an aggressive all-rounder, led to his participation in the tour of 1932–33. In its aftermath Allen attacked body-line as savagely as Warner. Elevation to the corridors of power followed. He was made an MCC Committee member when only 33, and when the tour of 1936–37 came along, Gubby Allen's nomination as captain was something of a formality. In the summer of 1936 Allen and Warner (with two fellow selectors) were soon busy picking the side.

The team was chosen piecemeal with a first announcement of just six names: Hammond, Leyland, Verity, Fishlock, Hardstaff and R. W. V. Robins. Hammond and Leyland were then considered the best batsmen in England and would both be touring Australia for the third time. Hammond, 33-years-old and at his peak as a classical batsman, was rated second only to Bradman himself. 'Put Hammond in an arena with 100 other batsmen playing the cover drive', wrote Jack Fingleton, 'and you would know him immediately.' Leyland, a most punishing left-hander, strong at driving and cutting, would be, at 36, the oldest tourist. His fellow Yorkshireman, Hedley Verity, a left-arm spinner in the classic tradition of Wilfred Rhodes, had already toured successfully with Jardine, but the other three choices were less expected. Fishlock and Hardstaff were both promising professional batsmen, in their early 20s, whilst the 30-year-old Walter Robins was the only amateur of the six.

There are uncanny similarities between Robins and Bosanquet. Both were dashing middle-order batsmen and leg-break and googly bowlers. Both played for Middlesex, their captain's county, had gained a cricket Blue at their captain's university, and were, as it chanced, exactly four years younger than their captain. Just as Bosanquet owed his selection to friendship with Warner, so also Robins with Allen. In both cases there was enough cheerful nepotism involved to make any self-respecting northern professional choke on his ale.

Four more professionals were named in early August: George Duckworth of Lancashire, now 35, a wicket-keeper on two previous tours; Bill Copson, a young, relatively untried Derbyshire seam bowler; Arthur Fagg, the Kent batsman, at 21 one of the youngest players ever to be chosen to tour Australia; and Stan Worthington, the Derbyshire all-rounder. Meanwhile, much discussion was going on behind closed doors about Bill Voce, Larwood's left-arm body-line partner. Allen and Warner did not want him, but the other selectors did, believing the English attack very weak without him. Allen was persuaded to have secret talks with Voce. Eventually the latter agreed to tour, signing a document in which he regretted any trouble that there had been in the past.

Voce's inclusion was announced with that of Jim Sims, the Middlesex leg-spinner, Charles Barnett, the attacking Gloucester batsman, and two amateurs, Errol Holmes, the Surrey captain, and Kenneth Farnes, a 25-year-old schoolmaster at Worksop College, whose appearances as a fast bowler for Essex were necessarily limited. The final, 17th place had been kept for Leslie Ames, Kent's wicket-keeper-batsman, who had been out of cricket for most of the season with back trouble. Finally, when Errol Holmes decided to withdraw for business reasons, Bob Wyatt received a deserved recall. He had captained England in 1930 and 1934 and had been vice-captain in Australia under Jardine. He was, therefore, the obvious candidate for the vice-captaincy, but no such appointment was made, Allen preferring to manage his side with absolute authority.

This absolutism, the fruits of a burning self-belief which fired Allen's whole personality, encouraged him to assimilate the duties of others. He undertook, for example, much of the manager's role. In earlier years this had been very competently filled by Fred Toone, the Yorkshire secretary, who had supervised the tours of Douglas, Gilligan and Chapman and had been knighted for his pains. Warner succeeded Toone in 1932–33 and may have been tempted to offer his services again, but he opted instead for Captain Rupert Howard, owner of a thriving textile business in

Lancashire, where he was the county's secretary. Howard, who was in his mid-40s, was a charming man, first-class at 'cementing', but, strangely, he had no previous experience of Australia. The MCC, it seems clear, was less interested in winning matches than friends.

Public reaction to the selections was predictably negative. It was considered to be one of the weakest ever to go abroad. The criticism seems more justified than that of Warner's team in 1903. The omission of Lancashire's Eddie Paynter weakened the batting, whilst the Surrey fast bowler, Alf Gover, who had taken over 200 wickets in the summer, might well have gone instead of Copson. Above all, the selectors had feared to take a chance on the 20-year-old Len Hutton and 18-year-old Denis Compton, whose quality was in stark contrast to the worthy but uninspired talents of Worthington, Fagg and Fishlock. The bowling lacked variety. Much depended on the pace of Voce, Allen, Farnes and Copson; the slow bowling consisted simply of the left-arm Verity and two leg-spinners, with no off-spinner at all. The batting was largely inexperienced and there was still no opening partnership to replace that of Hobbs, now retired, and Sutcliffe, now 41. All in all, the pessimism seemed justified and Allen unlikely to be bringing back the Ashes.

There was no lack of optimism, however, when Gubby Allen's team left Waterloo in September 1936, boarding the boat train in their dark three-piece suits, looking more like City businessmen than cricketers. 'I am always an optimist', said Allen to reporters, as trilby-hatted enthusiasts pressed densely around, 'and I think we shall do very much better than most people in this country seem to think. We are starting on a wonderful trip. I am sure we shall make many friends.'

Fittingly Plum Warner himself was amongst the large crowd of well-wishers, but of his Ashes-winning team of 1903–04 there were no other representatives. Several, like Tip Foster, Dick Lilley and Johnny Tyldesley were long since dead, whilst before

the tour was through Bernard Bosanquet and Bert Relf were to
die (the latter by his own hand).

Not all the tourists joined the boat train at Waterloo. Walter
Robins, for example, drove down to Southampton with his wife.
Several other wives went down to the port, including Mrs Arthur
Fagg, whose honeymoon had been cut short by the tour. Some
married couples coped better with the long separation than others.
Joe Hardstaff accepted it philosophically: 'It was my job and I had
to go where my job led me. My son was 21 before I spent a
winter with him.' By contrast, Walter Hammond's wife never
came to terms with the separations, always refusing to go to see
her husband off. Their marriage eventually broke up. Few of the
players faced the prospect of seven months of celibacy with much
resolution. One, asked how he spent his time on the long voyage,
remarked candidly, 'Chasing bints, mostly!' George Duckworth
in particular was reputed to be a ladies' man of infinite resource.
Wherever it went, the team attracted its fair share of feminine
admirers. Bob Wyatt, sensing Walter Robins's susceptibility to
their blandishments, tantalized him for many weeks with news of
a very beautiful, but wholly fictitious, admirer, whom somehow
Robins was never quite able to meet. Undoubtedly the tourists of
1936–37 were lucky to live in an uncensorious age, when privacy
was respected by the media.

Rain fell steadily at Southampton as the tourists assembled on
the deck of the P & O liner, the *Orion*, for a final flurry of
photographs. There followed a short reception, whilst the players'
luggage was being taken aboard the ship, under the watchful eye
of Bill Ferguson, the team's scorer and baggageman. Fergie, an
Australian, had first travelled to England with Monty Noble in
1905, and subsequently represented touring teams all over the
world, helping MCC with nine visits to Australia. His job had
begun this time when Allen's men had assembled at the Great
Western Hotel in London, consigning to his care their 180 pieces
of baggage. These included Bob Wyatt's precious wind-up
gramophone and collection of brittle 78s: popular dance songs,
Maori and Hawaiian music and a little Mozart and Beethoven.
Leaving nothing to chance, Fergie had travelled down to Southampton in a lorry with the baggage. Now all was safely distrib-
uted to the cabins: *These Foolish Things* and *Smoke Gets In Your*

Eyes were wafting from Wyatt's cabin and Fergie could relax, while the *Orion* eased her way out of her home port.

There were few more stylish ways of travelling in the 1930s than first-class on a luxury liner. The *Orion* was built on a grand scale, accommodating 1100 passengers and 460 crew. Only recently launched, she had cost over £1 million and offered immense comfort on eight decks, the first liner to have air-conditioned public rooms. Her fittings and furnishing glowed in brilliant Art Deco. At 23,000 tons she was eight times as heavy and many times more stable than Lillywhite's *Poonah*, yet well over twice as fast. In this floating luxury hotel many disparate lives would oddly coalesce; friendships, even love, might briefly blossom, for life on the *Orion* could be as romantic as the melodies of Ivor Novello which were danced to in the evenings. There was many a 'Glamorous Night', much 'Careless Rapture', as the *Orion* made her majestic way eastwards. Neville Cardus, making his first voyage to Australia, responded perceptively to the singularity of the whole experience: 'The distractions and responsibilities of the world for a while come to an end; as the hours go by we can almost count each pulsation of existence; consciousness and sense of personal identity become pure and absolute. And a strange sort of pathos falls on the little world we make for ourselves during the voyage.'

For Allen's team the voyage provided a most welcome holiday after a long English season. 'It was a saviour', commented Joe Hardstaff, 'a vital chance to get over things.' Little thought was paid to the impending Tests. Although the players met formally at two tables for all meals, the cricket ahead was largely forgotten. 'The team merged with the rest of the passengers', wrote one observer, 'until you scarcely knew where they were or which was which.' In this first-class and socially-aware milieu, where one dressed formally for dinner and where success could be equated with a seat at the captain's table, the amateurs moved more easily than the professionals and Allen and Robins were particularly in demand for cocktail parties. It was whispered by the ladies that the dapper MCC captain, with his sleek black hair and film star looks, was the most eligible of bachelors.

Allen was relishing his position. After spending much of the first three days in his cabin replying to 144 farewell messages (under the watchful eye of his mascot, a toy lion in MCC colours), Allen began dispensing goodwill in all directions and was deemed by the press a most popular captain. He and Robins devoted themselves to sports and games on the upper deck and it was noted with jealousy in some quarters how often Gubby Allen played the ship's captain at deck tennis. Robins was, like Allen, an all-round athlete. Of more mercurial temperament, Robins was a fine dancer, a rash chess player, an emotional golfer and an ambitious cards player; he never suffered from lack of self-belief. 'Robbie plays a cover drive past square-leg', it was remarked, 'with more confidence than any other batsman.' As Allen's confidant, he slowly drifted into the position of vice-captain. 'Birds of a feather', muttered one professional tersely.

The four amateurs were not, however, a homogeneous unit. Wyatt and Allen had become friendly on the body-line tour, but they were temperamentally very different. Wyatt was the more intellectual, always ready to indulge in serious scientific discussion, be it on the aerodynamics of powered flight or the art of photography. The latter was a passion he might have shared with the fourth and youngest amateur, Kenneth Farnes, but the latter was a shy and reserved personality, who kept himself very much to himself.

Gubby Allen made strenuous efforts to encourage good morale within the team. He would tour the cabins conscientiously, and sometimes played bridge and dominoes with the professionals in the cause of good relations. Unfortunately he tended to be overbearing in manner. 'He was always looking down, telling you', was the complaint. 'He was up there, talking down.' The social barriers, therefore, were never properly breached and some of the professionals found this hard to take. Their livelihood, however, was at stake. They knew that Allen had powerful friends and they held their tongues.

There were, of course, those who breached the amateur-professional divide, like Walter Hammond and Leslie Ames. Hammond had strong business interests outside the game, working on the sales and public relations side of a Bristol motor business. Shortly after his return from Allen's tour he became a director of a tyre subsidiary of Dunlop's, at a salary of £2,000 a year. He and Ames mixed much more freely with the tour leaders than the other professionals. Hammond played relentless deck games with his captain, Ames relentless chess with Robins. Yet both differed much in character. Whereas Ames was genial, Hammond was moody. The other professionals saw little of Hammond and it was not to him, the senior professional, but to Maurice Leyland that the younger men turned for advice.

Barnett and Verity also stood apart. Charles Barnett – he hated being called Charlie – was a model of gentility off the field, scrumpulously correct, serious and well spoken. Barnett and Verity would enjoy quiet, early-morning swims in the ship's pool, thereafter spending hours in each other's company, saying little, engrossed in books. There was great interest at the time in T. E. Lawrence, who had died only the year before. Verity read *The Seven Pillars of Wisdom* on the voyage out from cover to cover. Everyone respected the Yorkshireman. It was noted with some awe that he scorned idle gossip, ice-creams and the tote on the ship's progress.

The other professionals might well have been chosen for their amiability, good 'cementers' all. Jim Sims and his Nottingham friends, Bill Voce and Joe Hardstaff, were a particularly cheerful group. The two Notts players had originated from the same pit and played for the same colliery team. The charming Hardstaff, whose father had toured Australia in 1907–08, enjoyed himself off the field with the same flair which he displayed on it, whereas Voce was a quieter man, seldom laughing, though admirably modest and dependable. Derby's Stan Worthington, conspicuous for his broad, powerful build, was the team's pianist, more talented, it was said, than even Don Bradman. Worthington was also devoted to cards, dominoes, shove-halfpenny and darts.

Maurice Leyland and George Duckworth belonged to an older generation. Duckworth was the great character of the side, famous on the field for his loud, high-pitched appeals, most adept off it at dancing, eating and sleeping. No one talked more knowledgeably on carrier pigeons or Rugby League football. He was one of the few non-smokers and non-drinkers. Leyland, by contrast, seldom without a cigarette in hand or pipe in mouth would sit for hours in the café by the pool, the team's philosopher, delighting everyone with his fund of anecdotes.

Despite the dramas of the body-line tour there were still only a few journalists travelling with the team, most newspapers preferring to rely on Reuter's for their reports. The most distinguished were Neville Cardus and C. B. Fry. The 47-year-old Cardus was at the height of his powers, with a poet's imagination able to elevate even the most hum-drum of events to the sublimely heroic. C. B. Fry, striving for similarly purple prose, was also a first-time visitor to Australia. More than thirty years before, when he had been England's leading batsman, he had been unable to accept Warner's invitation to tour. Now 64 but as boyish as ever, Fry joined the ship at Toulon, with presents for all the players of special sun-helmets, and he provided non-stop entertainment thereafter. He was often to be found among the deck-chairs, eccentrically dressed, discoursing on his favourite subjects: cricket, astronomy, football, his training ship *Mercury*, books, athletics, politics, the League of Nations, Ranji, India and big-game hunting. It was not long before Fry and Cardus had fallen out. 'He talked all the way to Australia', complained Cardus (no mean talker himself), 'and all the way across Australia and all the way back home.'

Each tourist would have his own memories of the three-week voyage from Southampton to Ceylon. At Gibraltar, the first stop, there had been the sound of guns and the sight of starving, half-naked refugees, a reminder of the Spanish Civil War then raging. The second stop, at Toulon, allowed the amateurs and Hammond a round of golf at Hyères. There followed lazy days in the Mediterranean, with the *Orion* gliding slowly past the white cliffs of Capri. There was the fancy-dress ball, with Allen and Robins appearing as Australian umpires and Leslie Ames as Adolf Hitler. There was the merriment after Port Said when it was learnt that the astute Walter Robins had bought lense-less binoculars and a suit not properly stitched together. There was the uncannily silent passage through the Suez Canal, its sides picked out by the ship's searchlight. There was the heat of the Red Sea, too hot for deck games or swimming, yet with C. B. Fry still managing to give a demonstration of the latest dance steps on the promenade deck. There were the bare, mauve-brown cliffs at Aden, where the last rain had fallen six years before. There was the Indian Ocean, with the *Orion* following hard in the track of a monsoon. There were violent storms, whilst Ames and Robins still concentrated on their chessboard. 'Did you move, Leslie?' 'No, but I will if the storm doesn't cease.' There were several steamy days with no sight of land, until that first, exciting view of Colombo. 'A beautiful place', wrote Bruce Harris of the *Evening Standard*, 'this great seaport capital of Ceylon, with its wonderful Ocean Parade, its fine buildings, and tropical gardens of fresh verdure.'

The one day ashore at Ceylon began early (yet the sun was already quite high in the sky) native boys already diving off the ship's rails to seek shillings in the clear water, as members of the local cricket club collected the MCC for breakfast. By 11.00 the match was starting, the Colombo ground packed with a capacity crowd, predominantly native, black umbrellas at the ready for the day's sun and the evening's monsoon deluge. Ross Slater, in *The Cricketer*, reflected his delight to be again on dry land, as the MCC, wearing solar topees, came out to field: 'It was a thrilling moment and we were quite carried away with excitement. There was Allen, as immaculate and cheerful as ever; Hammond with his silk-coloured handkerchief; Farnes towering above the delightfully rotund Duckworth, and of course Wyatt, as business-like as ever. . . .' Farnes bowled the first ball of the tour, very gingerly, at half pace. There was great humidity, and sweat tended to blind the fielders' eyes. By the lunch interval most of the players looked as if they had been for a swim. On the featherbed wicket the home team prospered, declaring at 149–4 and it was something of an embarrassment for the tourists to slump to 23–3, but a stand by Gubby Allen (82 not out) and Joe Hardstaff (65 not out) ended the day satisfactorily. A dinner-dance at the Galle Face Hotel followed, a traditional delight for tourists at Colombo. The two-mile journey back by rickshaw could turn the toughest professional into breathless poet: 'The soft pit-pat of the rickshaw boy's feet was the only sound on the night, a night wrapped in stars and tied with a new moon.'

After Ceylon the tourists turned their thoughts to Australia, and the final run to Fremantle was marked with some nightly running and skipping. For ten days they saw only ocean and coral atoll. The sight of the Cocos Islands delighted them just as it had delighted Warner's team. 'All the adventure stories of my youth', wrote Cardus, 'sprang to life: here was Stevenson, Ballantyne, Defoe. On the little beach, silent and empty, there was surely Man Friday's footprint. . . .' Bill Voce responded more simply: 'It makes a lump come into your throat.'

At last, after a voyage of thirty-two days, the *Orion* reached Australia, exactly on time. It was mid-October and Fremantle basked in the clearest and hottest of early mornings. A tugboat-man cheerfully called out, 'Where's Jardine?' and reminded the tourists of a recent Bradman double-century. Meanwhile launches sped out to the liner, carrying Western Australia Cricket Association officials, together with reporters and photographers from all over Australia. There was an aeroplane leaving for Sydney shortly and pictures had to be sent of every tourist, so there was much bustle and flurry. When the tourists eventually disembarked, they made little concession in their dress to the heat. Many wore pin-striped, double-breasted, three-piece suits, with white silk hand-kerchiefs decorating many a breast-pocket. Charles Barnett, impeccable and idiosyncratic as usual, sporting a deep-brimmed felt trilby and smartly-cut tweed jacket, would not have been out of place in the paddock at Cheltenham. Gubby Allen's team were magnificent ambassadors for English tailoring. Through the customs they were ushered with alacrity – just a pause to give anxious officials their autographs – and into a posse of motor cars for the twelve-mile journey to Perth. 'You see that tree', Leslie Ames said to Farnes, squinting in the great glare, as they bumped along at 35 m.p.h. 'Well, it's a gum tree and you won't see any other sort for five months.'

Much had changed in Australia since the tour of 1903–04. There was the new confidence of a nation which had 'pledged its last shilling' for the mother country in the First World War and earned its independence with the blood of 60,000 Australian soldiers (including fast bowler Tibby Cotter). A new national consciousness was symbolized by the recently-constructed Sydney harbour bridge and the new Federal parliament building in Canberra. Nonetheless, ties remained very strong with England, which was still regarded as 'home' by many. 'Some of the

Australians may be a bit rough', remarked Bill Pollock, who was covering the tour for the *Daily Express*, 'but, by George, the British Crown means something tremendous to Australia.'

Spectacular conquests of the air had helped bring the two countries closer. In 1930, when Bradman first toured England, Amy Johnson became the first woman to fly solo to Australia. Now, in 1936, Gubby Allen's arrival had been less newsworthy than that of a young New Zealand flyer, Jean Batten, who had just created a new record with a ten-day flight from Britain to Australia. Only the year before, Imperial Airways and Qantas had begun weekly scheduled passenger services (the flights taking twelve days) and they were testing the possibilities of the flying-boat.

The growing ease of long-distance travel had enabled most touring teams to include Perth in their itinerary since A. O. Jones first called there in 1907–08; so Allen, in starting his tour in Western Australia, was following usual practice. It was still only mid-morning when his team arrived at the Palace Hotel, rose-scented, on the Perth Esplanade facing the Swan river. There was no time for unpacking, for a reception had been planned around tables laden with sandwiches and bottles of beer. Allen was soon speech-making: 'The Lord Mayor says he knows very little about cricket. Well, I know very little about Lord Mayors, but I shall know a great deal more about them before I leave Australia!' From the first Allen was careful to make his crusading message clear: 'We came here to play cricket but we realize too that we do bring the best wishes of the English people to you in Australia; if we can do anything to cement the bonds which hold us together, we shall regard it as our duty and pleasure. . . .'

Any hopes which Allen may have entertained that his manager might do some of the public-speaking perished at Perth. Howard had risen to his feet and was in the middle of a story about the difference between a lady and a diplomat when he was disconcerted to learn that all the speeches were being broadcast. Blushing to the roots of his short white hair, the manager sat down in great confusion. Allen was not a natural speech-maker and at the beginning of the tour tended to rely on a few phrases – he had brought a good lot of chaps – there was no member of the team who was a non-bender in the field – but with much practice he soon became proficient. He had already made six speeches before he played any cricket.

After three days of rest and acclimatization there were two matches at Perth which resulted in a victory against Western Australia (still, because of its geographical isolation, not a member of the Sheffield Shield) and a draw with a Combined XI, in which the Western Australians were augmented by Grimmett and Badcock of South Australia and Stan McCabe and Jack Fingleton from New South Wales.

These matches gave many tourists their first sight of hard Australian wickets. Cardus was amazed. He likened the strip to a pavement in London. 'If the Nelson monument had stood at one end, with a row of shops, I should have thought I was walking down the Strand.' Preparation of Australian wickets had recently changed and bulli soil was no longer used. As a result they were more favourable to spin, less encouraging to pace, but essentially in the batsman's favour. 'I would rather sweep the streets than bowl in this country', declared Cardus, after one look at the Perth wicket.

The large Perth Oval of the 1930s had a barren and bumpy outfield and the practice nets were very poor. Nonetheless C. B. Fry was regularly within them, pipe in mouth, monocle in eye (in readiness for his Australian début against the boys of Wesley College.) He was frequently bowled out but remained as exuberant as ever. Cardus too was in the nets, his off-breaks severely dealt with by Badcock, whilst hundreds of watching boys barracked rowdily, much to the bowler's annoyance. Both journalists could not but be impressed, however, with the setting of the Perth Oval. 'The afternoon sun', wrote Fry from the press-box during the first match, 'is shimmering on whispering gum trees. Eleven pelicans are fishing in the Blue Swan river, a long, low shot beyond cover-point.' Cardus too was fascinated by the river and musingly anticipated the arrival of Lohengrin on his white swan.

At Perth, as elsewhere, Allen's team were overwhelmed with hospitality which threatened to be to the detriment of their cricket. As a team they spent an afternoon on the Mount Yokine golf-links (Voce winning the trophy thanks to a generous handicap), an afternoon at the races and two evenings of trotting (two-wheeled chaises racing on a floodlit track of crushed oyster-shells); there was a trip down the Swan river with the sight of three acres of wool bales (waiting to be inspected by buyers from Bradford) and a drive to York through seventy miles of fertile agricultural land (with cocktails in an orange grove). At the theatre were productions of *Iolanthe* and *The Yeoman of the Guard* and there were several films. It was not long since *The Jazz Singer* had heralded the talkies and film-going was the craze of the time. Allen himself was a considerable devotee, known to have turned down a glittering banquet for a movie, and he was highly delighted with a gala night at the Capitol cinema, Perth, to see Ronald Colman's latest drama, *Under Two Flags*. There was also much private hospitality, groups of players being taken all over Western Australia by car. Farnes, for example, went on a kangaroo shoot in the bush, while Gubby Allen took three days off for some sightseeing and useful business contacts at the Kalgoorlie Gold Mines.

The warmth of their reception soon made the tourists forget that they were 12,000 miles from home and it alleviated the incessant insistence of their hosts that everything they saw was 'the best in the world'. It even made endurable the repetitious singing of 'Jolly Good Fellows' and 'Why were they born so beautiful'. It was with great sadness that the players left Perth after twelve very pleasant days. The city had charmed them as much as the people; they admired its spacious streets, its palm trees and 'the clean dignity that reigns everywhere'. But it was now time to cross the continent.

The journey from Western to Southern Australia, from Perth to Clare, began with a three-day train journey of 1,500 miles to Port Augusta. Much of the terrain was featureless red desert and the heat was intense. It proved easily the worst journey of the tour, but, even so, bore no comparison with what Lillywhite and, sometimes, Warner had suffered. Showers were available, dust storms infrequent; there was an air-conditioned observation car with writing-tables and a piano. It was, it is true, a temperance train, but the players had been forewarned and came well-stocked. For entertainment there was a travelling Gilbert & Sullivan company and the anecdotes of Arthur Mailey; for company there were the four Australian cricketers who had played for the Combined XI. Some of the players, like Clarrie Grimmett, quietly read cheap thrillers; others pored over English newspapers which told of the impending coronation of Edward VIII. Most were regaled by the opera company's Jack Point, a member of the Oxford Movement, who spent the journey distributing and discussing religious texts.

From Port Augusta the players were taken in a dozen cars high into the Flinders Mountains by way of a dusty, bumpy track, then down to the little town of Clare, in the heart of South Australia, a land rich in sheep, wheat and wine. On the 125-mile journey at every hamlet hundreds of children lined the route. There were constant stops for speeches of welcome. Allen made ten replies that day.

When at last the players reached Clare, they found themselves in the middle of its centenary celebrations. At once they were taken to the racecourse, as celebrity guests, Allen presenting a cup to the winner of the day's big race; then they went on to a dance, where they sampled the Australian equivalents of port, sherry, sparkling hock, chablis, burgundy and moselle. After a short night at Bentley's Hotel they somehow found the cricket ground (a very pretty one, fringed with gum trees), played their match in bitter weather, then journeyed eighty difficult miles to Adelaide. Lillywhite's men, observing this interlude from Valhalla, would surely have approved of its eccentricities.

Thereafter, however, Gubby Allen's team travelled more comfortably between the major cities – Adelaide, Melbourne and Sydney – to the first Test at Brisbane. In this period the team's results were as mixed as the weather; several serious injuries did not help. On the credit side, Hammond's batting flourished; on the debit, the first meetings with O'Reilly and Bradman boded ill for the Tests, as did the side's alarming vulnerability to widespread attack by leg-spin.

No touring team could have been worse hit by early injuries and illness. The most seriously affected were Robins (with a fractured finger), Wyatt (a fractured wrist) and Duckworth (a dislocated finger). With Leslie Ames suffering from serious back problems, the team had no wicket-keeper, but fortunately Tom Wade, the young Essex player, had worked his passage over on the *Orion* and was able to play in a couple of matches.

The Australian weather proved unreliable. At Melbourne it was cold enough for snow. On the fourth day of the match with Victoria the MCC could have played snowballs (but opted for bridge). 'We have had a sample today', wrote C. B. Fry, 'of every month of our English year – drenching rain, a whistling cold wind, sunshine, and finally hard round white hail. I picked up a handful and threw it at Neville Cardus. . . .' The latter's romantic notions of Australia, however, were not to be disturbed by a Fry snowball or a mere downpour of rain. 'Australian rain', he mused, 'is rather different from Manchester's. Here it is rain pure and undefiled – a natural element, not a chemical or dye.'

A defeat at the hands of New South Wales coincided with the team's first encounter with Australia's best bowler, Bill O'Reilly. Prematurely balding and therefore looking older than his thirty years, O'Reilly had already taken many English wickets cheaply in his Test career and was much feared for his leg-breaks, googlies and top-spinners, which he bowled at genuine medium pace off an ugly but rhythmical run: 'He hid his intentions with his fluent movements,' wrote Jack Fingleton, 'as the 6' 3" of him, elongated arms and legs flaying the atmosphere, bobbed and jostled on the long run to the wicket. He was a flurry of limbs, fire and steel-edged temper.' His final stride, straddling the bowling crease, was enormous. O'Reilly was at his most dangerous when his Irish temper was roused; batsmen tried hard to keep him cheerful, but usually in vain. 'He roared at the umpires', wrote Arthur Mailey, 'and scowled at batsmen. There was no sign of veneer or camouflage when he appealed nor were there any apologies or beg pardons when the umpire indicated that the batsman's legs were yards out of line with the stumps.' The tourists, meeting him at Sydney, were all duly impressed with his immaculate length and change of pace and flight. He aimed for leg stump, with two short-legs close in, two behind square-leg to save singles, a mid-on rather deep, and a wide long-on twenty yards from the boundary. To win the match, in the closing minutes, O'Reilly took 4 wickets for 4 runs in twenty-three minutes, hypnotizing not just the batsmen but also the umpires. All four victims were lbw. The louder O'Reilly's appeals, the higher, it seemed, went the umpire's finger. Allen was furious. 'We were unquestionably cheated', he wrote home to Warner; Hardstaff's lbw, with just two balls to go, was 'just a joke'. But this was a goodwill tour, so Allen lectured his irritated players on good manners and bit his tongue.

The very next match featured Don Bradman, playing for a Combined Australian XI at Sydney. He had been due to captain South Australia against the tourists, but had been prevented by the death of his one-day-old son. Bradman, at 28, was already considered by an admiring public to be the greatest cricketer of all time. He had first played against England eight years before and, despite the tactics of Jardine, his Test average against England was an impressive 89.51. His 334 was also the highest score ever made in Anglo-Australian cricket at that time. The drama of Bradman's first foray against Allen's team was well captured by C. B. Fry: 'So the Don walks in. Enormous cheers. As ever, drama is afoot. He has introduced himself with unwonted circumspection and looks rather pinched in his long sweater under the elongated peak of his green cap. Now Don has ceased from reconnaissance and opened his bombardment. Horizontal fire at Farnes. Farnes has withdrawn for Voce. Tea done, Don comes out without his sweater. He has slipped to 31 without our noticing it. He is, I vow, a curious performer. Without ever seeming to be in a knot, he seems to untie himself into an unwarrantably hard stroke. He swiftly shifts his neat feet and clouts the ball. Don at once hits four boundaries off Verity. On drives. The Don is swinging and clouting without disclosing any rusticity. But at last great Worthington clean bowls him. Or rather, Don misses an acrobatic trick *en tournant*. He has swept up 63 runs just as he pleases. I see no reason why he should ever get out, unless he tries an abnormal, impossible stroke. . . .' After Bradman's dismissal a large crowd of 36,500 rapidly lost interest and left the Sydney Cricket Ground.

The MCC's own champion, Walter Hammond, had a less Olympian Test average than the incomparable Bradman, a mere 54.93, but his 336 not out against New Zealand was the current highest Test score. Hammond began the tour with centuries in his first four innings. At Perth he had destroyed Clarrie Grimmett's Test chances. 'Another Hammond holiday,' wrote Fry. 'Walter at his best. Rarely has he played so well that lovely swinging back-stroke past extra cover, with the weight on the hind foot. His driving was exhilarating in all senses. One immense sixer went over mid-off's head into the car park. A prodigious, easy golf drive. . . . Finally Walter hit another huge straight sixer into the grandstand. . . . There is no doubt that our Champion is in cool, calm and superlative form and our hopes in him cannot be exaggerated.'

Despite the successes of Hammond, spin bowling was posing problems to most of the tourists. As Jardine's tour had been greatly influenced by fast bowling, so Allen's was by wrist spin. All the States possessed at least one googly bowler, following the trail blazed so successfully by Bernard Bosanquet. At Perth there was Zimbulis, at Adelaide Ward and Grimmett, at Melbourne Frederick, at Sydney O'Reilly and Mudge. On wickets which encouraged generous bounce and turn the Englishmen seemed flat-footed and nervous. In desperation friends of the team suggested that Jack Hobbs should leave the press-box (where he was representing the London *Star*) to coach them. 'I don't think I could do any good', wrote Hobbs (a modest statement by a man who had toured Australia no less than five times for MCC). 'A batsman must use his feet to get to the pitch of the ball and right forward to cover the break. Or he must play right back watching the ball onto the bat. . . .' Clearly the MCC batsmen were having some problems of very basic technique.

Allen's response to his batsmen's loss of confidence was to ask for more practices. He called several meetings demanding a harder approach, with less drinking and socializing. Writing home to Plum Warner from Sydney he confided: 'I wish you had been here this time, as it is a cricket brain which is badly needed at this minute: someone who could help Hardstaff, Fishlock, Farnes, Fagg, Sims and Copson; in fact all the newcomers.' Allen seems to have discounted help from the remote Hammond or the modest Hobbs. It is probable that already, even this early in the tour, Allen was unable to think completely clearly because of the great pressures he was under. It was not just a question of the heavy demands of public speaking. His manager tended to refer every problem to him. The result was that everything, from deciding on tips and arranging hotel rooms, to seeing doctors and undertaking the interviews, devolved on Allen. 'I have felt so tired and worried at times', he confided to Warner, after only five matches. 'I don't think any captain has ever had quite what I have had to put up with, as I really have had no one to help me off the field.'

The failures of the MCC against Australian spin bowling would today have probably brought the wrath of the media upon their heads. But the 1930s were gentler times. Jack Hobbs was typical. 'Let's keep our faith in them', he wrote. 'Encouragement at this stage will do far more good than harsh criticism. . . . Naturally we are disappointed but every team has their bad spasms. . . .'

The tourists reached Brisbane by way of a 700-mile rail journey from Sydney, a twenty-eight-hour ordeal in scorching heat in old wooden carriages with no refreshment facilities other than water from a tap. Along with Bradman, O'Reilly and several other Australian Test cricketers who were also travelling north, the tourists leapt out at the occasional stops to race along platforms in search of cups of tea, pieces of fruit or plates of soup. Rail travel in Australia in the 1930s was unimpressive. At a time when, in England, steam trains were setting new speed records – the *Princess Margaret*, for example, had just travelled from Euston to Glasgow in under six hours – the outlook of the Australian railways was distinctly conservative. Warner's team, over thirty years before, had taken barely two hours more than Allen's to do the same journey from Sydney.

At Brisbane the tourists were overwhelmed by heat and humidity. Although, at 90° in the shade, it was quite mild for the

Queenslanders themselves, sweat poured off the Englishmen day
and night. The only sanctuary was the air-conditioned dance-hall
of their hotel, the Bellevue. For many it was the first experience
of sleeping under mosquito nets in a sub-tropical climate. They
were constantly reminded of their proximity to the Tropic of
Capricorn by the many exotic birds and trees in the botanic
gardens by their hotel. Walter Robins might admire the man-
groves by the river banks and the profusely flowering purple and
white bohinia, Kenneth Farnes might enthuse about the exotic
dragon-trees and a poinciana of regal splendour, but most of the
team could well have done without the piercing screeches of the
gardens' inhabitants, particularly at dawn, when, said Cardus,
'the sun pierces us like a red-hot sword, even through the wooden
shutters of the bedroom.' Cardus complained that in five nights
he had achieved only five hours' sleep. He especially hated, much
more than Fry did, walking in the streets in the stuffy, heat-laden
evenings, when crickets chattered incessantly, and 'winged things'
flew into his face. Brisbane, the suffering Cardus believed, was
not the place for a Test match, for the climate was too much
against the visitors. 'Australians', he remarked, 'might, with equal
justice, be expected to play in a November fog at the Kennington
Oval. . . .'

Apart from the trying climate the tourists enjoyed their fortnight based in Brisbane. They were most hospitably entertained
and agreed enthusiastically that Brisbane's was the best beer in
Australia. They found it a prosperous city, full of wool-buyers,
reckless car drivers and lotteries for huge prizes, conservative
enough in outlook to allow the survival of numerous 19th-century
buildings. With many a neo-classical facade fronted by swaying
palms, Brisbane of the 1930s still had something of the aura of a
distant colonial outpost. Thus the tourists of 1936 might have
understood Plum Warner when he wrote of Brisbane in 1903:
'The MCC are ever ready to encourage cricket in the most remote
corners of the Empire.'

Gubby Allen's men certainly found the Woolloongabba cricket
ground remote, even primitive. With its ramshackle stands of
corrugated iron and asbestos, it was, said William Pollock of the
Express, more suitable for fat ladies and coconut shies than cricket.

He feared the arrival of Ned Kelly and his gang, galloping into the fields, firing pistols and carrying off C. B. Fry and his Wild West hat. Cardus similarly expected the arrival of Tom Mix and thought that this was cricket in Bret Harte's Roaring Camp. He noted with some irony that one side of the ground was called the Vulture Street end.

Although the outfield at the Gabba was as poor as the facilities for spectators, the actual wicket was good and looked a batsman's paradise. C. B. Fry compared it to a ballroom floor, 'glistening with light brown perfection'. Fry, who was always trying to outdo Cardus in vividness of imagery, also likened it to a Roman pavement – which surely would have encouraged variable bounce? – and 'a historic barrow containing the honourable bones of departed and disillusioned bowlers'.

The Australians, with Bradman, McCabe, Fingleton and Badcock most likely to exploit this pitch, were clear favourites. One Sydney bookmaker had laid £4,000 to £2,000 that England would not win a single Test and even the English journalists were pessimistic, Bill Pollock hoping that rain might come to England's aid: 'A pity we can't move the match to Manchester.' Nonetheless there were five newcomers in the Australian XI (one of whom, the tall all-rounder Mark Sievers, a Post Office employee, had learnt of his selection whilst working up a telegraph pole) and Fred Ward seemed a less formidable leg-spinning partner for O'Reilly than Clarrie Grimmett, who had been dropped.

The captains came out to decide innings, both smiling confidently enough to unsettle at least one Sydney bookmaker. Bradman tossed into the air a fourpenny bit, given him for luck by his wife. Allen called correctly and did a little dance, throwing up his arms as if in oriental prayer. 'Allen be praised', he smiled, and elected to bat.

There were 14,000 spectators at the first day's play but they made noise enough for ten times that number. Brisbane had drawn a queer assembly. City business men, heavily dressed in dark suits and waistcoats, collars sticking to their perspiring necks, mixed with sun-dried sheep farmers and exotically garbed sugar-cane workers. There were gaunt old men, heavily whiskered like Old Testament prophets, and young dark-tanned boys, who knew little of classrooms but much of herding cattle. All were drawn to the Woolloongabba by the name of Bradman. Many, on hearing that England were batting, bided their time in bars, for they had not come to watch a cricket match; they had come to watch Don Bradman.

Inside the Gabba the heat was stifling. 'The sun is a one-eyed tyrant', wrote Cardus, 'ready to afflict us with Ethiopic scorchings.' A sultry wind, bringing no relief, blew in from Vulture Street, as England's makeshift opener, Stan Worthington, received the first ball of the series. Victoria's Ted McCormick raced in, his slips lying very deep. A fast long hop! The burly Worthington sighted it briefly as it rose towards his left shoulder and tried to hook. The pace deceived him, the ball was merely edged and spiralled in the air. Oldfield ran in from behind the wicket to take a simple catch. Worthington retired, the crowd yelled in exultation and, high in the press-box, C. B. Fry groaned heavily. 'We are to be tried in the furnace for some hours!' he wrote.

The young Arthur Fagg appeared, hatless and innocent. McCormick and Sievers dug the ball in short, the former hitting Fagg in the stomach which halted proceedings. Allen, in the pavilion, watched with mounting irritation. This was not the spirit of 1936 but of 1932! He would speak to Bradman.

There was irritation too in the press-box, where the view of the pitch was heavily obscured by pillars and awnings and the space impossibly cramped. 'I write with somebody's knee in my back', scribbled Cardus, as Fagg essayed a leg-glance to McCormick and Oldfield held a good leg-side catch. The journalists had indeed been treated shabbily at the Gabba. They were not allowed in the pavilion; they had no washroom, merely the use of a tap at the back of the stand. The Australian journalists had amongst them some most distinguished names – Noble, Mailey, Woodfull, Ponsford, Macartney, Kippax – but it didn't seem to matter. 'Warwick Armstrong behind me', noted Fry, 'cannot see at all. Such is gratitude. . . .'

Hammond was at the crease now, receiving his first ball. It pitched short. 'A deliberate bouncer', muttered the watching Allen. Hammond played it off his left hip, awkwardly, and spooned a gentle catch to silly short-leg. Pandemonium at the Gabba. England 20–3 and the celebrations surely audible at Darwin or Cairns! In the press-box Fry adjusted his monocle and scowled darkly. 'I am not sure after all that I want to see much', he wrote. 'It is all too painful.' Shortly afterwards, Fry stumbled over Bruce Harris's typewriter in the cramped press-box and kicked the lid so furiously that it disappeared high over the heads of the crowd, never to be seen again.

The innings was rescued by Maurice Leyland, gritty and expressionless, risking very little, and helped for a time by Charles Barnett, as usual risking very much. Leyland was never pretty to watch and his innings did not initially please the purist Fry, who much preferred the bold classicism of Barnett to the dour brutality of the Yorkshireman: 'Maurice is still doing his stout little fight. But he never backs up an inch. Nor runs his first run fast enough to take a second in the outfield. . . . Still he has tidied us across to tea-time. His cover drive is in abeyance and he has hoicked too much at his straight drives. That front shoulder pulled away. Yet he is a stout little fighter and usually watches the ball. . . .' Despite incurring Fry's displeasure for technical shortcomings, Leyland turned the game around, eventually making 126, and by the close of the first day England had recovered to 263–6.

On the second day the score was taken to 358, thanks to Hardstaff, Robins and Allen, a marvellous recovery from the early disasters. McCormick was out of the match with lumbago and most of the bowling had been done by the two leg-spinners, O'Reilly (who took 5 for 102 in over forty 8-ball overs) and Ward. A record overflowing crowd of 30,000 flocked to see Bradman. Cardus described the atmosphere at the beginning of the Australian innings as the most frenzied he could ever remember: 'The roars were colossal when Badcock at once drove Allen straight for 3 and pulled him for 4. And when Badcock suddenly played on, the sky was split by the noise. I expected the lions and the Christians. Bradman was heralded by the trumpets and trombones of acclamation as he walked to the wicket and the whole multitudes of the orchestra crashed out as he cut Allen for 4 and pulled him gigantically for another. Then Voce missed the edge of Bradman's bat by a hairsbreadth and hysteria let out its shriek. It was a lucky escape. But heavens! What a game this cricket is in Australia! What a battleground, not to say shambles, is made of a cricket field. And how I shall greet the green peacefulness next year at Worcester and Horsham. I love the grandeur of Test matches here, the strain and power. But I am a man of peace and this is war. . . .' Bradman delighted only briefly, however, and after the trumpets and trombones there was surely only a solitary 'cello, playing the most doleful of elegies, when Worthington held a slip catch to dismiss him for 38. The day ended with Australia 151–2 and the match finely poised. The exhausted Cardus brought it to a gentle close: 'The roaring and the screaming subsided, and when stumps were drawn everybody departed, and the sun suddenly went down, and the lovely velvet of a Brisbane twilight concealed the battlefield.'

A rest day followed. Most of the English players motored fifty miles to Southport, where the Governor of Queensland, Sir Leslie Wilson, an old family friend of the Allens, offered hospitality. The England captain and the Governor tramped many miles along the golden beaches, discussing the game as the surf crashed nearby. They looked an odd couple, Allen in his long black trunks and singlet (men's bare chests were still not allowed on the beaches of most Australian States) and the Governor, in his bare feet, trousers rolled up at the ankles, but trilby hat still firmly worn. No doubt they discussed amongst other things the likely final Australian score.

It proved to be a mere 234, leaving England over 100 runs ahead on the first innings. 'For the past six weeks we have been very sympathetic and consoling to our visitors', wrote the car-toonist Renn in the Melbourne *Age* 'and then they turn round and do a thing like this!' Bill Voce's 6 for 41 was a vindication of Allen's determination that not a hint of body-line tactics should be adopted. The England captain had been coming under increas-ing criticism in some quarters for not allowing Voce to bowl leg-theory. Jardine himself was leading this lobby, commenting on the tour at home for the *Evening Standard*. Just before the first Test he wrote: 'It is little short of amazing to read that Voce has not yet bowled to a field comprising more than two square-legs. . . . Gestures are all very well in their place, but best left to politicians who delight in them.' Cardus, always a strong critic of body-line, now rejoiced in Voce's success, achieved through orthodox methods. 'Voce was superb; no short stuff, no modern theories, but correct length, much pace off the pitch and the deadly ball that leaves the bat a little.'

On the fourth day England, at 122–5 in their second innings, looked likely to have lost the game, but Gubby Allen saved his side with 68 precious runs. C. B. Fry, his temper now much recovered, watched admiringly: 'Our captain has scored 1 run, having promoted himself in the order at the urgent request of Robins. He is still in and has shaped far more like an English batsman than heretofore. That is, he shapes fit to go in first. Just style and confidence. He may make a score or not, but he looks worth 50 runs. . . .' Later on: 'Gubby still batting, with 20 to his name. Eton playing-fields have flooded back to him. He hears the school pro monotously admonishing, "Come forward to her, sir, come forward." No bad advice on this wicket. Anyway, Gubby is batting Lord's style and the old school tie with no small success. . . . Now Gubby has gathered 40. If anybody writes and gets printed "a captain's innings" I shall go home. But it is one.' By the end of the fourth day, the match was as good as won, barring Bradman. Australia, in their 2nd innings, were 3–1, needing another 340 for victory, and the wicket taking considerable spin.

The team was watching a film in a Brisbane cinema that evening when they first learnt that it had started raining hard. With the wickets uncovered and matches played out to a finish, this had to be in their favour. Later that night, in the Bellevue, Allen spoke to Verity: 'Put your left arm in a sling, Hedley'. It rained again during the night and Allen led his team out at a run the next morning, as the sun shone on their expectations. In the event, Verity was not needed. The ball reared unpredictably one moment and kept horribly low the next. Allen (5 for 36) and Voce (4 for 16) skittled Australia out for 58. Bradman came in with the score at 7–3, walking out to great applause, tight-lipped and full of determination. The crowd hushed to complete silence as Allen bowled to him. The first he blocked, but the second climbed high and he sent an easy catch to Fagg at gully. The

Australian captain smiled wryly as he left the field. Unlike Trumper, whom he outshone in all else, Bradman never coped with sticky wickets and tended to play recklessly on them. 'He had a bit of an ego', explained Joe Hardstaff. 'Didn't like to be seen struggling.'

Bradman was still smiling wryly when he left the Gabba, wearing dark glasses. Australia was stunned by the unexpected catastrophe, but the Prime Minister, Joe Lyons, was quick to send Allen a telegram to emphasize the political importance of the game. 'Feel sure', it ended, 'all Australians will accept defeat in the true spirit of cricket.' Bradman concurred. 'We hope to have further pleasant games with them.' Allen was suitably modest. 'The age of miracles', he said, 'is not past.' All in all, the politicians of both countries could not have been more delighted, for while the cricket had been fiercely contested, the acrimony of 1932–33 was pleasingly absent.

The politicians of both countries had more pressing worries than cricket, however, for the first Test was played out against a background of the Abdication crisis. The English newspapers gave the constitutional crisis the headlines, while including the Test match latest in the Stop Press:

PREMIER AND ARCHBISHOP AT BUCKINGHAM PALACE	England collapse, 20–3
BALDWIN GOES TO THE KING'S FORT	England 311–8
ULTIMATUM TO THE KING DENIED BY CABINET	Australia 176–4
END OF THE CRISIS: MRS SIMPSON: I AM WILLING TO WITHDRAW	England 82–3
PREMIER DINES WITH KING AT FORT BELVEDERE	Australia 41–8
ABDICATION IS FEARED	England win.

It was two days after the Test that Edward abdicated. Gubby Allen heard about it as he was travelling by sea down to Sydney. 'It does seem to me', he wrote home, 'that he has behaved disgracefully. I believe he thought he was so popular with British people all over the world that he could get away with anything.

If she had any decency she would have walked out when she saw what was going to happen.' It was a conventional view of the time and Allen could have been forgiven if he saw kingship in the light of captaincy. By abdicating Edward had let his team down, something which the highly competitive Allen could not begin to understand. Nor could he appreciate how easily an attractive woman might completely undermine a man's judgement and sense of propriety.

There were eight days before the start of the second Test at Sydney, with little for the MCC to do – such were the unhurried itineraries of the 1930s – but to play a friendly game at the small industrial town of Ipswich, twenty-five miles north of Brisbane, and then travel slowly back to Sydney. The Ipswich ground would have been familiar territory to Lillywhite and Warner – a tiny enclosure, holding a thousand spectators with difficulty, its facilities distinctly limited. Around the ground were drab, tin-roofed buildings (which echoed resonantly as Hammond peppered them with non-stop 6s). The outfield, devoid of grass, was covered in gravel, whilst the changing-rooms were inhabited by ants of enormous size. 'You looked down on feeling a tug at your bootlaces', said Farnes cheerfully, 'to find they were unlacing them!'

The only ants at Sydney Cricket Ground were the players, viewed from the heights of its amphitheatre, which could now accommodate 65,000 spectators. The cycle track on its perimeter had long since gone; there was a large, recently-completed stand and the giant scoreboard, now all-electric, gleamed from the top of the Hill. 'Without a doubt', murmured C. B. Fry, 'the proper field for Mars against the World at cricket.'

Sydney itself had also grown, to twice its size since Warner's tour, and was now the second biggest white city in the Empire with 1¼ million inhabitants. New buildings, including many skyscrapers, were erected in 1936 alone to the cost of £9,500,000! But Allen's team found Sydney brash, Americanized and fiercely parochial, its streets lacking law and order, its women treated with scant respect. In the evenings there seemed little alternative entertainment to the excellent cinemas, just one or two dull dance-halls and a few cafés in Kings Cross 'run on American lines of coffee and crooners'. There were no pubs; the bars all shut at 6 o'clock. 'Oh, for something to DO in the evening!' sighed some of the cricketers. 'Oh, for somewhere to GO!' There *were* compensations. Usher's Hotel in Castlereagh Street, with its superb cuisine, delighted everyone, especially Neville Cardus, when he had persuaded the musicians in the dining-room to adopt a more classical repertoire. Then there was the harbour, which affected Allen's team just as strongly as it had Warner's and Lillywhite's. They would stand for hours at Pott's Point in the evenings, smoking innumerable cigarettes and watching the lamplight dancing on the moonlit waters, the anchored battleships dreaming of war, the gentle ferries plying to and from Manly, the ocean-going vessels venturing through the Heads in search of rest or freedom.

The cricket, too, was the stuff of dreams. Whereas the rain had merely confirmed the likely result of the first Test, it decided the second. Walter Hammond, with 231 not out, magnificently led England to 426–6. Then the heavens opened and changed the character of the wicket, allowing Australia to be bowled out twice and Gubby Allen to take a surprising 2–0 lead in the series. The Australian public was stunned. The Board was roundly condemned for not looking after its team properly; the appointment of a manager was encouraged. Bradman's captaincy was queried and Vic Richardson suggested. Older hands smiled knowingly and bided their time. Amongst those specially invited to the match were J. J. Kelly (who had kept wicket in the series of 1903–04), 90-year-old Jack Tooher (who had batted fifteenth for the New South Wales XV when they had beaten Lillywhite's All-England XI in December 1876) and 79-year-old Tom Garrett, still a practising solicitor in Sydney, who had played in both the Combination matches of 1877. While the younger generation panicked and looked for scapegoats, their elders kept calm. Class would surely tell. Bradman would yet save the series.

At this crucial stage of the tour, with two months gone and three more to go, Allen's team began to suffer from a lack of proper match practice. In the nine days between the second Test at Sydney and the third Test at Melbourne there was only a friendly two-day game at Newcastle. Then, after the third Test (when rain this time favoured Australia and a Bradman double century led to a big home victory), the MCC went on a two-week holiday in Tasmania, which included just five days of gentle cricket. Thus, when they reached Adelaide, towards the end of January, their rain-affected match with South Australia was their first State game since they had played Queensland in November. It was not an itinerary to help out-of-form batsmen and bowlers.

The England selectors plotted their tactics for the fourth Test at a hotel at Seacliff, a small resort twelve miles from Adelaide. Although it was now 100° in the shade, here, at least, the air was fresher at night and the team could relax in the surf. Allen himself, in his desire to win the Ashes at Adelaide, was encouraging a greater sobriety within the ranks of his professionals, setting the lead by giving up all alcohol himself. This was probably not a great personal hardship. 'He never drank', observed Joe Hardstaff, 'except at official functions. At least I never knew him to come to the bar.' The team was still vexed by injuries and illness. In South Australia Fagg contracted rheumatic fever (taking no further part in the tour) and Fishlock broke a bone in his hand. Worst of all, Voce had back problems. Wyatt, however, was at last able to play again and took the place of Worthington, whose form with the bat continued to disappoint. 'Somehow I can't focus the ball properly out here', he remarked sadly. Despite the long deliberations, Allen left the final decisions of team selection very late indeed. 'I did not know I was going to play in the match until a quarter of an hour before it began', wrote Kenneth Farnes.

Things were also far from right in the Australian camp, for there were those who were not making things easy for Bradman in his first season as Australian captain. It was hard for the other Australian players not to feel twinges of envy. Bradman had an acute business sense which enabled him to make much money from the game. Few players by the age of 21 have given their names to bats, hats, boots, shirts, suits, gloves and pads! Moreover, Bradman tended to move in more exalted social circles than his team-mates, forming friendships easily with the English amateurs. He enjoyed much squash and golf with Allen in the course of the tour and during the Adelaide Test Walter Robins stayed at his home (reciprocating hospitality to Bradman in 1938). Bradman was also more abstemious in his drinking habits than most. 'I haven't had more than six glasses of beer in my life,' he admitted that summer, adding that he liked the occasional glass of sherry. He, in turn, considered some of the beer drinking of his team-mates irresponsible, and he said so to the Board. Thus on the day of Australia's victory in the third Test, four members of his XI – O'Reilly, O'Brien, McCabe and Fleetwood-Smith – found themselves called before the Victoria Cricket Association to be reprimanded. It all augured badly for a happy team atmosphere in Adelaide!

One of the four, Leslie O'Brien 'Chuck' Fleetwood-Smith, had come into the side after missing the first two games through injury. He was a powerfully built man, in his mid-20s, darkly handsome, with clipped moustache, and a hint of Laurence Olivier in *Wuthering Heights* about him. Like Heathcliff, too, he was a man of mystery, a left-arm bowler of googlies and chinamen, much feared by the Englishmen. Fleetwood-Smith was a big spinner of the ball, delivering it with a high action after a short, easy run. His stock ball was the chinaman, breaking from the off, but he also bowled, with imperceptible variation in action, a googly as well as a top-spinner which hastened straight on. On and off the field Fleetwood-Smith found it difficult to be solemn. He was capable of doing bird imitations as he ran in to bowl, even in a Test match. But his good nature was sometimes taken advantage of and from cricketing fame his life degenerated, through excessive drinking, to eventual vagrancy.

Fleetwood-Smith had been thought likely to cause Jardine's team problems in 1932, but early in the tour had been deliberately hit out of Test reckoning by Walter Hammond. Now there were only five survivors of the body-line series playing at Adelaide (Bradman, Oldfield, McCabe, O'Reilly and Fingleton), whereas seven of Allen's team had played in that memorably bad-tempered match at Adelaide in 1933, when Woodfull and Oldfield were hit by Larwood, and Woodfull had told Warner in the Australian dressing-room that only one of the two teams was playing cricket.

No such crises were likely this time. During the third Test the

MCC's President, Lord Somers, had arrived in Melbourne and had been busy doing his share of 'cementing'. His cheerful words on radio after the Australian victory were carefully chosen: 'Long may cricket be played as it has been played in this match! I bring greetings from England to all lovers of cricket! These representative games are great institutions, and will be played as long as there is cricket. While they are on, they assume vast importance. So much so that relations between two nations can be altered by a game. It is therefore a delight to me to see the game played as it has been played in this match . . .'

Lord Somers was also present at Adelaide, where sixty years before Jim Southerton had supervised a team of four horses pulling the corporation roller across the pitch in an effort to make it playable. Now it was perfect! 'On this turf', wrote Cardus, 'I felt a batsman would only get out by absence of mind or by that deep-seated periodic law of human frailty which causes even Heifetz to play a wrong note.'

Adelaide had grown in size since Warner's tour, tripling to half a million inhabitants, but its beauty remained. Farnes thought it the most charming of all cities visited, likening its climate to the south of France. He admired the spacious Adelaide Oval too. First there was the approach: 'It was most pleasant in the morning', he wrote, 'to leave the South Australia Hotel and walk down to the ground across the bright gardens.' Cardus also enjoyed this. 'I walked to the ground along an avenue which made me instinctively look for Carlton House Terrace on the right, for on the left was surely St James's Park.' One morning, to his delight, as the bees hummed in the heat, 'a number of men appeared from nowhere, removed their coats, waistcoats and watch-chains, sat down on camp-stools in the shade, produced trumpets and trombones, and proceeded to play the Egmont Overture . . .' Then there was the view. Sitting in comfortable leather chairs, Farnes and his team looked out across the turf, past the giant scoreboard, to the Mount Lofty range, bright with purples, blues and greens. Farnes remembered Albert Knight being similarly impressed. The old Leicestershire player had declared that the outstanding event of his career had been fielding in the deep at

Adelaide in 1903–04, 'taking in the beauty of the summer sky and the dreaming spires of the cathedral'.

On the first day of the fourth Test 34,000 thronged the Oval, many in trilby hats and dark suits. Sight and sound pleased the senses, as they waited. Strong sunshine had brought the far hills close to their eyes, as if a camera lens had suddenly found its focus. In the park behind the pavilion, where plane trees moved gently in a westerly breeze, tall grass was being mown by scythes. 'The sound', mused C. B. Fry, 'is of Midland meadows at home in July.' The bare wicket lay expectantly before him in its circle of close-clipped green: 'A long strip of yellow in the middle of an Oxford College lawn.'

Big crowds always attended Adelaide Tests. None was more partisan, however, than now, for only three years before, Bradman had moved to Adelaide, forsaking his native New South Wales to follow a career in stock-broking. Adulation was rampant, almost child-like in its devotion:

> 'Don, Don, lay the willow on;
> there was none like you before you;
> there'll be none when you are gone.
> Come and bat before us,
> till the arching sky that's o'er us
> rattles with the mighty chorus:
> "Don, Don, Don"!'

Everywhere he went, Bradman was instantly recognizable. When he walked down a road, rode in a street-car or dined in a restaurant, he was immediately acclaimed, his autograph sought and given. Bradman's every private detail was public possession: the house he had built in the suburb of Kensington, his billiard-room, his piano, his parrots, his love of dancing, ginger beer and tea, books on history and travel. . . .

Test cricket in the 1930s attracted much female support and it was the ladies, excited and vociferous, who now led the applause for the two captains as they walked out to toss in front of the pavilion, diminutive figures in white in the large context of the green oval. Both had shirts rolled to the elbow, as if anticipating a hard day in the sun; both wore baggy flannels, in the manner of the period. Bradman was wearing his favourite green cap; Allen was bareheaded, his short, well-brushed hair gleaming in the sun. To increase the excitement the crowd had been told that whoever won the toss would pick up the coin. Bradman's florin glinted in its high, arched flight, as if enjoying its moment of celebrity. Its owner retrieved it. The Australians would bat first and the crowd exulted. Bradman's wife, Jessie, looking pretty in a light flower-print dress, her hair close-bobbed like Clara Bow's, smiled with anticipation. Allen smiled too, though cursing inwardly, and went off to change hurriedly out of his black shoes. So keen, meanwhile, were the Australians to sample the Adelaide turf that their openers, Brown and Fingleton, came out too early and had to sit and wait at the gate for the English fielders.

Cardus, in the press-box, observed the scene with relish and admired its theatricality: 'The heat shimmers on distant hills, and the steeples of the cathedral are given the clear outline of a stage scene. In fact, I expected the crowd to applaud and call for the producer.' Later, as was his custom, he embellished this newspaper report for use in a book, considerably enlarging the imagery: 'The heat shimmered on distant hills, and the steeples of the cathedral were given the clear outline of an old-time stage setting. Nature in Australia confirms the school of nineteenth-century scene-painters; Hawes Craven was entirely true to life. The productions at Daly's held up the mirror faithfully.'

The first day's play, indeed, had an unexpected touch of musical comedy. There were charming duets which did little to advance the action. Wickets were ludicrously surrendered. There were humorous run outs and even the leading man tripped up on the scenery. By the close of play the expected big score had not materialized. Australia were 267–7 and had lost the initiative of the toss.

There were 33,000 for the second day's play, not nearly as many as would be expected on a Saturday if there was a prospect of Bradman batting. The day began badly for Allen, with the need to break the news to Ken Farnes of his mother's death at home in a car accident. Farnes, who had bowled magnificently on the first day, was a bowler of moods. Despite his height, which allowed him to bring the ball fiercely down from 8 feet, he was essentially a gentle giant, constantly in need of provocation, too amiable in temperament to be a great fast bowler. Now, however, he showed his mettle, going out in the fullness of his grief and helping England finish off the Australian innings quickly: 'Fleetwood-Smith', wrote Cardus, 'looking more like Hitler than ever, heard his off stump ejected by Farnes with a most Nazi violence.'

By the end of the second day's play England, at 174–2 in reply to Australia's 288, seemed on the way to winning the Ashes. Back in Britain, racked by bitter cold, cricketers were warmed by the news. Most propitiously, even the ball-by-ball broadcast of the last ten minutes of play came through their radios without interference. England's position was regarded by the *Observer* as a 'triumph'. However, one thing was overlooked. In scoring at little more than 2-an-(8-ball)-over England had simply concentrated on survival, eschewing all aggression. 'A bad ball is a bad ball', groaned Neville Cardus, 'whether bowled by myself, Arthur Mailey, Sydney Barnes, or by Charles Fry in mid-sentence.' Even Hammond had been strokeless.

This pusillanimous policy continued the next day. Barnett paid the price for a slow century by falling to the most dubious of lbw decisions. ('He ran out to drive a high-pitched ball from Fleetwood-Smith to mid-on,' wrote a commentator, 'but was beaten by the flight of the ball which hit his feet while he was several yards out of his crease.') In the end a very small 1st-innings lead resulted. Perhaps it was an outraged goddess of Fortune who allowed a Russian radio station to overlap the wavelength of the ball-by-ball commentary. At all events, when the BBC switched off the unintelligible summary of the day's play, it might have been turning off not merely the voice of Alan Kippax but the hopes of England. 'We had a really bad day today', conceded Allen irritably, 'and we will now have to put up a great performance if we are going to win this blasted match.'

In the event Bradman thwarted Allen. He came in with the score at 21–1, replacing Fingleton. As usual he looked supremely confident. Most new batsmen approach the crease with a grain of nervousness. Not so Bradman: his expression on arrival was always one of utter happiness. Having taken his guard, he looked about him, a wide grin showing his zest for the challenge ahead. He made a cheerful start, running quick singles with Brown to the unrestrained joy of a thousand female admirers. Allen had thought much about how to contain Bradman's genius. He began to offer him singles to keep him from the strike and meanwhile effectively closed up most routes to the boundary. Bradman responded responsibly and cautiously. 'It seemed to me', wrote Hobbs, 'that Don had made up his mind to score a 100 and nothing was going to put him off.' Allen showed some resourcefulness. Sensing there was more danger from bounce than spin, he removed Verity's traditional slip and instead posted two silly points. This most modern of field placings raised some eyebrows but Bradman was unruffled. Allen resorted to asking Verity to bowl over the wicket and down the leg-side. Bradman grinned and bided his time.

The innings spread to the fourth day and nearly 36,000 were there to watch him. The England pace attack of Allen, Voce and Farnes was roughly treated. Robins's few overs of leg-breaks were expensive. But Verity, conceding only 54 runs in 37 overs, kept Bradman in check. 'His loose, boneless action and his curving length lulled our senses', wrote Cardus. 'Verity is a patient student in quest of the absolute.' Later, he elaborated: 'He seems to bowl in a vacuum, for the quality of his art is not related to finite and vulgar things such as boundaries or wickets. Here is bowling for bowling's sake, seen under the conditions of eternity.' The battle between Verity and Bradman was cricket at its most skilful and antagonistic; Cardus, loving it, waxed lyrical. At one moment Bradman became Paganini, a virtuoso entertainer, and at another Atlas, carrying the world of Australian cricket on his shoulders. With Bradman on 199 Verity applied every aspect of Yorkshire cunning, resetting his field most lengthily, then bowling well wide of the leg-stump. Bradman smiled nonchalantly and waited, as relaxed as if at net practice, and, next over, hit Voce firmly to leg for 3. Appropriately Bradman's innings spanned Australia Day, the 149th anniversary of the First Settlement. A Bradman double century was a fitting culmination of the nation's celebrations, eclipsing even the message from London of Australia's new King. It had not been Bradman's easiest innings, the deep-set fields causing him to score 99 of his runs in singles. 'The journey was long for Bradman', admitted Cardus, 'but he travelled by Pullman, plush cushions and all.'

At the close of the fifth day England were 148–3, needing another 244 to win, with Hammond and Leyland not out. 'We still have a chance', wrote Hobbs loyally. The wicket, though worn, was still not taking huge spin. A big innings from England's champion might yet win the Ashes. But Fleetwood-Smith, who took 10 wickets in the match, bowled Hammond, stretching forward, in the first over of the day. The excited crowd roared out its joy and gave the bowler three resounding cheers; the Australians, with Bradman leading, ran up to the bowler and enthusiastically shook his hand. Some said that it was a googly, which had come in very quickly from the leg to hit the middle and off stumps, others that it was a chinaman. Hammond, back in the pavilion, merely described it as 'a humdinger to get early in the day' and Bradman, fifty years later, still remembered it as one of the finest deliveries sent down. 'If ever one single ball won a Test match, that was it.' Later, when the match was over, the crowd called for its heroes again. Bradman responded and made a modest speech – 'The result was in doubt right up to today. I hope you enjoyed it as much as we have' – but Fleetwood-Smith was in the bath. Forty-five minutes and a few beers later, he emerged to enjoy the plaudits of the Adelaide crowd.

Over three weeks elapsed between the fourth Test at Adelaide and the decisive fifth Test at Melbourne, during which the tourists played four matches, friendly games at Geelong and Canberra and return fixtures with New South Wales and Victoria. It was now five months since the tourists had left England and their travel-weariness showed, particularly at Sydney where the victorious New South Wales XI bowled them out for only 73.

The MCC had not played at Canberra before. The match against the Southern Districts of New South Wales was a fixture which Douglas Jardine had declined four years earlier and Allen's visit to the centre of Australian politics seems a symbolic act of reconciliation. He and the other amateurs stayed at Government House with Lord Gowrie, the Governor-General. Body-line would have been much discussed, for Gowrie had played a key part behind the scenes during and after the crisis. The Prime Minister, Joe Lyons (who himself in 1933 had put pressure on the Australian Board, for political reasons, to withdraw the word 'unsportsmanlike'), also took a great interest in Allen's visit and the whole team was invited to Parliament House for tea one morning. Several cabinet ministers also joined Gowrie and Lyons for the match at the Manuka Oval (where a weakened MCC side, which included Captain Howard, won a comfortable innings victory).

Canberra, which today has an overall population of nearly 250,000, was then a city of just 10,000 people. The decision to build a new capital had been taken at the time of Warner's tour but the seat of government was only moved there from Melbourne in 1927; ten years later the architect's intentions were still largely unrealized and the tourists found the unfinished city confusing and sometimes irritating. 'Of what use is the purple majesty of the hills?', asked Bruce Harris, 'when it is necessary to walk a mile and a half from one's hotel to buy razor blades?' However, from the vantage point of Red Hill they could look down and see the logic of the planners' intentions, a spacious, leafy garden-city, divided by a lake. Its development was costing millions of pounds and its detractors considered it a likely white elephant. Bruce Harris, however, despite the razor blades, disagreed: 'It is an extraordinarily attractive experiment in the building of a City Beautiful. Australia can be proud of it. Fifty years hence she will be prouder still . . .'

Canberra placed yet further off-field strains on Gubby Allen. A speech at the Grammar School was followed by another at a luncheon given by the Federal Capital Territory Country Association. He was speaking again and tree-planting at the new Commonwealth Sports ground, where his inexpert shovelling raised clouds of dust. 'That's the first time', whispered Leyland, 'I've seen the skipper do any work!' He spoke at Parliament

House and, the same day, to 700 guests at an evening garden party given by Sir Geoffrey Whiskard, the British High Commissioner, an impressive affair complete with military band, male choir and Chinese lanterns strung up between the trees on the High Commissioner's gracious lawn. The skipper certainly *was* doing his share of work.

Allen was now far from fit. Bowling flat-out on bone hard Australian grounds had taken its toll; he was suffering from strained thigh muscles and was physically drained. His natural enthusiasm for sight-seeing, driving long distances and meeting family and business friends had exacerbated matters. He had insisted, for example, on driving down from Melbourne to Canberra with Wyatt, a journey of 410 miles done in one very long day; Lord Nuffield's offer of a 25 h.p. Morris had proved irresistible. Above all, he was exhausted by the heavy demands of public-speaking and generating goodwill at every port of call. The smiles now came less readily to his face; the demand for autographs was less cheerfully met. By the end of the Canberra visit Gubby Allen had broken down with severe mental exhaustion. He found difficulty in controlling his temper. Inane remarks irritated him. In particular he became sensitive to the suggestions, now being made, that he had been very lucky to have won the first two Tests. He played no cricket in this period and even absented himself from the two State games. Robins and Wyatt captained the team in the four matches between the fourth and fifth Tests. Instead, Allen took to the roads, staying with friends for a time at Moss Vale and later driving in holiday fashion along the coastal route from Sydney to Melbourne.

Here, just before the final Test, the debilitated Allen fell out with Bradman. He had heard of bumpers bowled against the MCC by a Melbourne policeman, Laurie Nash, who had been recently drafted into the Victorian side and subsequently picked for the Test. Allen accordingly told the Australian Board that Nash should be dropped from its squad. Later he and Robins met Bradman over lunch. If Nash's selection meant the re-introduction of body-line, said Allen, he would hold Bradman personally responsible and feel free to retaliate. Unsurprisingly Bradman resented this interference in his team selection and its implication of bad sportsmanship. However, the captains did agree that neither side would bowl bumpers, an agreement which irritated many onlookers. 'The batsman who objects to bumpers, when no packed leg-side field is set,' complained Vic Richardson (Bradman's predecessor as Australian captain), 'ought to be packed in cotton wool and sent home labelled fragile.' Bill Pollock assented: 'Peace at any price may have its advantages, but I hope that a precedent for giving up fast bouncers in big cricket has not been established.' It hadn't! Nonetheless 'peace at any price' *was* the slogan of the day. At home, as the Test began, it was learnt that Stanley Baldwin was to give way to Neville Chamberlain as Prime Minister. Munich was not far away.

Gubby Allen had not wished to play in the fifth Test. Now as it got under way he heartily wished he had not allowed his fellow selectors to over-rule him. The Australians, inspired by centuries from Bradman (169), McCabe and Badcock, had reached 593–9 by the end of two days and the Ashes were as good as won! There was particular grief in the England camp, as Lord Nuffield had promised a Morris motor-car to every tourist if they won the series.

In England, tributes were paid to Bradman's continuing successes. Plum Warner, in the *Morning Post*, wrote: 'I can imagine W. G. Grace in the Elysian fields tugging his beard and muttering "This boy looks better than I was".' Overall, however, there was understandable disappointment. A losing England cricket team soon becomes a source of humour and on BBC radio the popular duettists, the Western Brothers, lamented the poor start:

Oh England, mother England, dear land of strange design,
Is it true Australia's 593 for 9?
Oh breathe it not in Manchester, in Sheffield or in Brum
Nor mention it in London town, that devastating sum.

T'is true, alas, you Englishmen, this heavy Aussie gross,
And in the streets of Nottingham they're talking sotto Voce.
The toss was lost! The catches missed! Old England on the run.
Young Gregory got 80, too, and he's not twenty-one!

A crowd of 70,000! What a lovely lot of bobs!
Think if we could only send a bat out to Jack Hobbs!
The sun shone down, our thirsty men pursued their heated way,
Thank heaven they had Worthington upon the field of play!

The crowd of 70,000 was no exaggeration. Melbourne had just
built its enormous outer stand and could now accommodate up
to 92,000 spectators. This Test, as indeed all the others, drew
gigantic crowds. Nearly a million people watched the series and
the profit which MCC brought back (£42,000) was also a record.
Jim Lillywhite would surely have approved.

Lillywhite's name was on many lips at Melbourne, for this was
the Diamond Jubilee Test and a bronze commemoration tablet
was attached to the new stand, whilst Gubby Allen found himself
involved in yet more tree planting. Tom Garrett's presence was
announced to the crowds. It was remembered that it was on this
ground sixty years before that Charles Bannerman had scored his
165, Tom Garrett putting on 43 runs with him, before Bannerman
retired hurt. Later Garrett had bowled out All-England's top
scorer, Harry Jupp.

These and other announcements were greeted with hearty
cheering, not least from the ladies who were said to have
outnumbered the men at the Jubilee Test. They idolized their
heroes with a fanaticism more usually reserved for film stars.
Indeed Don Bradman, Chuck Fleetwood-Smith and Ross
Gregory were even more admired – and a little more accessible –
than Clark Gable, Gary Cooper and Spencer Tracy. When Ross
Gregory, slim and inconspicuous, was spotted coming quietly
into the ground, hundreds of waiting female fans clapped and
screamed in ecstasy, whilst the nonplussed youth hurriedly
retreated to the safety of the dressing-rooms. The English players
came in for their share of adoration. 'Gubby's smile is positively
fascinating', wrote one lady to the newspapers. 'Charlie Barnett
has the most gorgeously determined chin and Kenneth Farnes the
most divine profile.' Farnes attracted particular attention. 'He's so
tall,' enthused an admirer, 'with such nice dark hair and such
melting gazelle-like eyes.' Joe Hardstaff, with his fair, curly hair,

was popular too, as was Walter Hammond: 'He has such big, broad shoulders and he's so graceful in his movements.'

Although both Hammond and Hardstaff pleased their adoring public with good innings, the team's luck continued to run adversely. After Australia's 604 had been made in perfect conditions, rain caused England to be bowled out to a humiliating innings defeat. Australian jubilation was matched by English disappointment. Allen's was excessively acute and his comments after the match showed it: 'I make no bones about it. I am a very disappointed man. . . . This is probably my last appearance in Melbourne. It has been a sad one for me.' Likewise, in a speech of thanks to the VCA (for a gift of onyx and pearl waistcoat buttons, shirt studs and cuff-links), he showed similarly undisguised feelings: 'I do think that captains coming here should be protected. I have been rather hard-worked and I think it tells on a man's cricket. If you look at the record of previous captains you will find that every one has been a flop. They should be protected from the amazing kindness. But I am grateful for it, even if it has killed my cricket.'

In his exhaustion he found little consolation in the fact that the goodwill mission on which he had been sent had been so successfully accomplished. George VI sent congratulations to the captains on 'the friendliest spirit' of the series. Lord Gowrie congratulated Bradman on the splendid way in which they had all demonstrated 'what is commonly known as playing the game'. The MCC secretary, Rait Kerr, sent out a significant cablegram to Allen: 'All here sympathise your disappointment result of rubber but success of tour fully recognized'. Indeed it was. 'This series,' proclaimed the Sydney *Referee*, 'has cemented Anglo-Australian Test goodwill.' All the damage done by Jardine's tour had been repaired. The destinies of the two countries were still inextricably linked, as the political situation in Europe continued to worsen.

The rest of the tour, after the fifth Test, was simply a glorious holiday. There were two final weeks in Australia, with inconsequential matches at Benalla and Sydney University. The touring party, however, was already breaking up. Walter Robins had exercised an amateur's right to independence by departing, before the conclusion of the final Test, to do some shooting in South Australia, after which he flew to Perth to catch the *Orion* home. Arthur Fagg, hospitalized since the last games in Adelaide, also sailed home early on the *Orion*. The Australian journalists now all went their separate ways – most had been with the team since Perth; some, like Mailey, had joined up as early as Colombo. Most English journalists also opted for early returns, Cardus and Hobbs among them, while Fergie, the baggageman and scorer, left the team to get married.

There were emotional farewells at Sydney, highlighted by a dinner at Usher's Hotel given by the New South Wales Cricket Association, where the tourists were presented with inscribed cigarette boxes of polished Australian wood. Many officials and past and present players were there, amongst them the irrepressible Tom Garrett. The speeches flowed like the wine. Bert Oldfield, who ran a nearby sports shop, made a simple and dignified speech, which typified the goodwill existing between the two sides. Oldfield, now 42, had just come to the end of a very distinguished Test career and probably realized it. His warm words were in harmony with the poignant atmosphere of the occasion. The imminent departure of a touring team always signals not just the end of another summer but of the illusion of permanence which the lengthy ritual of a Test series encourages. It is an emotional and unsettling moment.

Soon the remaining tourists prepared to sail for New Zealand, where they were to stay a fortnight, playing friendly matches at Christchurch, Wellington and Auckland. But their departure by ship was delayed a little on the initiative of George Duckworth, who had hurriedly organized a football match, England v New South Wales. England lost heavily despite the impressive, if rotund, presence of Duckworth in goal, of Walter Hammond, who had played professionally for Bristol Rovers, and of Laurie Fishlock, a current Southampton player. Allen, at right-half, was hampered by the most enormous pair of boots, loaned to him by a policeman and far too big, even when stuffed full of socks. Luck really had deserted the England captain.

So Allen's team sailed from Sydney. Like Lillywhite's at Glenelg and Warner's at Largs Bay, they left a grieving fraternity of friends behind on the wharfside. It was early evening. Most people in Sydney were settling down to the pleasures of Saturday night. The MCC had come and gone and Sydney carried on, business as usual. Inside Usher's Hotel the waiters, as usual, were delivering an abundance of oysters and chicken, whilst the two lady musicians, as usual, were entertaining in the dining-room. Outside, black taxi-cabs with orange tops and mudguards were hurrying down Castlereagh Street and neon signs were beginning to colour the shadows.

Aboard the *Wanganella* the players stood on deck, waving farewells and acknowledging cheers. As they moved slowly away from the wharf, the crew of a nearby vessel, seizing their moment, burst into a raucous rendition of 'Jolly Good Fellows'. It was a very different departure from Jardine's silent retreat. The *Wanganella* passed serenely under the bridge and along Port Jackson towards the Heads. The tourists, however, were still looking behind them, where the sun had set, in vivid red, as if in final salute, its deep glow silhouetting the black spars of the new suspension bridge. Allen, weary from the football, retreated to his cabin and firmly closed the door. 'I am so damn tired', he wrote to Bradman, 'that I don't intend to get up until we reach Wellington.'

In New Zealand there was much sight-seeing and a little cricket. Allen and Verity motored to the top of Mount Cook, the country's highest peak, during the match against Canterbury and Otago. Farnes climbed the summits of Mounts Ruapehu and Ngaruhoe, whilst the team took on a New Zealand XI at Wellington. All the players, en route to Auckland, went by charabanc to the famous valley of geysers, swam in the sulphurous waters at Rotorua, the showplace of the Maoris, and rubbed noses with Rangi, the famous woman guide. By the beginning of April they had won their match at Auckland's Eden Park and boarded an American liner, the *Mariposa*. After six months they were heading home.

There followed fourteen days of delightful cruising, with short stops at Fiji, Samoa and Honolulu. They docked at Los Angeles and spent a day sight-seeing at Hollywood as guests of the English film actor Aubrey Smith, now 74 and at the height of his popularity. Fifty years earlier he too had been touring Australia, as captain of the ill-fated team which Lillywhite, Shaw and Shrewsbury organized in competition with Lord Hawke's XI.

Gubby Allen and C. B. Fry lingered in Hollywood for several weeks, both playing for Aubrey Smith's Hollywood XI alongside Boris Karloff and other film stars in matches against Los Angeles and Pasadena Cricket Clubs. The rest of the party, however, took the Santa Fé express to Chicago and sailed home from New York in the *Queen Mary*.

They landed at Plymouth at the end of April, to discover the newspapers full of the speeches of Hitler, the latest plans of Amy Johnson, the impending marriage of the Duke of Windsor to Mrs Simpson and the Coronation of his brother. Many of those who had crossed the Atlantic with them had come for the Coronation: Lady Warwick, James Gerard (President Roosevelt's personal representative), the film star Gloria Swanson and the financier Pierpoint Morgan. Photographers and reporters buzzed round the disembarking celebrities, as if emulating a scene from Cole Porter's current musical comedy *Anything Goes*. Most theatrical of all was the Ranee of Sarawak, Lady Vyner Brooke, who had been giving advice in Hollywood for a film about the first white Rajah of Sarawak. She was met by her equally glamorous daughter, Princess Pearl, alias Mrs Harry Roy, wife of the famous dance band leader.

Less loquacious and quoteworthy were the MCC tourists. 'We've been told to say nowt', smiled big Bill Voce, 'and we're saying it!' The imperturbable Captain Howard was soon being pressed as to why the Ashes had been lost. 'I suppose it was because the Australians won three of the five Tests', he murmured blandly. As they posed for the cameras on the Plymouth quayside, their arrival blurred with their departure from Southampton seven months earlier. Perhaps George Duckworth and Walter Hammond looked a little travel creased, but mostly the team was still a credit to its tailors. Bob Wyatt was still carrying his camera around his neck and wearing his favourite felt hat. Maurice Leyland was still thoughtfully smoking his pipe, Hardstaff and

Sims still cheerfully drawing on cigarettes. A loud cry of welcome from Charles Barnett's 5-year-old son broke the spell, however, and soon a number of husbands and wives were reunited.

Nearly a month later, after eight months abroad, Gubby Allen returned, emerging at Southampton from *The Empress of Canada*, looking much more relaxed than latterly at Adelaide or Melbourne. 'I have had a wonderful holiday in America', he told enquiring reporters, 'which I needed a great deal.' The English season was well under way by now. Would he be playing soon? 'I shall be turning out on Wednesday for the MCC Australian Touring side against the Rest of England, but I very much doubt if I shall play in any other matches this season. I now have to get back to my work on the Stock Exchange.' What about 1938? Gubby Allen smiled modestly and began moving away. 'My ability to play next year will depend upon whether I am wanted, whether I am fit, and whether I can get away from my work as a stockbroker.'

As Gubby Allen made his way to London, he ran over in his mind the report he would have to submit to the MCC. The ultimate defeat he put down to three things. First, there had been an excess of cricket, as many as ninety days in all. This was more or less the same as on Jardine's tour, but was 30% more than the cricket played by Warner or Lillywhite. The ideal tour, Allen believed, should contain two months of travel and three of cricket. His tour had been two months too long. Second, there had been many batting failures. In particular, they could have won the Test at Adelaide, had they batted better. During the series only four batsmen had scored over 200 runs: Hammond, Leyland, Barnett and Hardstaff. It had been bad luck that Bob Wyatt was only available for two Tests but no excuses could be found for the batting failures of Ames, Fagg, Fishlock, Robins and Worthington. Third, he had suffered from a lack of accurate spin bowling. The Australians had taken 51 Test wickets with leg-breaks, chinamen and googlies. Verity, Robins and Sims had between them taken 17. England had relied on a pace attack, bowling three times as many such overs as the Australians on wickets which primarily suited wrist spin.

Despite the disappointing result, Gubby Allen always remembered the tour with fondness. Fifty years later, indeed, pride of place was still given in his drawing-room to an engraved silver cigar box: 'A token of appreciation from members of a happy MCC touring team, 1936–37. To our Skipper'. He was quick, however, to dismiss it modestly. 'We gave something like it to Douglas, I believe!' After fifty years the frustration of the Ashes' loss lingered on, but time had muffled most discords and memories of his fellow tourists were affectionate.

Hedley Verity? 'A splendid chap, knowledgeable too, pretty damn knowledgeable.' Leslie Ames? 'Leslie was a pretty damn good wicket-keeper; don't have any illusions.' Bill Voce? 'Bowled magnificently until he started having trouble with his back.' The verdict on Jim Sims was more surprising, in the light of the failure to match Australian leg-spin success: 'Jim was a bloody good leg-spinner; no, a world-beater.' Perhaps he should have persevered with him and played him in more than just two Tests? There was less praise for Hardstaff ('didn't do all that much'), which was unsurprising, as the two did not see eye to eye. It is arguable that, with more sensitive handling, the young Notts batsman, who found his touch comparatively late in the tour, might have succeeded sooner. Wally Hammond's off-side magnificence was given due credit. So, too, his technique on a turning wicket. ('All the great players have the better eyesight.') But the passage of time had not completely turned the complicated inter-play of seventeen cricketing egos into a picture of perfect harmony. Hammond's self-centredness was remembered ('not a characteristic of most great batsmen.'). Barnett was 'a fine stroke player' but 'wrapped up in himself'. Farnes was 'quietish. He got on pretty well. One or two didn't like him before the tour. . . .'

Who were his greatest helpers? This needed thought. The captaincy, it seemed, had been a lonely job. 'I had two or three quite intelligent chaps', he mused at last. 'Robbie. Robbie was intelligent, when he was paying attention. Bob Wyatt of course. Maurice Leyland was very good and Hedley. Ducky in certain ways.'

Essentially, as a captain, Allen was his own man, scornful of modern captains who tend to operate by consensus. Typically too he remained a bachelor, married, it was said, to cricket, and living in a most elegant house backing onto Lord's, a Bentley in the garage. After the tour of 1936–37 he played only intermittently. He might have returned against Australia in 1938, had Plum Warner not given the captaincy to Wally Hammond, who had recently acquired amateur status. For a time the Warner-Allen friendship waned in warmth. Allen did, however, captain the MCC, at the age of 45, on the tour of West Indies in 1947–48 and, like Warner, he was nearly 50 when he played his last first-class match. Later, he bore with great fortitude a whole series of painful hip operations, the legacy of his fast bowling days. Until his death in 1989 pronouncements on the game continued to be shrewd and trenchant, that 'velvety Etonian confidence', which C. B. Fry had so admired in Australia in 1936–37, always evident.

Postscript

FROM ALLEN TO BREARLEY

The advent of the Second World War meant that Gubby Allen's was the last MCC tour of Australia for ten years. Several of those tourists had distinguished war records. Leslie Ames and Wally Hammond ended as Squadron-Leaders and other professionals became officers: Captain Stan Worthington, Lieutenant Maurice Leyland and Captain Hedley Verity. Gubby Allen himself was a Colonel, doing intelligence work in the War Office; typically he had managed to play a little war-time cricket. Others were less lucky and amongst the many cricketers who perished were three who had played in the last Test at Melbourne – Hedley Verity, Kenneth Farnes and Ross Gregory.

Nevertheless, when Walter Hammond's party arrived in Australia in 1946–47, cricket still seemed much the same and, with Bradman and Hammond the captains, there was a sense of continuity. Hammond took along three members of Allen's old side, Bill Voce, Joe Hardstaff and Laurie Fishlock, and Rupert Howard was again the manager. Afterwards the four-year pattern was re-established, with subsequent teams led by Freddie Brown, Len Hutton, Peter May and Ted Dexter.

All these sides travelled to Australia by sea but returned by air. Thus Len Hutton, returning early from the tour of 1946–47 because of illness, was able to claim to have been the first tourist ever to fly between the two countries. Hutton suffered a long, tedious journey and at one stage his little plane had to return to Darwin with mechanical problems, alarming its passengers by circling the airfield for three hours whilst jettisoning fuel. Most of Wally Hammond's team of 1946–47 returned from New Zealand by a scheduled flying-boat service. The flying-boat gave the tourists an adventurous week, with stops at Bowen, Darwin, Surabaya, Singapore, Rangoon, Calcutta, Karachi, Bahrein, Basra, Cairo and Marseilles, before a final landing in Poole Harbour! In the immediate post-war period, therefore, the means of travel had altered considerably, yet the touring itself remained of similar scope and style.

In the 1960s and 1970s the introduction of more and more one-day cricket and the beginnings of sponsorship radically altered English domestic cricket but did not immediately affect the Australian tours. In 1965–66 Mike Smith's tourists were the first to travel both ways by air, yet he and his successors (Ray Illingworth in 1970–71 and Mike Denness in 1974–75) still undertook long, traditional tours of up to five months, which included no more than a single one-day International in Australia. Mike Brearley's tour of 1978–79 was the first to show any real signs of change. The duration was cut a little, to four months; and for the first time there was a sponsored three-match series of one-day Internationals.

There *were* big changes, however, in the 1970s and they were ones of mood, brought about by the greater availability of money. In 1977 the touring fee had been £3,000 and the fee for a home Test appearance £210. By 1978, thanks to sponsorship, the touring fee had been raised to £5,500 and home Test appearances to £1,000. Mike Brearley's tourists of 1978–79 would be far better paid than any of their predecessors. In addition to the basic £5,500, the tourists would receive an extra £200 for all their previous tours. The much-travelled Geoff Boycott, therefore, would receive £6,700. Moreover, both teams were eligible for prize money, organized by the Australian Board of Control through its sponsors, Benson & Hedges, whilst the TCCB offered a further £1,250 to be shared by the team for every Test which it won. Finally, the England players had appointed an agent to look after promotional activities on the tour (such as making advertisements for the Milk Marketing Board and doing press, radio and television interviews). Bob Taylor thought that each player made an extra £1,500 through promotional work and bonuses.

Most established Test players now had their own agents, exploiting their commercial potential to the full. Just before the departure of Brearley's tour, Bob Willis (and The Wickets) made a gramophone record about the winning of the Ashes; Willis reckoned to have spent most of the time between the end of the English cricket season and the departure in mid-October on commercial and promotional engagements. Ian Botham at this period had Reg Hayter as his agent, then editor of *The Cricketer*. It was not surprising, therefore, when articles about the tour started appearing in the magazine under Botham's name. Of course, later, Botham was to employ Tim Hudson as his agent, who included Hollywood stardom in his grandiose plans for Botham. Understandably, the players took these new-found commercial opportunities very seriously indeed. Hendrick and Gower spent much time on the flight out to Australia in 1978 debating the merits of turning themselves into limited companies. The book, *With Time To Spare*, which Gower, aged 21, produced with help from Alan Lee, was copyrighted 'David Gower Promotions'. At the time of Brearley's tour Gower was reckoned 'at a conservative estimate' to be earning £20,000 a year from his cricket.

All the Test players of the late 1970s, therefore, had much more to lose financially than their predecessors if they were dropped from international teams and it was inevitable that a greater ruthlessness should exhibit itself on the field of play. The style of captaincy adopted by Ian Chappell epitomized the new age; the abrasive 'macho' qualities of men like Lillee, Marsh and Thomson were widely copied. 'The Australians under Ian Chappell', wrote Bob Willis, 'performed a brand of cricket that involved hard-faced, unyielding attitudes on the field: unnecessary appealing to pressurize the umpires, refusal to walk if the batsman knew he was out and baiting of batsmen by some of the fielding side.' England's Dennis Amiss suffered more than most, the recipient of constant bouncers and much verbal abuse. 'Amiss, you're a xxxxxx', Lillee would snarl, 'and what's more, you're no xxxxing good as a batsman.' It was said that, by the end of the series of 1974–75, Lillee could have run up and bowled Amiss out with an orange.

Poor behaviour on the field exacerbated that off it. There was an early example of crowd problems in 1970–71 when Illingworth was forced to lead his team off the field at Sydney because of threatening crowd behaviour. The Hill, though never exactly a dry area, had become in the 1970s the haven for loud-mouthed 'ockers'. No less than 864,000 empty beer cans were removed from its precincts during the course of one Test. Sharp wit and repartee, so long a hallmark of Australian cricket crowds, turned to something less amusing: 'Kill, Kill, Kill!' became the cry as Lillee and Thomson ran in at the batsman. Forty years ago it had all been very different. Joe Hardstaff's memories of the Sydney crowd were of people after his own heart: 'I always liked to field down by the Hill. They were fair-minded. They'd barrack you, naturally, but if you'd do well, they gave you credit.' The only similarity now was the size of the crowds. Those in the 1970s were sometimes nearly as big as the record-breaking crowds of the 1930s. There were 77,000 at Melbourne on Boxing Day in 1974. But cricket was becoming very ugly, as it had fleetingly been in 1932–33; the age of the helmet was at hand.

Then suddenly, amidst all the turmoil, the names of Lillywhite and Bannerman were again on everyone's lips. It was the time of the Centenary Test at Melbourne. Tony Greig's MCC side, after touring in India, diverted to Australia, where, after one warm-up game, they played a five-day Test in Melbourne in March, exactly a hundred years since the Combined XI had beaten Lillywhite's depleted and travel-weary side. Quite remarkably, Greig's team, like Lillywhite's, lost by 45 runs.

Less than two months after the conclusion of the Centenary Test the Kerry Packer story broke in the newspapers. Thirty-five of the world's best players had initially been signed by the Australian millionaire, whose inability to gain exclusive TV rights to first-class cricket in Australia for his own Channel had led to the formation of World Series Cricket. Kerry Packer's ruthlessness certainly harmonized with much that was happening in the game: 'I will now take no steps to help anyone', he said after an abortive meeting at Lord's. 'Every man for himself and the devil take the hindmost.' He then inaugurated, at the reported cost of $12 billion, the first of three seasons of World Series Cricket, the second season of which would coincide with Mike Brearley's official tour. Brearley's tourists would be competing with the Packer Supertests for the favour of the Australian cricketing public.

One break with tradition went almost unnoticed during the continuing Packer revelations and controversies. The tourists of

1978–79 were the first to go to Australia under the aegis of the TCCB, the MCC having ceded its ancient sovereignty to a newly-formed Cricket Council. The diminished authority of the MCC and the problems of modern cricket would not have pleased those two pillars of the Lord's establishment, Plum Warner and Gubby Allen. The former, however, had died, at the age of 89 in 1963, but Allen's influence at Lord's was crucial for over forty years after the war. Like Warner before him he devoted himself to the administration of the game; both men were rewarded with knighthoods and the presidency of MCC.

Allen, for his part, accepted the inevitable advent of democracy within the game but fought energetically against the uncouth concomitants of big money. 'I can't see why they can't play to win', he used to say, 'without being absolutely bloody. It's gradually got worse. . . . with the one-day Internationals especially. . . . There's too much big cricket, too much appealing, too much looking as though you've been "done". We're definitely going to make an effort to change things.'

In 1978 few would have disagreed that change was needed. Poor standards of sportsmanship, wretched crowd behaviour, intimidating fast bowling, weak umpiring and the undue influence of the media were but a few of the problems exercising the minds of administrators as Mike Brearley led his team to Australia. Then there was Kerry Packer. The tourists of 1978–79, therefore, in their own way had as many problems and pressures to face as Jim Lillywhite's men a hundred years before.

5

MIKE BREARLEY'S TOUR

1978–79

In October 1978 the world was a confused, troubled place. In America President Carter was inaugurating a national austerity campaign and there were dark days ahead for Mr Bhutto in Pakistan, Ian Smith in Rhodesia and the Shah in Iran. At home unemployment was rising to well over a million, and Prime Minister Jim Callaghan was struggling; his 5% incomes policy was provoking a rash of strikes. Meanwhile, the tabloid press continued that particularly modern phenomenon, the eager pursuit of fallen idols. During the Brearley tour, Jeremy Thorpe, the former Liberal leader, and Don Revie, the former England football manager, provided breakfast-table entertainment for the masses, as did Bernard Bosanquet's son, the controversial TV newscaster Reginald, whose successful defence against a paternity suit brought him unwelcome attention from the media.

Confusion and discontent were rife in cricket too. Kerry Packer's World Series would surely embarrass the forthcoming Ashes tour by providing alternative entertainment featuring seventeen of the best Australians. Mike Brearley claimed that England would be missing four or five players and the Australians seven or eight. In reality there was a greater imbalance. England were minus Knott and Underwood, whereas Australia, lacking the Chappell brothers, Lillee, Thomson, Marsh, Bright, Hookes, Gilmour and Wessels, could be said to be fielding virtually a 2nd XI. Kerry Packer, confident that *his* Australians would win the public's support, was preparing to offer on his own TV channel over 250 hours of World Series Cricket, attractively packaged and ferociously advertised. The Australian Broadcasting Company, giving live coverage of the six Test matches, was uneasy about the impending battle. It was no wonder that, as the moment arrived for the departure of Mike Brearley's team, Alex Bannister was declaring in the *Daily Mail*: 'Since James Lillywhite started it all in 1877, no England captain in Australia has carried greater responsibility than Mike Brearley.'

John Michael Brearley, MA, PhD, looked anything but over-awed by his responsibilities as the team assembled at mid-day at Lord's for a farewell reception given by Cornhill Assurance, its sponsors. Lord's was an appropriate starting-point for Brearley, a Middlesex player like Warner and Allen before him. He had known Lord's since his schooldays when he visited its nets to be coached by Jim Sims, Gubby Allen's leg-spinner. After a success-ful time as a schoolboy cricketer (at the City of London School, where his father taught mathematics and coached the 1st XI), Mike Brearley had progressed to Cambridge; there, in addition to scoring a record 4,068 runs, he had taken a first in Classics and a second in Philosophy. By the time he was 19 he was playing for Middlesex; he toured South Africa and Pakistan with England in the 1960s but it was not until he was 34 that he was picked, as an opening batsman, for England. Tony Greig's defection to Kerry Packer had opened the way to the English captaincy and now, aged 36, he was leading his country to Australia, an unbeaten captain in his previous seventeen Tests.

Brearley, or 'The Cambridge Superbrain', as the *Sun* dubbed him, was a man of many parts. No previous England captain had hummed melodies from Beethoven's Rasoumoffsky Quartets when batting, had given up cricket for two years to lecture and study at university, had spent two winters working in a therapeu-tic community for disabled adolescents or taken on tour novels by Tolstoy, Henry James, Paul Scott, George Eliot and Iris Murdoch. An intellectual, single-minded man, Brearley had spent the weeks before departure examining and revising his batting technique in the indoor nets at Lord's, whilst his mental resources were sharpened by a week of solitude in Wales. His interests were not those of his team, who mostly would be looking forward to Australian beaches, parties and discos. The keen beer drinkers in the side – and there were a number of them – would not be seeing much of their captain in the evenings. Nonetheless Mike Brearley was not an aloof captain, an authoritarian figure in the mould of Gubby Allen. 'The idea of a captain twenty-five years ago', said Brearley in an interview shortly before flying to Australia, 'was of someone who wouldn't listen, who told people what to do. Of course you've got to tell people what to do, but I like to get people's advice, to hear what their views are, to give them a say. . . .' The distinction between amateurs and professionals had been abolished in 1963 and Brearley was proof of breached social barriers. 'He was intellectually remote from me', said Bob Taylor, 'but he never talked down.' Although Brearley's friends did tend to come from outside the game, he was a good communicator and well respected. The vice-captain, Bob Willis, with whom he shared the same agent, was one of his closer friends.

Perhaps it was in the common pursuit of commercial aspirations that Brearley most obviously identified with the rest of his team. In 1978, his benefit year, he had followed the fund-raising trail with great vigour, selling pontoon tickets in pubs and raffling autographed bats as to the manner born. In the weeks before the tour's departure, things had been busy; there was an end-of-season dinner-dance, with John Cleese providing the cabaret, a boxing-dinner night, with Benny Green and Tim Rice the speakers, a Stag night, with Brearley himself and Fred Trueman entertaining, and 'An Evening with Ian Wallace'. A benefit of £31,000 had resulted.

Mike Brearley, therefore, was a captain of wide interests and sympathies. Now, on a sunny afternoon at Lord's in late October, he seized the opportunity of combining business with pleasure and held the first of many team talks. In it he emphasised the importance of good communications. It was vital, said Brearley, for players to discuss problems with him. On a long tour it was easy for people to feel left out and for cliques to form. There would be enough pressures from the Australians without the creation of their own. Bob Willis, the vice-captain, agreed, cautioning the team about 'the Aussie press' which would seek out half-truths to create 'sensations'. Doug Insole, the tour manager, mentioned World Series Cricket. The best way to compete, he said, was to play tough but positive cricket. Brearley agreed. 'I certainly don't think we should try to jazz up our cricket. The important things are to get on with it. To get on with the over-rate, to look to be on top when you are batting, to look to be on top when you are bowling . . .'

Brearley's team was a strong one. The difficulty of keeping a touring team in practice and the ease of flying out replacements persuaded him to choose sixteen rather than seventeen players. He took out one fewer specialist batsman than Allen, but one more fast bowler. Like Allen he was taking three spinners, the left-arm Phil Edmonds being in the classic tradition of Hedley Verity, Wilfred Rhodes and Jim Lillywhite. However, whereas Verity was complemented by two leg-spinners, Edmonds was accompanied by two off-spinners, Emburey and Miller. All in all, Brearley's team was a splendid mixture of experience and youth. Gooch, Gower, and Botham were in their early 20s, at the beginning of their distinguished careers, and Miller, Emburey and Randall not much older. Hendrick, Lever, Old and Willis, a magnificently varied quartet of fast bowlers, were still in mid-career. Radley and Tolchard were widely experienced county players in their early 30s; Boycott, Taylor and Brearley were the elder (but very fit) statesmen.

There was also a strong management team. Doug Insole, although without previous experience as a tour manager, had played Test cricket himself and until recently had been Chairman of the TCCB, so he would be able to handle all World Series Cricket developments with ease. Insole, at 52, a former Cambridge Blue like Brearley, had strong opinions of his own and was very much an establishment figure. As captain of Essex for many years Insole had, said Trevor Bailey, 'an absolute conviction that he was invariably right'. Ken Barrington, who ran a garage business in Surrey, was his ideal foil as assistant manager, a man of immense touring experience. Barrington had gone out to Australia with both Dexter and M. J. K. Smith and had played eighty-two Tests in all, until a heart attack in 1968, when he was 37, abruptly stopped his career. Since then he had managed teams to India, Australia (for the Centenary Test), Pakistan and New Zealand. Insole and Barrington made a most efficient and understanding managerial combination. Brearley also had the expert help of Bernie Thomas as travelling physiotherapist, who had made his first Ashes tour in 1970–71. The twentieth and final member of the party was Geoffrey Saulez, the scorer, a retired accountant, who, like Thomas, travelled with many England teams.

Prior to their departure from Lord's the team went to the indoor school where a large assortment of free gifts had been gathered, including much cricket equipment. It was time, too, for them to put on their official travelling clothes. Soon they were smiling for the cameramen in their regulation dark blue trousers (flared as in 1970s style), striped touring ties, light brown shoes, blue socks, and light blue jackets, with the badge of St George as first designed for Plum Warner in 1903. All in all, it was a big improvement on previous attempts to produce a casual, corporate image.

There was nothing, however, that the TCCB could do to produce a uniform hair-style. Hair, lots of it, was still popular in the late 1970s. Derek Randall, Graham Gooch, Geoff Miller and John Emburey all sported early-Beatles cuts, whilst John Lever went for an altogether longer and slightly professorial look. Bob Willis's luxuriant Afro cut was particularly striking and in notable contrast to Geoff Boycott's more modest display. The greying Brearley and Taylor looked suitably distinguished, while the young Phil Edmonds, untouched as yet by any recession, displayed blond locks in plenty.

From Lord's the players went by coach to the Excelsior, Heathrow for their second reception of the day, an opportunity for the pressmen who would not be accompanying the team abroad to pen some final copy. Frank Keating of the *Guardian* was among them, noting that Willis looked 'keen and bushy-tailed' – he surely meant 'keen and bushy-haired'? – and the young Graham Gooch 'earnest and nervous'. While Brearley gave a headmasterly address, Radley and Boycott stood in attendance 'like elder prefects'. For Keating the most interesting personality was Geoffrey Boycott, at 38 the team's most senior player, who only the year before had reached the great milestone of a hundred 100s. Deprived of the England leadership by Brearley's expertise, he had very recently been stripped of the Yorkshire captaincy by a committee with which he and his supporters were now in a state of total war. His saga was providing excellent material for the tabloids and that very day the story headed YORKSHIRE CONFIRM DECISION TO REPLACE BOYCOTT was the *Times*'s second biggest front-page feature. He was, said Keating, 'an oddly vulnerable man', who even with a bat in his hand was 'as massively dominating, but still frail around the edges, as any of England's great cathedrals in a line from Hereford to Durham.' As at Heathrow, so on tour, Boycott would remain a man apart.

There was a considerable press presence on the tour. Since Gubby Allen's time numbers had risen steadily to a record thirty who accompanied Peter May in 1958–59, after which there was a gradual decrease, not unaffected by the closing of many provincial newspapers. Nonetheless the media men of 1978–79 could nearly have fielded two cricket teams. Excellent relations existed between press and players on this tour. They generally travelled as one party, using the same transport and hotels (which allowed the TCCB to obtain cheaper rates). 'There was a degree of trust', remembered Paul Fitzpatrick of the *Guardian*, 'between Fourth Estate and players that seems not to be there now. I doubt if a single journalist would look back on that tour with anything but pleasure.'

The departure of the team and its large entourage, economy class in a Qantas jumbo jet, lacked the style of Allen's in the *Orion* or indeed even that of Lillywhite in the *Poonah*. The statutory photographs were taken at the stairs of the jumbo on embarkation, but this small display of ceremony could not alter the fact that mass holiday air-travel had rendered such journeys as Mike Brearley's quite mundane. No one took much notice as his team quietly left England (two hours late, the Boeing 747B having shredded a tyre on the way to the runway). The two press conferences, likewise, were a poor replacement for the massive, spontaneous public farewells of earlier days at London railway stations. Nonetheless, for the departing players the excitement was as great as that of any of their predecessors. 'To tour Australia with the England team', wrote Graham Gooch in 1979, 'is every cricketer's dream. No other tour can compare with it.'

No sooner were they in the skies than Doug Insole was passing round team autograph sheets for everyone to sign. Mike Brearley managed around 2,000 on the flight. Most of the players were soon changing out of their official clothes into something more comfortable. Derek Randall was the only exception. He seemed, thought Brearley, to be drawing inspiration from his orange, red and navy-blue striped tie; the sight of St George and the Dragon on his blazer badge may well have conjured up memories of

Melbourne in 1977, when his 174 in the Centenary Test had brought him instant, uncomfortable celebrity.

A pontoon school started up amongst the keenest card players – Gower, Emburey, Miller and Botham – but the latter did not think much of the modest stakes. 'What little there was to win, I won!' he declared afterwards with cheerful immodesty. It was not long, however, before David Gower was asleep. Gower was the most successful sleeper in the side, and, whereas John Lever, who disliked air-travel, was grimly enduring it, Gower dozed peacefully. His calmness at all times, however, did not altogether win his captain's approval. 'I would like to see other feelings come through more obviously. . . . excitement, fear, anger. . . .', he wrote.

There were the usual in-flight films, which received a mixed response. Bob Taylor thoroughly enjoyed Peter Falk as the detective Colombo, but Geoff Boycott watched in some perplexity a kangaroo called Matilda boxing for the world heavyweight championship. David Gower tried a film too, but couldn't keep his eyes open.

Mike Brearley took advantage of the long flight for chats with Ian Botham and Geoff Boycott, two of his key players. Two days before their departure Botham, while having farewell drinks with some friends at his local, had put his hand through a glass partition and severed two tendons. His wrist was now in plaster and he was unlikely to play any cricket for two or three weeks. The incident had been much dramatized by the media; Ian's wife, Kathy, expecting their second child, had been harrassed at home. The 22-year-old Botham was beginning to learn the less pleasing aspects of being a public figure. Meanwhile Geoff Boycott, in addition to his problems with the Yorkshire committee, had suffered much from the recent illness and death of his mother. The last six weeks, he told Brearley, had been the worst in his life. Brearley was a sympathetic listener. Leaving England for a while, he suggested to Boycott, was the best possible antidote to his troubles. Scoring runs against the Australians would restore his morale. The two men were of very dissimilar backgrounds and cricketing abilities, but the talk did much to clear the air between them; Brearley nonetheless remained anxious for his senior batsman, whose crisis with Yorkshire had been so deeply wounding.

Brearley himself had much to reflect upon, in that he had suffered a dramatic loss of form that very summer, probably connected with the breaking of his arm in Karachi in January. When Alec Bedser, the chairman of the selectors, had offered him the captaincy for this tour, he had been unsure whether to accept, such were his doubts about his batting. 'It is an ordeal', he wrote, 'to undergo failures in public.' On the flight, however, he was able to keep his mind from such anxieties by the pursuit of an interesting theory. He had read an article which suggested that jet-lag was caused by dehydration. The body lost a quart of water in a thirty-hour flight. The England captain, carefully monitoring his extra intake of water, proved that the theory worked! 'I never felt better in my life', he remarked at the end of the flight.

After short re-fuelling stops at Bahrein, Singapore and Perth, Mike Brearley's Boeing arrived at Sydney airport at 7 a.m. on 25 October. A horde of newspapermen intercepted them as they changed planes for Adelaide, where they would be staying for the first two weeks. Insole's message to the Sydney press was one of cautious optimism: 'Yes, I would reckon we have come over here as favourites – which is not the greatest place to be. We don't know too much about your players, nor do you, but you are a very resilient lot and you produce players out of nowhere! No doubt you are going to produce players who are going to give us a hell of a good going over, and until we see who they are on the day I don't think either you or we know what the outcome is going to be.' Insole seemed determined to play down his own team's strength: 'We have got a side', he declared, 'in which only Geoff Boycott has had any real experience over here.' In fact fourteen of the tourists had played cricket in Australia before and several were on their second or third Australian tour. Mike Brearley was similarly cautious, singling out only David Gower for special mention: 'As good a timer of the ball as I have ever seen.'

As they flew on to Adelaide the team discovered that the Sydney papers were full of Kerry Packer. There was news of his intention to take his teams to the West Indies, of the installation of floodlights at Sydney Cricket Ground, of his offer to pay all the parking fines for spectators who attended night matches there and of a court battle being fought out between Queensland and his latest recruit, Jeff Thomson. They read too of a Packer pro-am golf tournament at Adelaide, which might minimize the impact of their own arrival. Clearly rivalry between the two forms of cricket was likely to be intense and, in the circumstances, it seemed strangely appropriate that Adelaide should at that moment be celebrating the Battle of Stringybark Creek, a shoot-out between Ned Kelly's outlaws and the traditional forces of law and order.

The players reached Adelaide twenty-nine hours after they had left Heathrow. They were met by the 70-year-old Sir Donald Bradman, who, with Lady Jessie, still lived in the suburb of South Kensington, a man of substance and influence, a director of several companies and friend of Prime Ministers. Bradman's opposition to World Series Cricket was strong and he wished to give the Ashes series every support.

The younger tourists had heard much of the beauty of Adelaide but the view from the coach as they sped along wide, dusty streets from the airport was initially disappointing, a garish kaleidoscope of motels, petrol stations, neon signs and corrugated bungalow roofs. The city had nearly doubled in population since Allen's day, to around a million, but its dignified centre remained as impressive as ever. Pennington Gardens were much the same as when a band had unexpectedly delighted Neville Cardus there with the Egmont Overture, and it was still possible to catch a tram from Victoria Square down to Glenelg, scene of the arrival and departure of Lillywhite's men, and where the Pier Hotel in Jetty Road was a reminder of the time when Harry Jupp mistook a window for a porthole. Less durable had been the gracious South Australia Hotel, where both Warner and Allen had stayed. Brearley's team, in keeping with more modern days, was based at a high-rise motel, complete with roof-top swimming pool and a park across the road for compulsive early-morning joggers like

Bob Willis. More pressmen were lurking at the motel and, while Insole and Brearley supplied patient answers, others wearily made for their beds.

Jet-lag was, of course, a problem. For a week to ten days the players woke up at 4.00 in the morning, unable to sleep further, and around 4.00 in the afternoon they felt extremely tired. There were, however, five days before the first match. During this period the team met up outside the hotel at 9.30 a.m. And then drove in cars, courtesy of Avis and Chrysler, to the Oval, where they ran and exercised under the expert guidance of Bernie Thomas. Nets followed, supervised by Ken Barrington and the vice-captain, Bob Willis, for an hour either side of lunch. These were taken seriously, proper dress insisted on, Barrington making sure that the chief batsmen faced the main bowlers. David Gower, for example, was given a preparatory dose of bouncers by Bob Willis: 'I hit one, nick one, and duck a couple more. I'm trying to discipline myself to playing on bouncy wickets, to organize the brain to leave the bouncers alone.' Local bowlers were also utilized for the tail-enders and there were sometimes a number of young Englishmen, such as Gatting, Agnew, Roebuck, Tavaré and Larkins, who were abroad on scholarships or coaching appointments and available to help.

It was no longer customary, of course, for the press to take part in net practices, as C. B. Fry and Neville Cardus had occasionally done, so happily, in 1936–37. One day, however, the English bowlers were exhausted and all the locals playing in grade cricket, so two journalists were hastily summoned by Barrington. Steve Whiting of the *Sun*, who had been involved in a violent dispute with Ian Botham on the previous winter's tour to Pakistan, had the delight of bowling to Geoffrey Boycott. 'For about one minute', wrote Whiting, 'I probed his weaknesses. For the next 119 he hammered me all over the Adelaide Oval.'

For many years the pattern of MCC tours had allowed for twenty-eight days of first-class cricket before the first Test. Brearley's itinerary, by contrast, allowed for only four 4-day State matches. In addition, there were four one-day up-country matches, neatly sandwiched between the State games. Brearley (and his fellow selectors, Insole, Barrington and Willis) decided to drop everyone from one State game, a policy which did not meet with total approval. 'Those who are considered certain to play in the first Test', wrote Geoff Boycott, 'should be allowed to play in every warm-up match if they want to.'

The first match was at Renmark, a small town, prosperous through its fruit and wine production, some 130 miles up the Murray River. This involved a day's excursion from Adelaide, flying in a forty-seater Fokker Friendship. After the aeroplane had landed – somewhat bumpily – on a red mud airstrip, the tourists were greeted enthusiastically by the Mayor and crowds of cheering children, for they were the first English cricketers at Renmark for nearly thirty years and their Fokker was the biggest aeroplane seen there for many years. Journalists, indeed, had received very odd looks from the Adelaide airport receptionist, when they tried to book an early flight to Renmark. 'No one's been there for ages', she said.

Such was Renmark's enthusiasm that 4,000 of the 6,000 population came to the Rovers football ground to watch the contest and empty their ice-boxes of copious cans of lager. Clive Radley was top scorer in a drawn game, played in brilliant sunshine. After some rousing post-match hospitality and presentations to the players of original paintings of Australian scenes, the tourists made a somewhat alarming departure, their plane guided to the runway by the back lights of a lorry and taking off between rows of kerosene flares. Fortunately they did not hit any of the kangaroos which, according to the *Sun*, tended to gather on the dusty runway for their love-making.

The match against South Australia introduced the tourists to fast bowler Rodney Hogg, a 27-year-old insurance salesman and former milkman. His tremendous pace and an unfortunate head injury to Clive Radley were the features of a match which South Australia, the weakest of the States, won by 32 runs. Mike Brearley's comments, in a subdued dressing-room, were typically controlled: 'If anyone thought this tour was going to be easy they now know it won't be. We didn't play well, but I have nothing more to say at this stage.' That evening, still feeling somewhat chastened, the tourists caught an early plane to Melbourne. 'They will need to be in better form', wrote John Woodcock of *The*

Times, 'if they are to settle on the winner for tomorrow's Melbourne Cup.'

The tourists travelled from Adelaide to Melbourne in just forty minutes. Lillywhite, by contrast, using an inter-State steamer, had taken fifty hours on seas rough enough to inhibit all but two of the fifty passengers from eating. Warner's journey by train had taken eighteen hours, Allen's slightly less, but still included one whole uncomfortable night. The Ansett Airways aeroplane was certainly an improvement.

The team found their new hotel, the Hilton, agog with every sport but cricket. It was full of golfers, such as Faldo, Ballasteros, Miller and Irwin, staying for the Australian PGA, whilst Virginia Wade and Sue Barker and the tennis girls of thirty-seven nations were expected in Melbourne shortly. Above all, the hotel was full of excited, wealthy racegoers. 'Champagne and exotic fruit cup were there for the taking at the Hilton', wrote Alex Bannister, 'as the smart set assembled.' Ian Botham was wearing a particularly wide grin a little later, having won $50 in the team's sweep and $250 in another bet. Most of the tourists went to the races, for playing cricket on Melbourne Cup day would have been pointless, since, as Steve Whiting observed, 'The English cricketers could have done handstands in Treasury Park in their jock-straps and had no chance of diverting attention from the big event.' It was not as Neville Cardus would have expressed it, but it was probably true.

There followed a one-day excursion, this time by coach, to Leongatha, eighty-five miles south-east of Melbourne, in a rich dairy farming area. It had been raining hard and the weather was still foul, but Willis, captain for the day, insisted on completing the match even though it was so wet that he could only bowl off six hesitant paces. Inspired, perhaps, by a school brass band playing *Rule Britannia* as Gooch and Miller opened the innings, England recorded their first victory of the tour. It was another enthusiastically supported up-country match. The crowd of 4,000 exceeded the town's population and the entertainment in a golf clubhouse afterwards was first-class.

England next beat Victoria in a dismal, slow-scoring game played on a poor wicket in a largely deserted Melbourne ground.

Over 110,000 empty places glared at Mike Brearley as he scored a painstaking century. His hundredth run was received in utter silence, apart from the shrill boos of a few thousand children, who had been invited to the game for pre-match coaching. Brearley himself was cheerfully unrepentant. 'We *were* pretty boring', he conceded, 'but Victoria were pretty boring too!'

From Melbourne the team flew to Canberra, where centuries by Boycott and Tolchard helped them win their one-day match against the Capital Territory XI at the Manuka Oval. Next morning the tourists flew on to Sydney, where Allan Border and Geoff Lawson were young members of the New South Wales XI. It was Ian Botham's first game of the tour and he was understandably cautious in his early overs. Bill O'Reilly, now a much-respected senior journalist, writing for the *Sydney Morning Herald*, wrote so dismissively of him that an infuriated Botham proceeded to bowl England to victory in the second innings, each wicket accompanied by a gesture to the press-box. John Woodcock's assessment of the young Botham was less critical than O'Reilly's, if only cautiously laudatory: 'He is built more like a life-saver from Bondi Beach than a cricketer from England. So was Keith Miller, who played a lot of his cricket in Sydney and still lives here. I am not saying that Botham is as good an all-rounder as Miller was, or anything like, but he has the same physical advantages and they would both have made splendid pirates.'

From Sydney the team flew to Brisbane, having first spent ten minutes at Sydney airport chatting to a number of WSC players who were themselves en route to Perth. No sooner had Brearley's team found their rooms at the Crest Hotel, Brisbane, than most of them were flying up the coast in another Fokker Friendship to Bundaberg for a one-day friendly. Bundaberg is famous for its sugar-cane and its rum, the latter known and drunk by generations of Queenslanders as 'bundy', and there was much 'bundy' drunk on the evening flight back to Brisbane after a successful game.

A further victory, against Queensland at Brisbane, meant that the tourists had now won six consecutive matches and could face the first Test at the Woolloongabba with confidence. They had been in Australia for the whole of November. During those thirty days they had played twenty days of cricket at eight different venues, made eight flights and one 170-mile coach journey. In the evenings they had attended the usual receptions, those given by mayors, cricket associations and governors-general now augmented by those of sponsors like Benson & Hedges and Perkins Diesel Engines. This was a hectic pressurized schedule. Tourists of earlier generations, however, might have pointed out that Brearley's men only stayed in the big cities, in air-conditioned, luxury hotels, that there were no interminable journeys in pitching and rolling inter-State steamers, nor across desert and scrub in hot, smoky, dust-laden trains. The old-timers would have viewed with some irony Graham Gooch's comment that the one thing he did not like on this tour was the time spent in aeroplanes.

The Crest Hotel, Mike Brearley's Brisbane headquarters, would have made the early tourists gasp, containing as it did 440 rooms, six bars, four restaurants, two swimming-pools and a night club. Brisbane itself bristled with skyscrapers. No longer could it be said, as in Allen's day, that Brisbane was merely a big country town. The city spread impressively in all directions, home to over a million people, its new, futuristic Cultural Centre the badge of its modernity. But the tourists did not detect in Brisbane the bustle of Sydney or Melbourne. Life in Queensland existed at a slower, friendlier pace. The Brisbane river, likewise, still wound its way gently through the city, searching without hurry for the Pacific Ocean twelve miles away, and on its waters the *Kookaburra Queen*, a replica paddle-steamer, was a reminder of the way of life which Lillywhite knew.

It was late November, but thoughts were turning to Christmas. From their hotel's terrace café, overlooking King George's Square, the players watched a huge, plastic Christmas tree, of gaudy green, gold and silver, being erected. With the temperature in the mid-80s there was an incongruity in the sight of plastic reindeers in the streets and the sound of *Adeste fideles* in the hotel lift.

The Woolloongabba had been totally altered in the past decade from the ground which C. B. Fry and Neville Cardus so condemned. The new press-box had a perfect view through smoked glass windows; from such a palace Fry could never have kicked out Bruce Harris's typewriter lid in fury. The Gabba was now a fine, modern stadium. One of its two new stands was named after Gubby Allen's friend and host, Sir Leslie Wilson. The members' pavilion was impressive; so too a new greyhound track on the perimeter. For the players there was a plush, boundary-side Cricketers' Club. The scoreboard would have been the only item which Fry and Cardus would have recognized.

As usual, the high temperatures in Brisbane were very trying. 'It was difficult', wrote the journalist, Alan Lee, 'to walk down a short street without feeling your shirt and trousers clinging to you and your hair growing damp with every step.' In the short period of calm before the Test only brief nets were taken because of the heat. More time was spent in the hotel swimming-pools or on the Royal Brisbane Golf course. Some tourists motored out to Surfers Paradise where, said Christopher Martin-Jenkins of the BBC, 'the bikinis would stir the imagination of the chasest monk.'

Meanwhile there was time to read of Kerry Packer's great success in a night match at Sydney, attended by 50,000, the result of dynamic advertising. In addition to TV commercials featuring the insistent theme-song, *C'mon, Aussie, C'mon*, a huge Packer air balloon floated across the city, where, down below, a plethora of tee-shirts proclaimed the message 'Big Boys Play at Night'. John Woodcock was present and viewed the match with a distaste which most English journalists shared: 'We saw', he wrote, 'what unlimited money and vast publicity can achieve. The match was a layman's picnic and a bigot's nightmare. The fact that Packer's Australians have made only one total over 200 in a dozen matches they have played in the last three weeks seems to mean nothing. The fact that most of them were discredited when they came back from England fourteen months ago has been forgotten. Mr Packer, for the time being, has made them into idols again.' For Mike Brearley's team it was a timely reminder of the importance of the first Test.

On the eve of the match the tourists met up, after an evening meal together, to discuss tactics. Although there was a lack of detailed knowledge of some of the Australians, they nonetheless made some decisions. They would bowl at Yallop's off-stump (as he tended to push towards cover with the bottom hand), they would be especially vigilant in trying to prevent Kim Hughes's first run (because he was such a nervous starter), they would attack Laughlin with short-pitched deliveries around the hip (where he looked weak), they would ply Maclean with leg-stump yorkers and keep Carlson, a good driver, on the back foot. The meeting broke up around 10 o'clock, with Brearley uncharacteristically depressed. In the discussions the players had been niggling each other; he himself had lost his temper; tension was high. So, instead of an early night, he went for a walk with Doug Insole through the streets of Brisbane.

In a similar situation in 1936, on the eve of the Brisbane Test, Gubby Allen had filled his car with the first journalists or players he could find and had gone for a drive through Brisbane's suburbs, talking of everything else but cricket and seeking some cool air and a distraction from the joint cares of captaincy and team management. Brearley was much luckier, both in his close relationship with his manager and in the management's broader brief; Doug Insole's role was so much greater than that played by Rupert Howard forty years before. Like Howard, Insole was in charge of financial matters, but he also looked after travel and hotel arrangements (bills, meal allowances and laundry), the media (making a point of visiting the press at tea-time on match days) and invitations (carefully vetting all acceptances, sometimes splitting the party up between two or three different functions). He kept in touch with the TCCB at Lord's, chaired the selectors and was responsible for discipline. In short, the work of the manager now allowed the captain to concentrate on cricket.

The Test match had an odd prelude, Packeritis encouraging the Queensland authorities to celebrate Brisbane's fifty years of Test cricket on a grand scale. Accordingly the team were driven to the Town Hall for a pre-match reception in a formal procession of vintage cars and, as they were only staying on the opposite side of the square, they were taken somewhat ludicrously on a tour round the block. There followed a champagne breakfast at the Gabba, a march-past of 1,000 schoolboy cricketers to a Gurkha pipe band and the descent of three sky-divers, trailing orange smoke and waving the flags of Australia, Queensland and Great Britain. Commemorative medallions from the sponsors, Benson & Hedges, were presented to the two teams by the Governor. Older spectators, unimpressed with Packeritis, quietly chatted of the time, fifty years ago, when a country boy called Bradman had played his first Test at the Woolloongabba, batting at number 7. His lack of runs that match had encouraged one famous English bowler to tell him that he would never be a success in England. . . .

As the sky-divers landed, the two captains, Yallop and Brearley, came out to toss; the former, at 26, ten years younger than the Englishman, was smiling and dark-tanned, a wide moustache lending him the hint of a musketeer; the latter, grey-flecked and self-contained, looked thoughtfully about him. One of the sky-divers proffered Yallop a special silver coin, Brearley called wrongly and Australia chose to bat.

There was much nervousness in the England dressing-room. 'We had no idea', wrote Bob Taylor, 'how good the new breed of Aussies were. Brears said the first hour would be vital and that it was a good toss to lose because our out-cricket was excellent.' The usual Brisbane sunshine had given way to cloud. The atmosphere was heavy and humid, conditions most favourable for the England bowlers.

Bob Willis had been expected to give the Australians a torrid time with bumpers, but this did not happen. 'I did not bowl terribly quick', he wrote. 'The conditions demanded that I concentrated on line and length. It was the sort of morning you had to keep the batsman playing all the time. If you were off line or bowled bouncers it would have been a sinful waste of the conditions.' With the ball swinging dangerously, Australia collapsed to Willis, Old and Botham. From a humiliating 26–6 they struggled to 116, still a decisively low score, for, despite centuries from Kim Hughes and Graham Yallop in the second innings, England won the match comfortably by 7 wickets. Kerry Packer was delighted at the news.

It was in this Brisbane Test that helmets, already in use in World Series Cricket, were more widely adopted. The tourists had been taken aback by the severity of the bounce at the Gabba in the Queensland game and when Max Walters was hit in the face it was the fifth head injury which the tourists had met in their last three days of cricket. Mike Brearley had been experimenting for some time with special protection under his cap and now, with the help of Queensland's Ogilvie, he organized a net practice for the testing of helmets, followed by a sales drive in his hotel room. Most players decided to buy a helmet. 'If it helps my confidence', said David Gower, 'what have I got to lose? Every now and then an unplayable bouncer arrives and you're in trouble.'

In the 1970s bouncers were common currency. John Snow had led the way on Ray Illingworth's tour and the era of Lillee and Thomson had followed. By 1978 things had become bad enough for Gubby Allen and Leslie Ames, lively septuagenarians both, to take the initiative in trying to persuade the ICC to limit bouncers to one an over. 'Some of today's bowlers', explained Allen, 'aim to hit, and batsmen are so prone to pushing forward on the front foot, often prematurely, and that doesn't give them the best chance to avoid the bouncer.' Geoff Boycott was a staunch supporter of this call for reform: 'There is more to cricket than hooking and ducking. If the batsmen have to frame an innings with the fear of being hit lurking at the back of their minds, the game loses a great deal of its charm and attractiveness.'

England had come to Australia well provided with fast bowling. The first net practices at the Adelaide Oval highlighted their capabilities and in their first game at the Oval Willis's initial spell had Rick Darling ducking and weaving, in all kinds of trouble. (Later, in the fifth Test, a ball by Willis might well have killed Darling, but for John Emburey's prompt first-aid). Since this first State game an unmistakable policy of intimidation by the tourists was apparent. The Australians, though shorn of Lillee, Pascoe and Thomson, were well able to respond through Hogg, Hurst and Lawson. AUSSIES DECLARE WAR IN BOYCOTT BUMPER ATTACK ran one typical tabloid headline. On the fast Gabba wicket the situation was particularly bad. In the Queensland game Bob Willis was constantly sending the ball head high in a frightening way. Brearley, in his turn, was considerably angered as bouncer after bouncer flew past his head. John Woodcock observed it all in mounting despair: 'Bouncers are the curse of the modern game and fast becoming the death of the old one.'

Curiously enough, most of the tourists would have disagreed with this view. In retrospect they could see nothing wrong with the constant use of short-pitched bowling by both sides in 1978–79 and indeed (with a few exceptions, such as Bob Taylor and Geoff Miller) they thought that such intimidating bowling had not been on the increase. A pragmatic opinion prevailed: if one was lucky enough to possess real fire-power, it was foolish not to use it. Mike Brearley himself supported the Ames-Allen initiative of limiting short-pitched deliveries, yet could see nothing inherently wrong in them: 'The occasional bouncer', he wrote, 'is an ornament to, and an enrichment of, the game.'

No sooner was the Test over than the tourists were flying the width of Australia, from Brisbane to Perth, 2,500 miles accomplished in just seven and a half hours, which included a stop at Melbourne, long enough for Bob Willis to try on a new pair of boots. On the flight there were the usual games of cards. The captain, as often, spent time in deep tactical discussions with Willis, Insole and Barrington. Boycott was quietly composing yet another long letter attacking the Yorkshire committee. But all was not peace and quiet for long. Unless the air hostesses remained unmoved by the team's blandishments and were very severe, things always degenerated fairly rapidly into boisterousness, the aircraft full of noise and schoolboy pranks. Now, en route for Perth, Ian Botham was causing mayhem with his ubiquitous water pistol, and suddenly Derek Randall startled fellow passengers by bursting into a rendition of *Rule Britannia*. Randall's behaviour was less predictable than Botham's. The crowd's favourite clown lived in a world of his own, a lonely and often very homesick figure, a man of much emotion. The *Observer*'s Scyld Berry told of Randall sitting quietly at Brisbane airport, reading a book, waiting for the Perth flight. A mother, with two young children, came up and asked him for his autograph, which he gave. She then presented him with a book, a pictorial guide of Australia. Derek Randall thanked her and then, as she walked away, ran up and asked the younger boy for *his* autograph in the book.

The tourists settled very happily into Perth. David Gower, who had played grade cricket there the previous winter, was able to use the one free day for showing his friends the most lively beaches and bars before the match with Western Australia began; the latter were now the strongest of the States, unbeaten in their last thirty-one matches and winners of the Sheffield Shield in five of the last seven seasons; yet they were bowled out for just 52 and 78, giving Mike Brearley his eighth consecutive victory.

A one-day excursion to Albany, 250 miles away, followed. This involved leaving the Sheraton Hotel at 8.00 in the morning (Mike Brearley waving them a cheerful goodbye from the foyer), taking a coach to Perth airport, flying for an hour in a Fokker across huge fields of wheat, landing on a red gravel runway and playing a 40-overs match against six farmers, two clerks, a council worker, a real estate agent and a stock farm manager.

No previous England team had played at Albany (though it was still remembered that Ranjitsinhji had lunched there with Stoddart in 1896 en route for Adelaide). Western Australia's oldest settlement, Albany started life as a coaling station. Lillywhite had stopped there for just such a purpose in 1876, when Tom Emmett, delighted to make re-acquaintance with dry land, had run at full speed towards the nearest green field and exultantly rolled head over heels in it. Later, Albany became a whaling station and now it was a seaside resort and the commercial centre of Western Australia's southern region. The tourists, briefly seeing the town from the coach window as they were driven to the match, were very impressed. Albany's main road sloped gently down to an eye-catching harbour. There was a glimpse of jetties, silos, wharf sheds and yachts. The Old Gaol and Post Office of pioneering days were pointed out to them. At the ground a crowd of 6,000 (from a total population of only 16,000) was waiting on what was said to be Albany's hottest day for months. Flies abounded, but the pavilion was extremely civilized and there was an unending supply of tea. Just before Graham Gooch went out to score a spectacular 112, Derek Randall, now recovered from the early rise after a late night, entertained the crowd with a rendition of *Good*

day, Sunshine over the PA system. After the match (the tourists'
ninth win) there was a barbecue at an Albany hotel with good
food and plentiful beer. It was 11 p.m. before they returned to
their Perth hotel. It had been a long, fifteen-hour day. 'Gruelling'
was the commonest adjective bandied around. By Lillywhite's
standards, on the other hand, it would have been a comparatively
restful day.

From Perth the team journeyed back to Adelaide and a return
fixture with South Australia, which was described by the local
press as 'pointless' and attended on the first day by a mere 936
people. Much more exciting was the storm through which the
team flew afterwards to Melbourne, where they spent Christmas
before the traditional Test match in the New Year. They tried to
capture the Christmas spirit with some carols in the coach on the
way from Melbourne airport, Derek Randall conducting from the
front. But Christmas Eve was fairly quiet, the Hilton empty of
its previous animation and many players feeling homesick. Bob
Taylor's low spirits were typical; it was his sixth Christmas away
from home in the past eight years and this time even his wife's
Christmas card had been delayed in the post!

On Christmas Day the press and players had drinks together,
in the manager's suite, as was the usual custom, after which the
team changed into fancy dress for a private party and Christmas
lunch. Geoff Miller, the team's social secretary, had organized
festivities with the help of Lever and Hendrick. The fancy dress
was taken seriously and several of the players had hired costumes
from an Adelaide theatre, including Ian Botham, who was
perspiring heavily in a gorilla outfit. 'Guy, this is meant to be
fancy dress!' he was frequently reminded. Most appreciated was
Bob Willis, as a blind umpire, wearing dark glasses with a white
stocking over his head. Doug Insole, however, won the first prize
– a toy duck – with his impersonation of Inspector Clouseau.
Despite much jollity from Botham and John Lever (the latter
causing some genuine alarm with his joke-shop jelly) there was a
sombre undercurrent to proceedings, for Christmas on tour was

essentially a time for remembering absent families and looking forward to reunions.

In this respect the modern tourists were more fortunate than their predecessors. Allen's team had signed a contract stating that 'no player shall be allowed to take with him any member of his family without the permission of the MCC committee'; permission would not have been granted in the unlikely event of its being requested. The 1978–79 contracts, in contrast, stated that wives would be welcome, though the TCCB let it be known that it favoured the last few weeks (by which time it was anticipated that a firm team spirit would have been fostered) and put up much resistance to Ian Botham's request that his wife should join him for the early weeks as she was pregnant, only acceding under threat of his withdrawal from the tour. By the final weeks of Brearley's tour thirteen of the twenty members of the party had either wives or girl friends with them, a state of affairs which would have shocked earlier exponents of male exclusiveness like Monty Noble. Graham Gooch was convinced team spirit was unaffected: 'We went to *work* from nine in the morning until seven in the evening. Then, if it were possible, we spent a quiet, relaxing time with our wives.'

Things had not always worked out so smoothly. In the preceding tour of Mike Denness there had been so many little children around that it was rumoured some fathers were more involved in making crèche arrangements than playing cricket and one wife was said to have made such a nuisance of herself that she put her husband's career in jeopardy. It had not been a happy tour and the arrival of the families only served to confuse things.

Now, four years later, Mike Brearley's team were eagerly awaiting the arrival of wives and girl friends in the New Year, an anticipation which did not, however, inspire them to victory in the third Test, for Australia won at Melbourne, which was a good thing for the series and a bad thing for Kerry Packer. It was also a relief to Graham Yallop, whose rash predictions of a 6–0 whitewash had already been made to look very silly. Now that he was only 1–2 down, he insisted that Australia would recover to win 4–2. Yallop no doubt made these forecasts to help stimulate public interest, but he seemed to be inviting disaster with this apparent hubris.

Yallop, an articulate man, who was grammar-school educated and from an affluent background, had been hailed, on his appointment as captain, as a knight in shining armour. 'The presence of Yallop as captain', wrote Paul Fitzpatrick in the *Guardian*, 'will mean a clean series. He is very much a disciple of Simpson's and would not tolerate foul language or vulgar behaviour. The behavioural excesses of Ian Chappell's days as captain seem to have disappeared . . .' In any less difficult situation Yallop might well have succeeded in raising the tone as the *Guardian* had predicted, avoiding Chappell's abrasive manner of leadership in addition to producing good results. But, as it was, Packeritis ensured that the media put unrelenting and unfair pressure on him, a novice captain leading an inexperienced XI. The result was a series which was far from 'clean'.

For England the defeat at Melbourne highlighted some off-field problems. The early run of total success had understandably led to a certain relaxation. 'It seemed to me at Perth', wrote Christopher Martin-Jenkins, 'as the second Test victory neared completion, Christmas approached and pretty girls, sunny weather, beautiful beaches and good food all beckoned temptingly, that there was a danger that all the rigorous work at the start of the tour might be wasted.' Insole and Brearley, in being anxious not to treat the team like naughty schoolboys, were perhaps in danger of too much complacence. It was a familiar problem, one which Lillywhite had experienced.

The fourth Test at Sydney started almost at once, the day after the team's flight from Melbourne. With the series at 2–1 the touring party knew that it was a crucial match; they arrived tired and tense. The sight of the Sydney Cricket Ground with its enormous floodlights, installed for Packer, caused considerable feelings of alienation amongst the more experienced players and press. The six towering, grey pylons, each 240 feet high with ninety-six lights, seemed to have sprung up out of the earth and to be leering over the Noble and Bradman Stands like the foul targets of some Herculean labour. 'Wherever you look', complained John Woodcock, 'these monsters catch you in the eye.

Gone, I'm afraid, is the charm of one of the world's great grounds, crushed by the advancing tide of commercialism.' To make matters worse, the old Brewongle Stand, whose attractive, green wrought-ironwork Lillywhite had known, had been torn down and a modern six-tiered replacement was noisily being constructed. There was an ugly mark, too, across the ground where wiring for the Packer microphones had been recently inserted.

Despite all these developments the tourists thoroughly approved of Sydney itself. It was Brearley's favourite city and Boycott's too. He liked its life, its bounce, its beaches and its quiet nooks and crannies. David Gower, similarly impressed, commended the views and restaurants. But the British press were less happy. They noted that strikes had left rotting garbage in the streets. They lamented the city's vulgarity and ostentation. Sydney's traffic, with its screeching tyres, jarred their sensibilities, as did the fact that this was Kerry Packer's empire, where that fallen archangel, Tony Greig, was living like Lucifer in the most affluent of life-styles.

The Sydney Test started badly for England. Boycott was soon out and when Randall, rashly hooking, fell to a brilliant catch by Wood at short square-leg, England were 18–2. It was tremendously hot; 100° had been forecast; the partisan crowd of 20,000 was exultant. In the dressing-room Randall was quietly sitting, towel over head, monk-like. 'The hook gets me lots of runs. I'm in form so I play it.' He repeated the words quietly to himself, as if paying some early-morning, monastic penance. 'It doesn't matter how many xxxxing runs you've picked up', replied Ken Barrington sternly, 'You've got to look at the xxxxing wicket a few overs before you try a hook.' Randall mopped the sweat from his brow vigorously, unconvinced. 'The hook gets me a lot of runs. I play the hook, I play that shot well.' Barrington wandered back towards the balcony. 'Not to your second xxxxing ball', he said.

Ken Barrington was a compulsive watcher, nervously following everything, smoking innumerable cigarettes in the process. He had that day, as usual, been up since dawn, part of his job being to telephone the players on match mornings, reminding them to be ready promptly in the hotel foyer at 9.15. As assistant manager he was in charge of most off-the-field cricketing matters. Very professional and good-humoured, Barrington was respected enormously and all the tourists were to mourn his early death two years hence. 'Kenny was a terrific person', said Bob Taylor. 'He was a kind, considerate man', agreed John Emburey, 'wanting every touring member to do well.' Clive Radley, 12th man at Sydney and in many other big matches, saw a great deal of him on the tour. 'I probably learnt more about cricket and touring from him than anybody else', he commented. His greatest asset as a manager was the way he identified so very much with his team, so the first day's play at Sydney was particularly trying for him, for, by its close, England had been bowled out for 152 and Australia were 56–1. It looked as if Australia were about to square the series.

Mike Brearley, on the advice of Mike Hendrick, summoned the team together at the end of play. There was a small inner room off the team's changing-room, where sweaty clothes and towels hung from lines. Cloistered in this cramped, unprepossessing cell, the team received a quiet but very critical lecture from the captain. They had played, he said, in a blasé spirit, without any sense of responsibility. Later on they had looked depressed instead of determined. 'I want 110% effort from you tomorrow', Brearley concluded; no one smiled. Mike Hendrick then made a heated condemnation of the team's poor showing. Bob Taylor was similarly impassioned. 'We must forget what's happened today, and play each day as if it's the first day of the Test.' It was good advice, which was to become an axiom for the rest of the tour. The end-of-day meetings, too, became a regular feature and a great help in maintaining team morale and concentration as the tour lengthened and everyone grew more ready for the journey home.

Afterwards Doug Insole gave Derek Randall a lift back to the hotel and *en route* delivered a lecture on the folly of getting out hooking at both Perth and Sydney. Insole, an executive in the City for a big building company, knew how to put over a point forcefully and Derek Randall was listening, a little cowed. 'It's your *responsibility* to have a look at the bowlers', said Insole, 'to get the pace of the wicket before you start hooking.' Insole was a notoriously dangerous driver and Randall, sitting next to him in the Sydney rush-hour traffic, looked a distinctly unhappy young man. 'Another thing', continued Insole, applying his brakes heavily before accelerating away, 'You've simply got to remember to play your innings in segments! You've got to be there at lunch! You've got to be there at tea! You've got to be there at the close!' Randall screwed up his eyes, his manager mistaking anxiety at a narrow avoidance of highway disaster for disagreement. 'Maybe you'd better give some serious thought to the way you play', he muttered acidly.

Next day there was no immediate miracle. England bowled more tightly and fielded with flair and Australia made a total of 294, Allan Border prolonging the innings with 60 not out. Australia now had a comfortable lead of 142 and, when Geoff Boycott was lbw to Rodney Hogg first ball, the match still seemed to be slipping away. To fight back from this dire position would need much character.

Mike Brearley had had a wretched Test series so far. Here at Sydney in the first innings he had made 17 and in the first three Tests he had only managed 37 runs from six innings. The Australian press had demanded that he drop himself for this match, something which his predecessor, Mike Denness, had done when similarly out of form. Australian cartoonists were mercilessly enjoying the England captain's discomfiture.

The score was 0–1 as Derek Randall joined the out-of-form Brearley and it was nearly 0–2, Dymock being unlucky not to have Randall lbw straightaway. 'It pitched middle and kept low', complained Yallop. 'It would have knocked the middle stump out of the ground, half way up the stick!' Randall agreed that he was lucky still to be there. 'Rags', he muttered to himself as he fidgeted at the crease, 'Rags, you've got to get stuck in. You've got to get forward, forward.' The stand slowly prospered. In the middle of the afternoon it was Brearley's turn nearly to get out, this time to the leg-spinner Higgs. 'Come on, skip, a bit loose', said Randall reprovingly between overs. 'We've got to be here at t'close.' Perhaps another nightmare car ride with the manager loomed large in his mind. There was a need for *responsibility*. At tea, England had moved to 74–1 and the Australians were red-faced from the sun. Frustration was beginning to mount. As they went off for tea Brearley left his helmet and gloves out on the wicket to dry, and, as he moved off, he noticed that Wood gave the helmet a gratuitous little kick. What the fielders would have done to Randall's helmet, had he left it behind, one cannot imagine, for he was the focal point of Australian displeasure. Yallop was expressing his whole team's dislike when he wrote: 'He's a clown and that's putting it mildly. He sounds like an idiot always talking to himself. A lot of people think his talk helps him concentrate in his batting. I disagree. . . .' To the Australians it was simply gamesmanship, designed to put them off.

Tea for the batsmen consisted of a shower, another change of clothing and a cup of tea. It was too hot to eat anything. Afterwards the struggle continued; the heavily padded Brearley (wearing under his shirt, as protection against Hogg, what looked like part of a mattress) suffered in the intense heat, constantly removing his new helmet to mop his brow. When the 5 o'clock break for drinks arrived, the players took it sheltering in the shade of one of the new Packer-inspired pylons.

Eventually, with the score at the traditionally dangerous figure of 111, Brearley was bowled by Allan Border for 53. It had been an innings of great determination and it especially delighted Ken Barrington, who had given him much moral support during the barren patch, quietly trying to persuade him to play a little straighter.

After Brearley's departure Gooch joined Randall and the two were together at the close with the score still anything but safe at 133–2. Randall came in exhausted, 65 not out, his clothes soaked in sweat. As he sat slumped in the dressing-room Insole entered quietly and silently shook hands. Words would have been superfluous. It had been an innings quite out of keeping with Derek Randall's natural inclinations and talents, but, in the context of the match situation, it had been ideal.

Dudley Doust, who collaborated with Mike Brearley on his book of the tour, gave a detailed account of the rest of Randall's day. He went back to the hotel, without even stopping for shower or tea. 'There he soaked in a hot bath, drank two pots of tea and half-heartedly watched television as he waited for room service to send up his dinner. He dined alone on onion soup, steak and chips, strawberries and ice-cream. Soon he was fast asleep.'

Others meanwhile were having a merrier evening. Many went to see Warren Mitchell's one-man show, *The Thoughts of Chairman Alf*, and were delighted with some typically trenchant comments about 'that bloody Kerry Packer'. The next day was a rest day and Randall spent it quietly with Brearley, Willis, Hendrick and Lever, entertained in the suburban home of a Sydney doctor. Somewhat alarmingly, however, David Gower spent his day in bed with a sore throat and a temperature of 102.

It was even hotter on the crucial fourth day – the ground already 100°, inhibiting practice – when the tourists arrived, all cheerful, except a very pale David Gower, who was nursing a temperature of 101 and preparing to go in at the fall of the next wicket. Meanwhile Graham Gooch continued to support Randall, while tensions on the field soared with the temperature. Randall, who earlier in his innings had regularly stopped to ask the umpires to dab his face with ointment, again irritated the Australians with his delaying tactics. Time and again he stopped, just as the bowler was beginning his run, to ask the umpires for fly-repellant. Although he was not averse to umpire Bailhache's aerosol can, he preferred umpire French's cream, which took longer to apply. 'Randall is hard to cop at times', said an exasperated Yallop. The heat intensified around mid-day and a cameraman, overcome by it, was badly injured when he fell from a perch in the Bradman Stand. Randall, aware of the incident and genuinely upset, suggested that the game be temporarily halted, but Yallop, understandably incensed at Randall's many ploys and believing this to be mere play-acting, raced in from cover, waving his arms angrily and ordering him to get on with the game. Gooch meanwhile had gone, but Gower stayed on for 100 minutes and England's score steadily improved.

Randall's running battle of words with the Australians continued. Yallop was beside himself with irritation when his field-placing was queried. 'Wouldn't put him there, mate', said Randall, waving to a fielder whom Yallop had just positioned at fine-leg and motioning him elsewhere. 'Put him there! More use to you up there!' At lunch, with yet another segment gone, England were 191–3, Randall not out 87. Slowly he moved to 95 in the afternoon, still mumbling to himself. 'Come on, Rags, don't throw it away. Keep forward, Rags, keep forward.' The day was at its hottest, 105°, when Rodney Hogg was goaded by his captain into letting 'the son-of-a-bitch' have one more skull-crusher. With a swivel and a swat of the bat, Randall dispatched it to square-leg for 4. He was now one short of his century. Yallop again encouraged his man. 'C'mon, Hoggy, c'mon!' Fires of hate were kindled anew beneath the fair, matted thatch of hair, and, making a supreme effort, Hogg sent down another angry bouncer. Randall, however, pirouetted neatly in front of the stumps and struck it firmly to the legside boundary to reach his century. It had taken him 411 minutes and it was the slowest 100 in the history of the Ashes. 'The boundaries', remarked Paul Fitzpatrick laconically, 'came at intervals distant enough to be milestones!' Yallop (who frequently complained that the tourists never drank with his team at close of play) walked up to his tormentor. 'Seeing you've done so well, Derek, are you going to have a xxxxing drink with us after the game?'

Randall, still thinking of Doug Insole's segments and the next cup of tea, wearily carried on. It was a flawed innings with many chances given and not accepted. 'The gods were on Randall's side', wrote Paul Fitzpatrick, 'but goodness knows he worked hard enough to avoid being fried alive. To bat for almost ten hours is remarkable enough, to do so in the withering heat of the past two days has been a feat of endurance that would have impressed Lawrence of Arabia.' There were more fly-spray incidents after tea, more verbal clashes with Hogg and, when leg-spinner Jim Higgs opted to bowl round the wicket, Randall was able to ask for the sight-screen to be moved. 'If you're fussy about it', he had confided, 'you can waste a whole extra half-minute.' Eventually, with only half an hour to go that day Hogg exacted a deserved revenge, trapping Randall lbw with a ball which was not particularly special. Randall was by now so tired that he simply missed it. After an unfortunate display of petulant dissent at the decision, Derek Randall retreated wearily to the pavilion, booed all the way, just as he had been slow-handclapped during most of his innings. His score was exactly 150 and it allowed England to end the day 162 runs ahead with 4 wickets left.

The match, with one day to go, was now very evenly poised. But Yallop, suffering as much from Randall as from heat and frustration, made some foolishly unguarded comments at the press conference. 'I couldn't understand their tactics. I would have played for a win, but they didn't seem interested. Some balls were there to be hit, but they didn't hit them. I always attack, whatever the situation!' Randall in particular came in for enormous criticism in the Australian press. DEREK SO DEADLY! complained Peter McFarline's headline in the *Age*. Randall, the hero of the Centenary Test, was now an 'anti-hero', playing pat-a-ball, ignoring long hops, full tosses and half volleys. 'The side that came to Australia three months ago as a winning, confident combination', wrote McFarline, 'is obviously playing for a draw in a match it could have won.'

But the next day England bowled and fielded magnificently and Hendrick, Emburey and Miller turned the anticipated draw into a 93-run victory. In the wake of the Australian batting collapse Graham Yallop's cries of 'I always attack!' suddenly sounded very foolish and Ian Botham was quick to nickname him 'Banzai Yallop'. Certainly the Australian batsmen's proclivities towards death and glory had hinted of the Kamikazi.

The England team received much adulation. At home in wintry, strike-torn Britain, the victory was cheering news. SUNSHINE BOYS ran the *Daily Express* headline. 'It doesn't put the trains back on the tracks or the Brussels sprouts in the larder. But in early January 1979 there was still some fight left in the old country.' Mike Brearley's captaincy came in for tremendous praise, and rightly so. He was a 'Master Magician', a 'Captain Marvel' and a 'Napoleon'. 'In 1978–79', wrote Brearley with a wry smile, 'I knew what it was like to be regarded as a liability to the team one week and as the Duke of Wellington a week later. . . .' Graham Yallop was left to claim, with justice, that of the last ten days of Test cricket, his side had had the better of nine and yet England had just won the Ashes.

Shortly afterwards Kerry Packer had another triumph at Sydney, where a night game between Ian Chappell's Australians and Clive Lloyd's West Indians was attended by over 45,000 people. Mike Brearley, in dark glasses and upturned collar, was one of their number, as he had opted out of going to Tasmania with the team and was staying behind in Sydney. For him it was a night-out to remember. The ball was white, the sight-screens black, the West Indians in shocking pink and the Australians in custard-pie yellow. Plastic posters 50 feet high portrayed the captains of the three World Series XIs, like hoardings at some fascist rally; loud-speakers blared Sydney's current number 1 song, *C'mon, Aussie, C'mon*:

> 'You've been training all the winter
> and there's not a team that's fitter
> and that's the way it's got to be.
> 'Cos you're up against the best you know,
> this is Supertests you know
> you're up against the best the world has seen –
>
> C'mon, Aussie, C'mon!. . . .'

Packer had quadrupled his popular night matches this year and all his cricket was most effectively packaged. Boys were encouraged to attend by the offer of free coaching, special autograph sessions, free posters, caps and white balls (which were handed out at the turnstiles). WSC merchandizing covered most eventualities, from eyeshades to beach-towels, from soap to cushions and from overnight bags to plastic Dennis Lillee figurines.

The match which Mike Brearley watched was not without its problems. Six male streakers and one topless lady were, with some difficulty, restrained by the long arm of the law, for someone had forgotten to order enough policemen and only a handful were present. There was much drunkenness and, when rain interrupted play, the sport of can-throwing flourished. Next morning Ian Chappell castigated the mindless lager louts: 'If we arrest a few of these gorillas and charge them, it would soon stop.

It's becoming a bloody disease.' David Frith suggested that many of the crowd behaved as if at the zoo.

Predictably the English press hated the match. Pat Gibson of the *Daily Express* considered it a contest as meaningless as tag team wrestling at Scunthorpe Baths and conceded its popularity with ill-grace: 'The screaming discomaniacs, intoxicated by the psychedelic lights and colours, not to mention a few dozen tins of Toohey's, loved it.' David Frith stressed his feelings of alienation as he sat in the packed ground: 'For the first time in my life I did not feel at home at a cricket match, did not feel part of the occasion.' Australian Test players of different generations were also critical. Bill O'Reilly described the 'Supertests' as 'Superficialtests' and Rodney Hogg likened the West Indians' pink kit to 'a Sheila's underwear'. But, whatever the criticisms, the match was an undeniable commercial success. 'From now on', wrote Steve Whiting, 'cricket ignores Packer at its risk – just as a previous generation tried to ignore Hitler!'

Mike Brearley didn't stay to the end, but had seen enough to believe that it would not be long before some form of agreement was worked out between Packer and the establishment. Shortly afterwards he was amused to receive an invitation from Kerry Packer to play the WSC Australians for A$50,000, winner take all. After a quick telephone call to Insole in Tasmania and the TCCB at Lord's, he politely declined. Meanwhile an enormous party for everyone connected with WSC celebrated the success at Kerry Packer's home. Alan Lee asked one West Indian how it went. The cricketer rolled his eyes. 'It had everything, man, just everything.'

The England team had travelled to Tasmania after a game at Newcastle (which put Roger Tolchard in hospital for two weeks with a broken cheekbone and necessitated the summons from England of a replacement, David Bairstow). Cricket in Tasmania was now taken very seriously, flourishing under coaches like Jack Simmons and John Hampshire; the 18-year-old David Boon was one of its hopes for the future. The matches at Launceston and Hobart, in consequence, were much harder than those of Gubby Allen and the atmosphere in the spectators' enclosures less friendly. Gone were the days when the local bandmaster had struck up *The Lady In Blue*, having noticed George Duckworth chatting up a young lady in an azure dress! Gone too was the holiday-making. Warner's and Allen's teams had many free days to explore the beauty of the island. Brearley's had just one day before flying back to the mainland.

After Tasmania came a series of one-day Internationals, all played at Melbourne, for a Cup supplied by Benson & Hedges. It was won, 2–1, by Australia. The games were played very much in the same abrasive spirit as the Tests, but they were not successful in attracting huge crowds, an average of only 12,000 attending. The English attitude to this new competition was not totally wholehearted. David Gower, despite scoring a memorable hundred in the second match, reacted less than enthusiastically afterwards: 'A shame we lost – it means we've got to play again in a decider.'

Success in the Benson & Hedges Cup was a relief to Yallop, but it did not continue in the Tests, the fifth and sixth (played at Adelaide and Sydney) both being won by England, allowing them a remarkable 5–1 success in the series. Mike Brearley thus became the only England captain to win an Ashes series on tour by four clear victories, an achievement which has only been equalled by two Australian touring captains in England – Don Bradman in 1948 and Allan Border in 1989. Understandably, the Australian public grew more and more disenchanted and at Sydney a mere 22,600 people attended the sixth Test over the four days, the lowest ever attendance in that city for a match against England. The armchair cricket public likewise had long since begun to transfer its affections to Kerry Packer's more successful team of Australians. When a Supertest competed in prime viewing time with an ACB one-day International, the former rated 19–8, a conclusive victory for Kerry Packer's Channel 9.

The tour ended with the sixth Test, in mid-February. Brearley's team had been campaigning for three and a half months and the strain was certainly telling on both tourists and hosts. Yallop declared at the end of the match that he was mentally and physically exhausted. The English press, he said, had savaged him almost as soon as the first coin was tossed, and, later, only the Victorian press had remained fair-minded. As the season progressed Yallop found the off-the-field pressures intolerable. There was no Australian manager to help him handle the many conflicting demands: 'I was wanted on call morning, noon and night. This was not just the specialist cricket writers – there were radio talk-back shows, current affairs shows on TV, feature writers, magazine writers and gossip columnists. Eventually I had just to go for a walk to get peace and quiet and escape the avalanche of telephone calls at home, at the office and wherever the team stayed.'

Towards the close of the tour there were indications that Mike Brearley, despite his strong management team, was similarly beginning to feel the strain. In one of the one-day Internationals he had lost his temper with Ian Botham, who had insisted on retaining six fielders on the on-side, despite bowling the ball more regularly on the off. Botham, who had just heard of the birth of his second child, was in a euphoric state and not amenable to criticism and soon, with several fielders joining in, Brearley was enveloped in a raging debate. 'It was the only occasion', said Gower, 'when Brearley came close to losing control on the field.'

There were several off-the-field moments when Mike Brearley similarly lost his customary self-control. A bad umpiring decision in the fifth Test (when he was given out, caught off his sleeve) led to a long outburst in the dressing-room and, after the second Benson & Hedges defeat, Brearley found the heckling of drunken home supporters too much to take during the presentation ceremonies. 'If you lot shut up, you might learn something. . . .' was followed by 'If we'd won the toss . . .' and, finally, 'I don't think I'll say any more.' His abrupt departure from the presentations was interpreted by some as the act of a bad loser.

It was in the sixth Test at Sydney that Brearley's tiredness showed through most clearly. After expressing dismay at both the poor nets and the noise which the builders were making with their cranes, he was so exasperated to lose the toss yet again that he stalked away, leaving Yallop alone to answer the TV commentator's questions. Finally, after a tense match, came one final piece of over-reaction, when, with England set just 34 runs to win and with the wicket taking spin, Yallop requested the use of an old ball. Mike Brearley was beside himself with anger and Doug Insole was given the job of proving with the rule-book the illegality of the request. Yallop and the umpires were shown to be technically in the wrong, but England duly won the match, against the old ball, with the loss of only one wicket. Brearley's anger, in all the circumstances, seemed excessive.

All the team were ready for the journey home well before it came. In the latter days of the tour all talk of England was banned and no remarks about jumbo jets allowed. After the last Test there were three free days before departure. 'No more cricket!' sang Willis and Botham delightedly, as they drove down to a Sydney beach. 'It gets to the stage', said Willis, 'where I think Australia would be a great place without any cricket.' Brearley, like Allen before him, thought that the touring had gone on too long. 'A five-Test series over three months would be about right', he said. As it was, they had flown some 10,000 miles since their arrival, and, out of 115 days in Australia, had travelled on twenty-five and played cricket on sixty-nine, a much more concentrated schedule than that of Lillywhite, Warner or Allen and one which left players, management and journalists thoroughly drained. 'Everybody had had enough', wrote Alan Lee.

There was, accordingly, little euphoria in the final dispatches of the English journalists, little of the nostalgia which earlier writers like Cardus had felt for their Australian summers. Pat Gibson's last message from Sydney to *Daily Express* readers dwelt on the need for some rebuilding in the England team in the coming season, a somewhat surprising topic in view of the 5–1 victory! Paul Fitzpatrick gave the *Guardian* a very thorough, almost headmasterly, report on the players' performances. Michael Melford concluded for the *Daily Telegraph* with a final polemic against Kerry Packer.

There was just time for some last-minute sunbathing on the Sydney beaches and the buying of souvenirs. Clocks were presented by the team to Doug Insole, Ken Barrington and Bernie Thomas. But even the last moments were darkened by the Packer shadow. At a big, celebratory dinner Geoff Boycott, leader of the players' anti-Packer lobby, tried hard to persuade Mike Brearley to make a strong statement against World Series Cricket. Brearley, always a moderate on this issue, declined, but he did point out publicly that he, like the rest of the team, had turned down the offer which Kerry Packer had recently made to them all. Just as they had arrived in Australia, talking of Packer, so they would depart.

There were no big scenes of farewell. On the whole the Australians were relieved to see the last of the team which had beaten them so decisively. Doug Insole had the difficult job of making the peroration to those members of the Australian press who had dutifully made it to the airport. It was hard not to sound patronizing. 'There's obviously talent in the Australian team', he said. 'It's just a matter of putting it together and having a bit more experience. . . . It was a great deal closer than the 5–1 result might suggest. We could easily have lost at Sydney and Adelaide and, had we done that, we could have been 2–3 down going into the last Test.' This was true, but it didn't make for much comfort to the vanquished.

Modern touring parties fragment very quickly. Graham Gooch and his wife had already reached Perth, where he had a coaching assignment. Bob Willis and his girl friend were off to New Zealand, while Geoff Boycott, Clive Radley and John Emburey, plus their entourages, were staying on in Australia. The Qantas Boeing, meanwhile, carried the remainder into the skies of New South Wales, where the sun was setting dramatically, a brilliant orange glow through the windows on the port side. Twenty-four hours of flying were ahead of them, as they journeyed westwards, lightened a little by cans of Tooheys, games of cards, and a Sylvester Stallone movie. There was more fragmentation at Singapore, where the Gower, Taylor and Thomas parties alighted for a holiday stop. Mike Brearley, similarly intentioned, chose India. For the remainder the long night continued, with a pause at Bahrein which was barely noticed. Outside the cabin the air grew cooler, as Europe approached 570 miles nearer every hour. Finally, on a freezing February dawn the Boeing touched down at Heathrow, Ken Barrington doing a hasty check that all eight survivors of the touring party were freshly shaven, with St George and the Dragon once more on display.

They quickly learnt of blizzards paralysing Britain and a 'Minister of Snow' appointed by Prime Minister Callaghan. Bahrain and Bombay, Singapore and Sydney suddenly sounded very attractive again. It had been an English winter of discontent, in which the Labour Government's fortunes had plummeted. Ahead in the polls by 5% on the team's departure, it was 19% behind on their return. Industrial strife, which had stilled *The Times* since November (and caused an early return from Australia for John Woodcock), was more rampant than in Australia, where discontented airport workers had often made internal flights an anxiety to the tour management. Only one man sounded as if he had had a good winter, Trevor Francis, the first English footballer to be worth £1 million, who had pocketed £50,000 as his share of his transfer to Nottingham Forest. This made the tourists' earnings of around £7,000 seem a little puny.

An encounter with a group of Punk Rockers lent a bizarre touch to the tourists' return. The punks, their faces smeared with imitation blood, were carrying placards demanding BOYCOTT FOR POPE and BREARLEY MUST GO. 'We are here', said their spokesman, Captain Sensible, lead singer of The Damned, 'to show that punks are the only true cricket fans. Geoff is the hero of punks across the country and he can have a free ticket to one of my concerts any time he likes.' A young, female punk from Nuremburg added: 'We are going to camp out here until we catch a glimpse of Geoff. We may even chain ourselves to the railings.' After a while, however, the punks came to the sad realization that neither Brearley nor Boycott had landed with the party. Quite how long they maintained their Heathrow vigil is not recorded.

It was left to Insole to say a few words to the more conventional reception party of journalists before the tourists completely disbanded. Inevitably, the chief topic was World Series Cricket: 'Yes, it remains a real threat to Australia and perhaps to all', Insole conceded. 'It is on TV all the time. I do not think Packer's is the sort of game which would take on here in England – or at least I hope not. Nor do I think that the two sides are any closer to a compromise than they were when we left four months ago. . . .' In this, in fact, he was wrong.

As the weeks went by, any bad memories of the tour receded.

The tourists gradually forgot the bad wickets. Even the best, at Adelaide, was described by Boycott as 'not the sort of pitch you'd queue up to bat on', whilst the worst, at Melbourne, he likened to an open-cast pit at Barnsley. They forgot too the crowds' foul-mouthed minority (with their 'Piss off, Pommies, piss off', sung to Packer's tune). They forgot the mutually abusive behaviour of the sides on the field of play which had led to the resignation of one of the umpires. They forgot the losses of temper (most notably when Phil Edmonds had to be dragged away from his captain after a slanging match in the dressing-room). They forgot the bouncers ('still the untamed monsters of Test cricket', according to one observer) and such unsolved mysteries as the disappearance of Brearley's favourite bat at Brisbane and its reappearance, in mutilated condition, in a Gabba dustbin.

Rather, it was the many good things which were being remembered as, two months later, the tourists were reunited for a celebratory dinner given by the London Press Club. Each player had his own particular memories; for some it was the grandeur of Adelaide, the friendliness of Perth, the yachts on the Derwent river, *The Merry Widow* at Sydney Opera House, breaking 80 at the Royal Melbourne Golf Club, the tropical fruit of Queensland, the views of Australia from the air, the comradeship of touring or the hospitality of so many clubs and families. For others it was a particular hotel; there had not been a poor one. All had admired the Sebel Town House, high up by King's Cross, Sydney, boasting a clientèle of rock and film stars, with its fine view of the yachting basin and with a restaurant claiming to prepare whatever a guest requested. Then, close to Collins Street, Melbourne, there was the Hilton, its nightclub offering international cabaret.

There were a number of presentations and speeches at the London Press Club dinner. Mike Brearley, the hero of the evening, was presented by the chairman of Perkins engines with a double-headed coin, to help him to more success with the toss on future occasions. Brearley replied with a speech full of jokes at his own expense. 'I don't want to boast', he declared, 'but I must say that I was very gratified to be the person to score the winning run in the final Test'. He paused and smiled. 'Indeed, I was gratified to score any run!' He recalled with some amusement the considerable barracking which his batting had attracted and he particularly cherished one remark: 'Come on, Brearley, f'gawd'sake, you make Denness look like Don Bradman!' Then there was the occasion he was batting as a friend rang the pavilion with a message. 'Don't worry', said one of the tourists, taking the call, 'Mike'll be back in five minutes.' It was a splendid speech, hugely enjoyed by the tourists themselves, but Frank Keating could not resist the observation that 'Mike Brearley is a really outstanding leader. The team is trained to laugh at his after-dinner jokes as if it is the first time they have heard them!' If so, it was his ultimate triumph!

It was appropriate that the tourists should be honoured by the Press Club, for the tour of 1978–79 was notable for the harmonious relations between press and players, a harmony which was soon to be lost in the 1980s. On Brearley's tour, however, press and players still travelled together and stayed in the same hotels. The cameraderie had been exemplified by a presentation by the players at the end of the tour to Alex Bannister, who was just completing his final assignment abroad for the *Daily Mail*. But in the next decade, as the players' earnings from Tests rose sharply, so also their sensitivity to even minor public criticism grew. It had not been helpful when the regular cricket writers were augmented by news reporters sent out purely to spy and report on players' private lives. Leading players, like Ian Botham, now spread a preference for keeping all cricket writers at a safe distance; Bob Willis's tenure of the England captaincy was marked by a deep-rooted suspicion of the press. Don Mosey has described this withdrawal of friendship between tourists and reporters as 'a new kind of apartheid'.

Another cause for the breakdown in good relations was the pressure on players and press alike, which the new 'instant-cricket' of the aeroplane age has encouraged. Indeed, a remarkable feature of Mike Brearley's tour was the high quality of reporting, despite the very busy travelling schedule, though that highly allusive prose of Cardus and Fry, the product of more leisurely days, has disappeared. In the reporting of modern tours there simply is less time available for the selection of the *bon mot*. The advent of the aeroplane and the eclipse of the luxury liner have also taken away not just much of the romance of travel but also much of the time when writers could ply their trade. Neville Cardus, for instance, finished *Australian Summer* when sailing home on the *Orontes*. He could scarcely have polished off his account of Gubby Allen's tour so well in the cramped confines of a jumbo jet. Would he have been able to turn his thoughts back to Sydney, amid the clamour of duty-free sales and inflight movies, and let his imagination play on the ferry lights at Manly, the water lapping round the old *Captain Cook*, or the tug 'which rests in the curve' at Watson's Bay, where at night beauty comes out of the sky and the water holds it'?

6

EPILOGUE

THE LILLYWHITE LEGACY

In more recent years the tours have continued to be on a four-yearly basis – that of 1990–91 following those of Bob Willis (1982–83) and Mike Gatting (1986–87) – but the pattern has been obscured by the proliferation of additional meetings between the two countries, a proliferation which was encouraged by a peaceful settlement between Kerry Packer and the cricket establishment, reached only months after Mike Brearley's return. Once the World Series had been abandoned and the players had been returned to their rightful owners, the Australian Cricket Board cast around for immediate ways to replenish its coffers, severely depleted both by the $500,000 it had guaranteed the TCCB for the tour of 1978–79 and the losses which poor gates during that series had caused. Mike Brearley, to his surprise, found himself again leading England to Australia just a year later, for three Test matches and a triangular one-day series with fellow visitors, the West Indies. Ironically, the tour included Packeresque matches under floodlights. Cricket's Boards of Control were clearly keen to put some of the Packer ideas into money-spinning practice, but this hastily-organized tour was badly timed, the emotions of the Packer revolution not yet having subsided, and for Mike Brearley the whole venture was something of a nightmare.

This was just one of a number of additions to the four-yearly pattern in the 1980s. A visit to India, for example, ended with a diversion to Australia (for one-day Internationals with Australia, Pakistan and India), while in 1986–87 (when the winning of the Ashes was confused with the winning of the Perth and Benson & Hedges Cups) yet more one-day cricket was played against Australia at one of the less traditional homes of international cricket, Sharjah, in the United Arab Emirates. But the nadir was reached in the winter of 1987–88, when England set off on three separate tours, which included a meeting with Australia in the World Cup; this was the winter of the confrontation between Mike Gatting and umpire Shakoor Rana, surely a fable devised by the gods as a warning to over-zealous cricket tour planners. In all the helter-skelter of off-season money-making, pressures on players had become ludicrously intense. 'They'll soon not have a team', mused Joe Hardstaff, 'if they go on with those itineraries. Nobody can keep it up.'

The post-Packer explosion of commercialism in top cricket is, of course, only a very elaborate variation on a well-known theme, a heightened expression, in fact, of the Lillywhite legacy. Those 19th-century pioneers did not travel so dangerously and uncomfortably out of pure messianic zeal for the propagation of a noble game and the greater glory of the British Empire. They travelled because they were being very well paid to do so. The large financial rewards which players like Botham and Gower have reaped from the game are probably no more than George Ulyett or Harry Jupp would have enjoyed, had they been living today. The tourists of Lillywhite's time may have been more robustly passionate about their cricket than many of today's somewhat anxious performers, but they seem to have been no less commercially minded.

The history of the Australian cricket tour, like that of ancient Rome, seems to fit neatly into three phases. First, there was the period of the Kings, free-spirited souls like Lillywhite, Shaw and Shrewsbury, untrammelled by any rules, regulations or codes of conduct, who mounted their own expeditions and chose their troops with care, usually reaping rich rewards. Then, in 1903–04, came the Republic, a long and steady period of development under the Senatorial MCC, an oligarchic but benevolent body, which regularized the irregular and spread a code of rules and conduct ever more widely. Its consuls were men like Warner and Allen, Douglas and Dexter, Jardine and May, patricians to the last thread of their togas, men born and educated to rule. They might not necessarily have won all their battles, but their troops were well-disciplined, of sound technique and tolerably well-paid. Then came the third phase, the Empire, with the rise of a new bureaucracy, the TCCB. This powerful secretariat has been confronted with many problems. There is much unrest abroad, whilst at home the old Republican virtues of honour, loyalty and duty seem no longer fashionable.

Despite these changes of control and emphasis, the Lillywhite legacy remains as strong as ever, its future offering as much scope and interest as its past. There will be new generations of tourists, some with the greatness of a Jupp, a Hayward, a Hammond or a Boycott, who will also feel the pulse quicken as the shores of Australia approach. Perhaps the tourists of 2090, as they fire the retro-rockets over Adelaide in their inter-continental travel-capsules (with the badge of St George and the Dragon emblazoned on the nose-cones), may never even have heard of Lillywhite, Warner, Allen and Brearley; perhaps they may compete for the Ashes in a series of fifty half-day Internationals; perhaps they may go out to bat at Sydney wearing all-enveloping, protective suits of supple plastic and wielding bats of (dare one say it?) aluminium, painted in patriotic red, white and blue. Nonetheless, however bizarre the differences, the tourists will *still* be making summers out of winters, *still* have travelled 12,000 miles to represent English cricket in the vast and unchangingly attractive country of Australia. Their memories afterwards, one hopes, will be as happy as those of their many predecessors, for few indeed are the tours which are not remembered with affection. 'Enjoyed the beaches', wrote Geoff Miller recently of his visit in 1978–79, 'enjoyed the oysters and the fish. Team spirit was excellent. The Test result was the icing on the cake.' Long may that cake, iced or not, continue to be baked!

APPENDIX

SOME COMPARATIVE STATISTICS
OF THE FOUR TOURING TEAMS

Results

	Played	Won	Drawn	Lost
1876–77	23	11	8	4
1903–04	20	10	8	2
1936–37	28	8	15	5
1978–79	25	17	4	4

Batting Averages, all matches, whatever status

	Innings	Not Out	Highest Score	Runs	Average
W.R. Hammond (1936–37)	27	2	231★	1,547	61.88
C.J. Barnett (1936–37)	25	0	259	1,375	55.00
T. Hayward (1903–04)	25	1	157	1,181	49.21
R.E. Foster (1903–04)	28	5	287	1,056	45.91
R.W. Tolchard (1978–79)	11	3	108	357	44.63
M. Leyland (1936–37)	34	6	126	1,197	42.75
R.E.S. Wyatt (1936–37)	24	2	144	880	40.00
D.W. Randall (1978–79)	30	5	150	978	39.12
J.T. Tyldesley (1903–04)	27	2	127	926	37.04
L.E.G. Ames (1936–37)	29	1	109	1,017	36.32
G. Boycott (1978–79)	32	6	123★	905	34.81
J.M. Brearley (1978–79)	29	5	116★	827	34.46
W.R. Rhodes (1903–04)	22	10	49★	411	34.25
D.I. Gower (1978–79)	28	3	102	851	34.04
B.J.T. Bosanquet (1903–04)	24	3	124★	711	33.85
A.E. Knight (1903–04)	25	2	109	766	33.30
J. Hardstaff (1936–37)	38	3	110	1,146	32.74
G. Hirst (1903–04)	26	2	92	774	32.25
P.F. Warner (1903–04)	29	1	79	805	28.75
A. Fagg (1936–37)	19	1	112	512	28.44
G.O. Allen (1936–37)	21	3	88	505	28.05
I.T. Botham (1978–79)	18	0	74	488	27.11
L.C. Braund (1903–04)	25	2	102	620	26.96
G.A. Gooch (1978–79)	33	2	112	823	26.55
T.S. Worthington (1936–37)	33	2	89	820	26.45
A.A. Lilley (1903–04)	22	4	102★	432	24.00

	Innings	Not Out	Highest Score	Runs	Average
L.B. Fishlock (1936–37)	27	4	104	528	22.95
G. Ulyett (1876–77)	35	1	95	768	22.59
G. Miller (1978–79)	24	3	68★	455	21.67
C.T. Radley (1978–79)	18	2	64	344	21.50
H.R.J. Charlwood (1876–77)	35	1	66	694	20.41
R.W.V. Robins (1936–37)	20	0	61	375	18.75
A.E. Relf (1903–04)	19	3	39	298	18.62
C.M. Old (1978–79)	10	3	40	126	18.00
P.H. Edmonds (1978–79)	15	4	38★	195	17.72
J. Selby (1987–77)	34	1	88	589	17.28
R.W. Taylor (1978–79)	18	2	97	257	16.06
A. Greenwood (1876–77)	35	1	66	530	15.59
W. Voce (1936–37)	26	11	53★	228	15.20
E. Arnold (1903–04)	16	3	34	192	14.76
H. Jupp (1876–77)	17	1	63	233	14.56
T. Emmett (1876–77)	33	1	48	420	13.13
H. Strudwick (1903–04)	11	0	42	142	12.90
E. Pooley (1876–77)	20	3	39	210	12.35
J. Sims (1936–37)	24	1	43	281	12.21
H. Verity (1936–37)	28	3	47	293	11.72
R.G.D. Willis (1978–79)	14	4	24	117	11.70
W. Copson (1936–37)	15	7	19	90	11.25
A. Hill (1876–77)	33	5	49	312	11.14
A. Shaw (1876–77)	32	2	86	326	10.87
J. E. Emburey (1978–79)	16	3	42	140	10.77
G. Duckworth (1936–37)	13	4	15★	91	10.11
T. Armitage (1876–77)	32	3	38	286	9.86
J.K. Lever (1978–79)	10	0	27	96	9.60
M. Hendrick (1978–79)	14	6	20	70	8.75
A. Fielder (1903–04)	15	4	23	88	8.00
J. Lillywhite (1876–77)	33	6	30	179	6.63
J. Southerton (1876–77)	32	13	16	95	5.00

Bowling Averages, all matches, whatever status

(Excluding the 1936–37 fixture at Clare, in which Farnes took 2 for 23 and Copson 2 for 13)

	Balls	Runs	Wickets	Average
A. Hill (1876–77)	2,415	394	111	3.55
A. Shaw (1876–77)	5,181	883	231	3.82
J. Lillywhite (1876–77)	2,786	631	138	4.57
J. Southerton (1876–77)	1,582	463	99	4.67

	Balls	Runs	Wickets	Average
T. Emmett (1876–77)	1,462	291	58	5.02
T. Armitage (1876–77)	238	117	13	9.00
G. Ulyett (1876–77)	1,070	312	30	10.40
M. Hendrick (1978–79)	1,940	596	40	14.90
W.R. Rhodes (1903–04)	2,919	1,181	76	15.54
G. Miller (1978–79)	2,653	798	51	15.65
W. Copson (1936–37)	1,557	626	39	16.05
L.C. Braund (1903–04)	2,487	1,161	72	16.13
R.G.D. Willis (1978–79)	2,059	795	45	17.66
C.M. Old (1978–79)	1,200	569	32	17.78
E. Arnold (1903–04)	2,323	954	53	18.00
A. Fielder (1903–04)	1,483	605	33	18.33
J.E. Emburey (1978–79)	2,425	703	37	19.00
A.E. Relf (1903–04)	1,457	539	28	19.25
I.T. Botham (1978–79)	2,161	1,004	49	20.49
W.R. Hammond (1936–37)	1,675	705	33	21.36
P.H. Edmonds (1978–79)	1,911	670	31	21.61
G.H. Hirst (1903–04)	2,569	1,007	45	22.38
K. Farnes (1936–37)	2,405	1,086	48	22.63
G.O. Allen (1936–37)	2,253	1,103	46	23.98
J. Sims (1936–37)	2,904	1,408	57	24.70
B.J.T. Bosanquet (1903–04)	2,026	1.317	53	24.84
J.K. Lever (1978–79)	2,143	643	25	25.72
H. Verity (1936–37)	3,383	1,056	41	25.76
W. Voce (1936–37)	2,819	1,246	47	26.51
R.W.V. Robins (1936–37)	1,523	808	24	33.66

Time Spent Playing Cricket

1876–77   66 days of cricket out of 133 in Australia/NZ
1903–04   62 days of cricket out of 130 days in Australia
1936–37   89 days of cricket out of 171 days in Australia/NZ
1978–79   69 days of cricket out of 115 days in Australia

Age of Players at Beginning of Tours

21   Fagg (1936–37)
22   Botham (1978–79), Gower (1978–79)
23   Strudwick (1903–04)
24   Ulyett (1876–77)
25   Foster (1903–04), Bosanquet (1903–04), Rhodes (1903–04),
      Farnes (1936–37) Hardstaff (1936–37), Gooch (1978–79)

26 Arnold (1903–04), Fielder (1903–04), Barnett (1936–37),
    Emburey (1978–79), Miller (1978–79)
27 Selby (1876–77), Braund (1903–04), Copson (1936–37), Voce (1936–37),
    Edmonds (1978–79), Randall (1978–79)
28 Armitage (1876–77), Charlwood (1876–77)
29 Greenwood (1876–77), Tyldesley (1903–04), Relf (1903–04),
    Fishlock (1936–37), Lever (1978–79), Old (1978–79), Willis (1978–79)
30 Hill (1876–77), Warner (1903–04), Knight (1903–04), Ames (1936–37),
    Robins (1936–37), Hendrick (1978–79)
31 Verity (1936–37)
32 Hayward (1903–04), Hirst (1903–04), Sims (1936–37), Tolchard (1978–79)
33 Hammond (1936–37)
34 Jupp (1876–77), Lillywhite (1876–77), Shaw (1876–77), Allen (1936–37),
    Radley (1978–79)
35 Emmett (1876–77), Duckworth (1936–37), Wyatt (1936–37)
36 Lilley (1903–04), Leyland (1936–37), Brearley (1978–79)
37 Taylor (1978–79)
38 Pooley (1876–77), Boycott (1978–79)
48 Southerton (1876–77)

Average Age of Team

1876–77	32
1903–04	28
1936–37	30
1978–79	29

Numbers in Party

1876–77	12	plus none
1903–04	14	plus a manager
1936–37	17	plus a manager and baggageman/scorer
1978–79	16	plus a manager, assistant manager, scorer & physiotherapist.

SELECT BIBLIOGRAPHY

Among the many books consulted the following were of particular relevance:

General:

Bailey/Thorn/Wynne-Thomas: Who's Who of Cricketers (George Newnes 1984)
Frith: England versus Australia (Lutterworth Press 1977)
Various Wisden Almanacks and Lillywhite Companions and Annuals
Wynne-Thomas: Cricket Tours at Home and Abroad (Paul Hamlyn 1989)
Whitington: Illustrated History of Australian Cricket (Pelham Books 1974)

1876–77:

Pullin: Alfred Shaw Cricketer (Cassell 1902)
Wynne-Thomas: Give Me Arthur (Arthur Barker 1985)
Conway's Australian Cricketers' Annual 1876–77
Pollard: The Formative Years of Australian Cricket (Angus & Robertson 1987)

1903–04:

Warner: How We Recovered the Ashes (Chapman & Hall 1904)
Lilley: Twenty-four Years of Cricket (Mills & Boon 1912)
Howat: Plum Warner (Unwin Hyman 1987)

1936–37:

Swanton: Gubby Allen (Stanley Paul 1985)
Cardus: Australian Summer (Jonathan Cape 1937)
Harris: 1937 Australian Test Tour (Hutchinson 1937)
Farnes: Tours and Tests (RTS Lutterworth Press 1940)
Pollock: So this is Australia (Arthur Barker 1937)

1978–79:

Boycott: Put to the Test (Arthur Barker 1979)
Brearley & Doust: The Ashes Retained (Hodder & Stoughton 1979)
Frith: The Ashes '79 (Angus & Robertson 1979)
Lee: A Pitch in both Camps (Stanley Paul 1979)
Martin-Jenkins: In Defence of the Ashes (Macdonald & Jane's 1979)
Taylor & Gower: Anyone for Cricket? (Pelham Books 1979)
Yallop: Lambs to the Slaughter (Outback 1979)

INDEX OF PEOPLE

INDEX OF PLACES

247